ELIZABETH BISHOP
Her Poetics of Loss

ELIZABETH BISHOP
Her Poetics of Loss

Susan McCabe

The Pennsylvania State University Press
University Park, Pennsylvania

Library of Congress Cataloging-in-Publication Data

McCabe, Susan, 1960–
    Elizabeth Bishop : her poetics of loss / Susan McCabe.

        p.   cm.
    Includes bibliographical references and index.
    ISBN 0-271-01047-9 (alk. paper) — ISBN 0-271-01048-7
(pbk. : alk. paper)
        1. Bishop, Elizabeth, 1911–1979—Criticism and interpretation.
    2. Women and literature—United States—History—20th century.
    3. Loss (Psychology) in literature.   4. Psychoanalysis and
    literature.   5. Lesbians in literature.   6. Poetics.   I. Title.
    PS3503.I785Z77   1994
    811'.54—dc20   93-30390
                                                              CIP

Published by The Pennsylvania State University Press,
University Park, PA 16802-1003

It is the policy of The Pennsylvania State University Press to use acid-free paper for the
first printing of all clothbound books. Publications on uncoated stock satisfy the mini-
mum requirements of American National Standard for Information Sciences—Permanence of Paper for Printed Library Materials, ANSI Z39.48–1984.

In memory of my beloved mother
Ruth Langer McCabe

Contents

Acknowledgments

I first of all thank Stephen Yenser for his unfailing encouragement and sensitive criticism. His faith in my book from its inception to its completion has been a source of great inspiration. Calvin Bedient's passionate devotion to poetry and literary criticism has been an invigorating presence in my own work. I appreciate Anne Mellor's honest and wise advice in the early phases of my manuscript's development. I also thank Kathleen Komar and Ross Shideler for their conscientious reading and suggestions in the initial stages of planning.

I also thank Alice Methfessel for her help and permission to quote from the published and unpublished material of Elizabeth Bishop. I am grateful to Frank Bidart for his permission to quote from Elizabeth Bishop archives. Thanks must be extended as well to Elise Pritchard of Farrar, Straus and Giroux for her permission to quote from *The Complete Poems* and *The Collected Prose*. Thanks to Nancy S. MacKechnie, curator of Rare Books and Manuscripts, Vassar College, for permission to quote from unpublished material from the Elizabeth Bishop Collection, and to Rodney Dennis, curator of Rare Books, Houghton Library, Harvard University, for permission to quote from the unpublished letters of Bishop to Robert Lowell.

For other kinds of support, I thank Luke Carson for our days of poetry reading and endless *caffelattes*. I must thank Wendy Welch for her delightful collages (and for her whiskey on the porch in some difficult moments of my toil). I am grateful for Brian Lizotte and his kindness through all these years. And especially, I thank Billy for her generous dedication to my book; her sensitive comments and proofreading along with her loving support have been indispensable. I cannot thank Marilyn McCabe enough for her never-ending love and belief in me.

I thank again and again my dearest mother, Ruth Langer McCabe, who makes everything I do possible.

Introduction

We can be grateful that Elizabeth Bishop has finally begun to receive the critical attention she deserves. Investigations into the life of this great poet, including the recent full-length biography by Brett C. Millier, attest to Bishop's prominence in both academic and popular circles.[1] I began this book at a time when there was but one study of Bishop available. Why, I struggled to understand, was there such a dearth of criticism on this brilliant poet, who received the Pulitzer Prize in 1956 long before she would even write her best poems, who was consistently welcomed and adored when read? Why was she so acclaimed by other poets yet ignored by most studies of both modern and contemporary poetry? Her relative exclusion from serious academic exploration signifies the critic's inability to assign her to a movement and, finally, to articulate the subtle unsettling quality of her poems. I do not believe we have been critically equipped for Bishop—seemingly so conservative in her aesthetic wonders but so inventive and, as it were, in advance of what we could perceive. The recent interest in Bishop has emerged, in part, from a growing sensitivity to politicized canon issues and the underrepresentation of women writers. It is with new lights and, specifically, with a greater understanding of the postmodern and its relationship to gender that we can begin to appreciate Bishop's troubling yet exhilarating uncertainties and questions of reality, knowledge, sexuality, and self. In spite of increased recognition of Bishop, however, to date there has been no full-scale investigation of her that adequately reflects both her postmodernism and her feminism. This work will constitute the first such serious exploration.

I offer a detailed examination of Bishop's work—poetry, prose, and selected unpublished material—to show how her writing unsettles any notion of integrated selfhood and places us in touch with a sense of loss at the core of our attempts to fix ourselves through language. Such a model of the self is distinctively postmodern, as I shall discuss. Since personal loss guides many of her concerns, I emphasize the importance of autobiography to her poetry of uncertainty and flux. Thus Chapter 1 explores Bishop's early experience with loss and its impact upon her poetics. The subsequent chapters chart related interests, each linked to a conception of the self as essentially unstable, fragmented, and soluble, faced with the prospects of loss. Art, love, travel, and memory are the topics of these chapters and represent a circular movement away from the self and then back to it, redefined, as the variable but vital source for the processes of imaginative remaking. Throughout, questions of gender and sexuality infuse how Bishop uses language and her experience of loss.

Randall Jarrell's comment on Bishop's first volume of poetry, *North & South* (1946), that "all her poems have written underneath, *I have seen it,*" points to Bishop's richly detailed language but implies an ability to record objectively immediate experience, as if words could transparently describe the world, a recurrent error in modernist assessments of Bishop.[2] On the contrary, she vigorously discloses throughout her work that she has only apparently "seen it." Bishop's early formalism in the 1930s and 1940s, and the continued tendency among critics to characterize her style as impersonal, reticent, or as merely, if brilliantly, descriptive have led to categorizing Bishop as a modernist, in lieu of a better label. The postmodern implications and currents within her work have thus far been either ignored or minimized. Thomas J. Travisano's *Elizabeth Bishop: Her Artistic Development* (1988), the first book-length work on Bishop since Anne Stevenson's short critical study in 1966, underrates Bishop's self-scrutiny and dismantling of "objective" poetry.[3] Travisano approaches his task of chronicling the poet's artistic evolution with ingenious modesty, calling his method "eclectically traditional," brushing aside any theoretical excursions into the work as inappropriate: "I have left to others the exploration of Bishop's work in the light of poststructuralist aesthetics, an approach that sometimes threatens to make criticism more esoteric and obscure than the work itself" (13). Yet isn't traditional exegesis in fact obfuscatory and even reductive when it assumes a stable subject and seeks unity, closure, and coherence in a poet so often disruptive of these features?

Since so much of Bishop's poetry defies coherence and placement in a snug tradition, Jerome Mazzaro in *Postmodern American Poetry* (which devotes a chapter to Bishop) wisely discusses her as a postmodernist, but only as she continues Auden's "new kind of poetry" where feeling and personal experience are not divorced from poetic technique.[4] And it cannot be, as Mazzaro suggests in echoing Frost, that Bishop's poetic project functions as a "temporary stay against confusion" (178); instead, it is a site where confusion and uncertainty are allowed. Yet even as Bishop has been called postmodernist, the implications of this terming have not been fully developed. Lynn Keller, in her important book establishing postmodern trends in contemporary American poetry, recognizes how Bishop's life forms a continuum with her writing and that her poems look discontinuous with what has gone on in poetry before; she decisively shows where Bishop's debt to Marianne Moore and modernism breaks off, and unabashedly directs us to the poet's self:

> In Moore's work the object described is the genuine focus of interest; in Bishop's work the interest lies less in the object itself than in the narrator's relation to what she describes and in what this relation reveals about her. Bishop appears to be trying, in Modernist fashion, to see external things truly, while in fact what she scrutinizes is herself.[5]

Keller appropriately characterizes Bishop as introspective, skeptical, self-reflexive. The implications of these qualities in Bishop's poetry need to be further pursued in light of Bishop's entire career. In her 1991 *Elizabeth Bishop: Questions of Mastery*, Bonnie Costello addresses the poems primarily in terms of visual art, as attempts at mastery, and while she acknowledges postmodern tendencies in Bishop, the focus of her study prevents describing them in detail.[6]

Until now, then, there have been no book-length studies that primarily acknowledge Bishop as a postmodern or that develop the dynamics of her self-scrutiny. Even as I do not wish to overshadow analysis of poetic text or to be theoretical foremost, this book is necessarily informed by an implicitly postmodern bias, one that I would like to clarify at the outset. *Postmodernism* is, of course, itself a debatable and polysemous term, itself subject to interrogation.[7] And the category of modernism does not neatly break down with some grand advent of the postmodern; in other words, neither classification corresponds with chronological and historic periods—where either begins or ends is questionable since the postmodern can be read as an ongoing process, to which modernism belongs, deconstructing the mythic legacy of the Western metaphysics of full immediate presence and Enlightenment values of objectivity, reason, and empiricism. Modernism should not be considered as a seamless, unquestioned entity.[8] However, notions of the art work as autonomous, with an aestheticism resistant to foregrounded social, political, personal, and ordinary "mass" experience, belong largely in the domain of literary modernism.

Even though a single definition of postmodernism cannot be fixed, attributes associated with it—in contrast with but not independent from those surrounding modernism—resonate in a reading of Bishop. Most of Ihab Hassan's keynote and usable terms of postmodernism in "The Culture of Postmodernism"—purpose, design, hierarchy, mastery, presence, center, hypotaxis, metaphor, depth, determinacy, phallocentrism, transcendence— are countered by Bishop through play, chance, anarchy, silence, absence, dispersal, parataxis, metonymy, surface, irony, androgyny, indeterminacy, immanence.[9] If modernism and postmodernism have shared a similar excitement in language for itself instead of for mimesis, the former, even in its vibrant experimentalism, still possesses a faith in the power and adequacy of words that the latter more insistently questions or denies. Keller's book offers cogent summations of the character of contemporary poetry and—of particular interest here—alerts us to its doubt about "the precision of language" and its subsequent attempt "to work within the flat and worn language of our immediate experience"; she emphasizes the postmodernist's mode of writing about the "dynamic present" as a rejection of any established reality: "Focusing on the processes of epistemology rather than on achieved knowledge, they portray the mind engaging itself in the world and attending to events, without imposing fixed interpretations on that experience" (12). It is this kind of focus—upon uncertainty and the dubious processes of perceiving the world—that adumbrates Bishop's approach.

Surprised by Anne Stevenson's assigning her a closeness with a "philosophy," that of Ludwig Wittgenstein, Bishop proceeded, Millier's biography informs us, to read him "faithfully and unhaltingly" (366). Stevenson was quite perspicacious to see the later Wittgenstein's forerunning postmodern investigation of the precarious status of language, knowledge and belief in Bishop, whether or not she had read him.[10] Bishop is, almost above all, an epistemological poet who reminds us at every turn that we cannot know anything fully or absolutely, and that the activity of writing cannot save us with its "magical powers," but reveals our "grave difficulties" as in "12 O'Clock News" (arranged into two columns, objects on one side and signification on the other, in the style of Derrida's transgressive *Glas*) where she defamiliarizes an ink bottle on a writing desk:

> a *numen*, or a great altar recently erected to one of their gods, to which, in their present historical state of superstition and help-

lessness, they attribute magical powers, and may even regard as a "savior," one last hope of rescue from their grave difficulties.[11]

She will describe the water in "At the Fishhouses" as "like what we imagine knowledge to be," positioning us in a zone of provisional understanding; we can never know—we can only compare and imagine. Bishop's juxtaposition of the everyday and material with the numinous dislocates us as in "Questions of Travel," for example, with "the broken gasoline pump" made into a "bamboo church of Jesuit baroque," and her questions in that poem direct us to the "lack" that impels most of her self-reflexive unraveling of location and "home": *Is it lack of imagination that makes us come / to imagined places, not just stay at home?* The "playful, paratactic, and deconstructionist" character of postmodernism (in Hassan's terms) make it "in McLuhan's sense . . . hospitable to kitsch" and evidences itself in Bishop with her Jesuit gas pump or with the bad paintings of her uncle that at least two of her poems address, or with the "comic books," "the big dim doily," and "a big hirsute begonia" of "Filling Station," a poem with the wry and evasive "Somebody loves us all," pointing us to an unnamed figure remaking environments, present most in absence. Language always appears as a subject for Bishop, as in "Anaphora," where she quotes, without reference, "'Where is the music coming from, the energy? / The day was meant for what ineffable creature / we must have missed?'" We are slouching towards Bethlehem, but our words interfere, as we must begin, anaphorically, again and again. Throughout, we will have misses, departures and arrivals that never culminate in full articulate revelation, "every day in endless / endless assent." We go places but we never arrive or see them immediately: the landscape of "Florida" is "the poorest postcard of itself." Refuting any harmonious completion and plentitude along with an ability to transcend our texts, "Over 2,000 Illustrations and a Complete Concordance" offers us a speaker, frustrated over illuminated religious narrations as "the gilt rubs off" a "heavy book," who must declare entrapment in parataxis, signaling barely differentiated, nonhierarchical linking: "Everything only connected by 'and' and 'and'" (The unquoted *and* tells much.) Bishop's play between a metaphysical hope and worldly cynicism points to a mystic streak or crack (like the effect of the lightning bolt on the church in Santarém), but she demands that we pay attention to the restless linguistic surface that we never quite move beyond. She looks toward transcendence and knowledge, but in every volume refuses any assurance or possession of them.

I do not, however, simply want to pinpoint the ways Bishop adroitly plays against and with modernism; rather, I wish to show how her impulses toward absence, dispersal, and metonymy, for example, constitute a very personal poetics of loss. While Bishop is by no means a confessional poet in the manner of Sexton, Plath, or even Rich, she questions and tests the boundaries that would separate life from her art and makes loss a theme around which her self-interrogation constellates. She cannot, therefore, but disrupt an aesthetics of impersonality, autonomy, presence—those features extolled by a largely masculinist modernism. Brett Millier supplies the most complete biographical record of Bishop to date; *Elizabeth Bishop: Life and The Memory of It* is a work of vast importance to Bishop devotees and scholars, divulging information about Bishop's lesbianism and alcoholism hitherto unavailable, but its purpose and scope necessarily lead to an approach more journalistic than critical. The biographical pressures upon Bishop's work have been explored in David Kalstone's brilliant posthumously published *Becoming a Poet*, where he reveals how significant her personal life is in shaping her art, but as with others who do take into account the poet's life, little is done with the way her poetic project takes her early losses—her father to death and her mother to madness—and shapes them into an awareness of the instability of the very concepts of selfhood or place through a rhetoric of indeterminacy and irony.[12] Her poetry dismantles the notion of the traditional self as it confesses to a disunified self, and it is such a reexamination of the self that takes on major importance in my work.

Bishop's gender questions and sexual orientation as they inform her poetics have been even more blatantly resisted than the recognition of her work as postmodern. And these aspects of Bishop's writing need to be considered together if we are to come to a richer understanding of the poet's vision. I think, finally, Bishop resituates primal loss through a feminist poetics that appreciates an interdependency of a mobile and transilient self and reality. In his article "The Discourse of Others: Feminists and Postmodernism," Craig Owens recommends that the two strands of criticism in his title that have not been persuasively seen as related be brought together as he thinks that "women's insistence on difference and incommensurability may not only be compatible with, but also an instance of postmodern thought."[13] His plea is one I pursue here: Bishop's mostly undocumented postmodernism evidences her unacknowledged feminism (and vice versa). But feminism, like postmodernism, comes in many versions.[14]

The interrogation of the relationship between language, representation, and perception cannot but problematize the status of self, sexuality, and gender. As products of a lesbian poet, Bishop's texts seem particularly engaged, if often covertly, by the difficulties involved in gender definitions and labels. In her excellent essay, "Postmodernism and Gender Relations," Jane Flax discovers, like Owens, a compatibility between postmodernism and feminism, and refines these concepts in a manner that allows for better understanding of Bishop's implicit feminism.[15] Flax concretely summarizes beliefs that postmodern philosophers "seek to throw into radical doubt" (41): "the existence of a stable, coherent self"; "an objective, reliable, and universal foundation for knowledge"; "Reason itself has transcendental and universal qualities"; "Language is in some sense transparent"; "There is a correspondence between word and thing"; "Objects are not linguistically (or socially) constructed; they are merely made present to consciousness by naming and the right use of language," to cite the most pertinent here (41–42). Even as she recognizes "an understandable attraction to the (apparently) logical, orderly world of the Enlightenment," Flax asserts that "feminist theory more properly belongs in the terrain of postmodern philosophy," both approaches similarly subversive and deconstructive of "notions of reason, knowledge, or the self"; armed with postmodern discourse, feminists have begun "to reveal the effects of the gender arrangements that lay beneath their neutral and universalizing facades." With postmodernity then, "gender can no longer be treated as a simple, neutral fact" and "gender relations are complex and unstable processes" (44). Along with other postmodern feminists, Flax points to the limitations of feminists who do not consider the backfiring danger of universal categories, those attempts to fix a monolithic concept of the feminine. Nancy Fraser and Linda J. Nicholson in their "Social Criticism without Philosophy" further warn against "the heterosexist bias of much mainstream feminist theory" in its continued essentialism and universalism.[16]

While I find satisfying features in the work of many feminists, including Nancy Chodorow, whom many postmodernists, including those cited above, find essentialist, I am particularly alert to such a bias, sensitive to the ways Bishop's homosexuality inevitably inflects her work and her questioning of gender categories. Bishop must have been affected by the negative image of the lesbian as helpless invert, "a man trapped in a woman's body," promulgated by early sexologists and current during the years Bishop was coming of age, notions Lillian Faderman documents in her illuminating sociological study, *Odd Girls and Twilight Lovers: A History of Lesbian Life in Twentieth-Century America*.[17] And it does not seem merely coincidental that Bishop expatriated to Paris in the late 1930s and lived with her lover in Brazil for most of the 1950s, both eras when hostile assessments of the lesbian, as either psychotic or inherently evil, were at their height, as Faderman informs us; Bishop's *apparently* thoroughgoing silence and secrecy about her sexuality in her writing stem, at least somewhat, from the position of someone "in hiding." For instance, the speaker's urgent and manic injunction in "Pink Dog" (a poem in which a depilated dog is the ostensible subject but which addresses all those figures stigmatized or persecuted by a conventional society) to "'Dress up! Dress up and dance at Carnival!" bespeaks the lesbian's internalized command to mask her identity in fear for her very life. As Adrienne Rich's groundbreaking essay "The Eye of the Outsider" makes evident, Bishop's great attention to those marginalized by a patriarchal society demands that we examine the poet's work from a perspective that takes Bishop's own status as outsider, as lesbian poet into account.[18] While she avoids overtly political statements in her poems and even eschews them as unsuitable, thorough examination of her work leads to a sharper sense of her commitment to the marginal and silenced, a strategy that, I argue, is ultimately both feminist and aesthetic.

Another significant recent study, Judith Merrin's *An Enabling Humility: Marianne Moore, Elizabeth Bishop, and the Uses of Tradition*, assumes a feminist position, but it does so only on a limited scale: her subject is not Bishop foremost.[19] She takes up the issue of influence in terms of these two women poets and argues that their "enabling humility" helps them to revise tradition for their individual enterprises. Her analysis makes a substantial contribution to Bishop studies. But while Merrin's last chapter tries to answer the question her first sentence proposes—"How does a gifted woman enable her own literary work in the midst of a male-predominant culture and in response to what was and still is a male-preponderant canon?"—most of the book skirts this compelling question and barely mentions Bishop's homosexuality. Merrin calls for a recognition of the "intricate intertextual and intersexual literary reality" that informs all poetry (133) and of tradition as "folded and refolded as an Appalachian geosyncline" (137) rather than as linear progression or Bloomian agonism; she applauds Moore and Bishop "for their thoroughgoing (if sometimes subtle) resistance to *all* forms of egocentricity and domination" (139). Such assessments reaffirm my own sense of the significance and necessity of gender questions to Bishop. My study, however, considers Bishop's feminism as more pervasive, if paradoxically less trackable: I am concerned less with the male influences—Herbert and Hopkins and Wordsworth, though these are important—and more with the ways Bishop does inscribe and investigate her own gender experience and what serves as the "feminine" as she rejects impersonality and anti-confessionalism. Betsy Erkkila addresses similar issues of literary influence in *The Wicked Sisters: Women Poets, Literary History and Discord*, and her chapter on Bishop and Moore extends discussion of race, class, and other cultural impacts upon the creation of a feminine literary history: significantly, she contends that women's literary history is not only one of supportive affiliations, but again her discussion of Bishop is limited by her wide scope and focus upon many other poets.[20]

As one of the most recent critical books in this tide of urgency to acknowledge Bishop, Lorrie Goldensohn's *Biography of a Poetry* carries forward what Kalstone began in providing unpublished material previously unavailable, and reflects an awareness throughout of gender issues; in this way, it is truly a revolutionary and admirable contribution, though it does not (as no single book can) exhaustively analyze Bishop's work in either postmodern or feminist light.[21] Furthermore, none of the criticism thus far foregrounds, as I do, loss in connection with gender and poetics. The number of exciting works on Bishop as of late testifies to Bishop's significance and her growing reputation. Much reevaluation has been necessary to see her not simply as a token canon member but as one rigorously subverting what might appear only as modernist sheen or impressive craft. More is yet to be written on Bishop as we come to appreciate her multiplicity.

The organization of this book will appear roughly chronological, though less developmental and more thematic. Chapters 2–5 take up her consecutive major volumes, each published a decade apart; but the guiding premise of recovery and loss introduced in Chapter 1 becomes descriptive of all her work: pieces of earlier work resonate later. And as Chapter 5 on remembering indicates, linear time is a fiction, but one Bishop relies upon to undercut in all her questions of loss, love, travel, history and memory.

As the theoretical sources of my book range widely, I should call my work eclectically untraditional. In fact, I try to assume the *bricoleur* or assemblage sensibility—of making do with what is at hand and partaking of diverse materials—that I ascribe to Bishop in my chapter highlighting her metapoetics. A psychoanalytic perspective toward loss is invoked through Freud; with Lacan, I am able to link the experience of loss with writing. I supplement my use of the French postmodern feminists Kristeva and Cixous, who invoke the possibility of a distinctively feminine writing, with a variety of Anglo-American feminists such as Chodorow, Ostriker, Miller, Gilligan, Butler, Flax, as they diversely approach issues associated with women's writing and feminist philosophy.

In Chapter 1, I argue that a sense of personal and primal loss infuses and governs all Bishop's work and leads her to a more autobiographical stance than critics have suspected, to a writing that mourns, and to a language as sharp as it is unstable and proximate. Moreover, I contend that woman (as she becomes inscribed in phallocentric language) experiences loss in a unique way. Psychoanalytic writings, as already stated, allow me to consider the connections in her work among language, the experience of loss, and gender.

Chapter 2 moves beyond the experience of personal loss and examines Bishop's implicit model of the homemade—inspired by loss and the search for what will suffice, not for what will stand or overcome—which locates her in a struggle between isolation and independence as a lesbian poet and an art that testifies to the interdependence of objects and the world, artists and their artifacts, readers and texts: a collagist poetics that contends with more virile modernist conceptions of the art object as autonomous. Especially in *North & South* (1946) Bishop will reveal a struggle with sexual identity, creating images of the artist as male and encoding the divisions these images produce in herself and in her readers.

Critics miss the point, as I have said, when they praise Bishop's expert naturalism above all else. Her poems write about themselves—how they try to hold disparate details together (her interest in Joseph Cornell and box art makes much sense here), how they can only do so because they are made out of words. As she seems to become more the landscape poet in *A Cold Spring* (1955) than the naturalist, she shows herself being held back from immediate contact with "things in themselves" through metaphor. Chapter 3, then, treats the rupture opened up when Bishop undoes the correspondence between mind and nature as she introduces a vulnerability and personality not explicitly present before. More emotionally inflected poems reveal her confronting lack and dislocation when "art" and language fail to provide correspondences between the self and world. Poems of desire and longing for an Other emerge and test the limits of the self. If loss is the subject of Chapter 1 and her aesthetic of Chapter 2, the exploration of the possibilities of love becomes the main theme here.

Chapter 4 is concerned with travel and Bishop's continued questioning of the boundaries between exterior and interior, a place and how it is imagined, kinship and uprootedness. It examines the poet's commitment to homelessness, difference, and her continued interest in the complex relationship between her imagination and experience. The emphasis of this section will be upon *Questions Of Travel* (1965), which must be read in the light of her fourteen-year residence in Brazil prior to the volume's publication. The questions of the volume work against the resistance of boundaries. But instead of the desire for homogeneity, there is an openness to difference as revealed through her attention to the disenfranchised members of society—and here in particular, the conquered and displaced original settlers of Brazil. She suggests in "Brazil," the first section of *Questions of Travel*, that there must be a way to get beyond isolating differences as they show up in *A Cold Spring* without trying to convert them into sameness.

While Chapter 4 studies Bishop's relation to communities and cultures, Chapter 5 concentrates upon questions of identity and selfhood, as they are constructed and taken apart by memory; I deal primarily with the "Elsewhere" section of *Questions of Travel* and *Geography III* (1976). Without a mythic history, she turns to personal history (we have come full circle to the proposition of an originary loss I introduced in Chapter 1) as to a changing map that actively reshapes and transforms it. Memory binds us to our losses and our rewriting of them as it irredeemably widens the space between ourselves and immediate experience. Chapter 5, then, illumines Bishop's sense of self as unstable and only arbitrarily bounded: she locates the space for language to articulate the self, the "I" as it emerges from primal loss; at the same time, I contemplate how this "difference" might suggest a particularly feminine appreciation of the self as dependent on its relationships with others and the world.

While I think the language of the postmodern and feminist is pertinent here and will be implicitly present in this book, I enact close and meticulous explications of poems and stories in an effort to illumine the poet's work, her play enlivened and not drowned by too much theory. Perhaps the tendency to see Bishop as an anthology poet of discrete pieces derives from her own resistance to the labels available: feminist, socialist, lesbian, poet. She does not wish to be subsumed or pinned down nor does she "desire to get everything in its place."[22] Yet while she cannot be assigned to any "movement," the postmodern and the feminist permeate her work and become, in their own right, categories to be questioned. I want to place her; at the same time, her poems reveal self-displacement, evasion of settlement, and a critique of the very language that constitutes them. Clutching certainties produces small-mindedness, shortsightedness, uncharitable politics: loss of security can spell personal, literary, and social liberation.

1

Writing Loss

The art of losing isn't hard to master;
so many things seem filled with the intent
to be lost that their loss is no disaster.
            —Elizabeth Bishop, "One Art"

A loss of something ever felt I—
The first that I could recollect
Bereft I was—of what I knew not
                    —Emily Dickinson, Poem 959

I

In Chekhov's *The Seagull,* when asked why she only wears black, Masha responds, "I'm in mourning for my life." One mourns for life in order to live it, to understand its limits. Elizabeth Bishop knows this. She also knows that writing helps us raise and recall our losses so we can move ahead. If every word is an epitaph, as Emerson has said, and later Eliot in *Four Quartets,* each one encodes our passing; each one is "filled with the intent to be lost." All texts, in a sense, write loss, and moving from one word to the next and in between them, we never settle down. But the process of losing, for Elizabeth Bishop, is not an art like any other; it requires that we let go to gain mastery, that we neither monumentalize our experience nor fix what is always in the process of dissolution, that we recognize how inseparable our living is from our art. Poetic form and the lyric have been historically assigned the role of masking or denying the power of loss, instability, time.[1] In Bishop, however, writing is a way, not to overcome, but to come to terms with loss. Through a psychoanalytic reading of her autobiographical story "In the Village" along with some of her more rarely considered prose pieces (including a diary she translated from the Portuguese), and finally with "One Art," I show how writing becomes a means of mourning and how for her, a poetics of loss imbricates a writing of a fluid and unfixed self.[2] My use of Freud, as well as some poststructuralist and feminist responses to him that conclude this chapter, allows for an understanding of Bishop's grieving and poetics as constructing an identity that appears particularly "feminine." While I think no reader of Bishop would deny that a sense of loss informs her themes, its primacy in relationship to her interrogation of gender and of language itself has not been adequately elucidated.

Though born early in the century, Elizabeth Bishop produced most of her work after World War II; by default, she has been often read as a vaguely transitional figure, known primarily for a few regularly anthologized poems.[3] Ordinarily, Bishop's poetry (too frequently read at considerable distance from her prose) is characterized as impersonal, reticent, anticonfessional. But while she is assuredly not confessional, as are, say, Berryman, Plath, Sexton, or even Rich, she disrupts an aesthetics of impersonality and autonomy by an interlacing of her life with her art, or rather, by her *revealing* the difficulty in disentangling the two.[4] In one of her earliest essay-reviews, of a biography on Shelley, quoted by Thomas Travisano in his recent and provocative presentation of Bishop's *Blue Pencil* juvenilia, she herself assesses the inextricable relation of the poet's life and work: "The only real way to understand poetry is to know the life and beliefs of the poet, and this is especially true of Shelley whose poems are all written either to further his ideas of philosophy or to express one of his subtle changes of mood."[5] The prominence she gives to the writer's experience and moods cannot be denied. Yet at the same time, she will recognize the distance language automatically imparts to speakers, how it generates more language and reinstates the very separation from the world and immediate experience that it tries to erase or disempower. If a confessionalism, Karl Malkoff's refinement of the term is useful.[6] For him, confessional poets do not simply speak of taboo and daring subjects, but are "attempting a redefinition of the self" that takes into account unconscious impulses; they would expand through words the boundaries (that language itself sets up) of the self so that it becomes "impossible to isolate as a discrete entity." From this perspective, to confess the self is to lose it. To paraphrase Bishop's own words, a distinction between biography and art can never be completely clear; to discuss them as separable, especially in the case of a poet like Bishop, proves untenable, as recent criticism of her work proves.[7] Early loss of her father to death and her mother to madness initiated for her a lifetime of uprootedness and a poetics shaped by an awareness of instability and homelessness, an ability to perceive and question boundaries of all kinds—especially those marking the self.

While residing in Brazil with her lover Lota de Macedo Soares for a period that spans some fifteen years, her most continuous relationship with a place and person, she writes "In the Village" (1953), a story that recounts some episodes of her Nova Scotian childhood, tinted by the loss of her parents and by the emergence of her poetic temperament, and she translates *The Diary of Helena Morley* (1957), a record of an adolescent girl living in a pre-industrial Brazilian town during the changing of the centuries. They are mirror pieces in some sense, as the diary, like her own story, deals primarily with unavoidable loss and how the very writing we use to confront mortality and transitoriness becomes itself an act of loss and displacement. And with "One Art," a poem from *Geography III*, written after the death of Lota in 1967, these pieces together can figure forth a cycle of grieving, a process that for her calls into question the boundaries between self and world, living and dying.

Bishop's apparent objectivity and naturalism really represent an absorption of the self in the environment and a dismissal of any sense of a unified self: her "I" can never be absolutely pinned down; it reflects what Nancy Chodorow would call the "more permeable ego boundaries" of feminine identity, a fundamental paradigm informing the assertions in this book.[8] In brief, Chodorow contends that because females do not have to separate from their mothers in a resolution of the Oedipal complex, they are more susceptible to dependency and open to relationship than males. A less rigid sense of self must color the experience of loss and makes it both more acute and tolerable. To lose a loved object, in such a lubricious economy, can reveal both the lack of an autonomous and integrated identity, and the inevitable exponentiality of allegiances and substitutions. Marvelously lucid, "In the Waiting Room" *(Geography III)*, recounts Bishop's inauguration into gender and identity; as child, she both wants to turn away and to continue to fixate upon the "awful hanging breasts" of the Africans in the *National Geographic*. Her terrifying, yet homoerotic, identification with other women signals the loss of an ungendered, atemporal being in the world, but she also discovers that the self is always a matter of shifting, and that to define where it begins and ends is an act of language, self-naming.[9]

Bishop begins with loss. Born 8 February 1911 in Worcester, Massachusetts, she was eight months old when her father died. As "In the Village" retells, her mother could not lay aside her mourning clothes, and professionals apparently could not help her to successfully work through her grief. After the visit memorialized by Bishop's story, Bishop never saw her mother again. Her mother was considered irrevocably insane and hospitalized in a sanatorium at Dartmouth, Nova Scotia, where she died in May 1934. Elizabeth was brought up by her maternal grandparents and much-adored Aunt Grace primarily in Nova Scotia (with visits to Worcester) until she was six, when she moved to live with her paternal grandparents in Worcester, where she suffered intense loneliness and homesickness as well as multiple physical ailments, including severe asthma, bronchitis and eczema. She then went to stay with her Aunt Maud, her mother's older sister, in Boston; apparently in better spirits, her health temporarily improved. She attended Walnut Hill boarding school for girls in 1927 before enrolling at Vassar in fall 1929. Her childhood, unquestionably, was characterized by traumatic loss and dislocation. Bishop continued her movement by inhabiting diverse locations—New York, Paris, Spain, Florida, Mexico, Seattle, Boston—and never making of any except Brazil in 1951, a long-term home. Her movement was not only a matter of chosen travel but of necessity, namely, her frequent stays throughout her life in hospitals for the treatment of her alcoholism and asthma, and in hotels and at the homes of various friends while she was in transit from one place to another.[10]

The prose pieces I examine appear more overtly personal than her poems, linked as they are with these events of loss and travel, but can be read as a blueprint or gloss for her poetic projects. Her finished poems often, puzzlingly, refuse to show the link between her as subject and direct experience.[11] While her obfuscation of the self is, in part, due to the then-current New Critical disdain for the personal, it also comes from a resistance to the limiting "I." The diary she translates, for example, shows her attraction to the homey and the personal, without closing out her ability to operate through other voices. As her prose, then, helps us to understand her poems, an examination of the formal, even hard-boiled "One Art,"—which makes most explicit the way writing, loss, and the self intersect—makes Bishop's prose more visibly autobiographic.

"In the Village" seeks to stake out a past, neither ideal nor absolute, but brittle and transitory. And in fact the Nova Scotian world signals an awakening to language and to pain, an awakening narrated in the other prepositioning piece, "In the Waiting Room." The story opens with the memory of her mother's scream, a sound both illegible and limitless in significance, both hollow and substantial, carrying within it lack and silence (as it is a scream that sends the mother, after all, back to the sanatorium and forecloses her recovery to sanity); the scream converts the landscape into a synecdoche of eternal, entire loss:

> A scream, the echo of a scream, hangs over that Nova Scotian village. No one hears it; it hangs there forever, a slight stain in those pure blue skies, skies that travelers compare to those of Switzerland, too dark, too blue, so that they seem to keep on darkening a little more around the horizon—or is it around the rims of the eyes?—the color of the cloud of bloom on the elm trees, the violet on the fields of oats; something darkening over the woods and waters as well as the sky. The scream hangs like that, unheard, in memory—in the past, in the present, and those years between. It was not even loud to begin with, perhaps. It just came there to live, forever—not loud, just alive forever. (*CPr*, 251)

What persists "forever" in this prose poem paragraph is the "stain" of duration, a signature of transitoriness that colors and invades all of perception. Synesthesia displaces the traumatic experience of her mother's breakdown upon returning home from an asylum, and the child "sees" the scream: it "hangs" as mark of severance and separation. Her story reveals the desire to cover over her mother's hysterical articulation—avoid and repress what returns and echoes throughout the landscape's very texture; the absence of an "I" here underlines the way "it," loss, subsumes everything—even the existence of a self. She will recognize that she cannot obliterate "the frail almost-lost scream" identified in the end among all those other "things damaged and lost, sickened and destroyed" (274).

The moment of the scream is "almost-lost"—an "echo," "no one hears it"; a sign of its own passing and absence, and recounted once as memory, it keeps resurfacing and returning without materializing as sound throughout the narration: the child watches "it settling down" (254) and anticipates: "We are waiting for the scream" (260). And throughout, identification with her mother will haunt the child as she tries to incorporate the scream into her consciousness without being obliterated by it. A dressmaker (Miss Gurley) attempts to fit her mother into a purple gown during the sick woman's brief homecoming. But to be fitted, to remove her black garments, is too much for the bereaved who remains impacted in grief; mourning reproduces itself in the child even as she discovers the necessity of process and change, of donning the purple cloak of her own bishopic identity. Throughout, adults try to distract her, whisking her away from any possible "scene." But impending chaos and loss become more acutely sensed because of these measures. The scream, at one point, shades into the child's own shriek as she wakes up to a fire (268). Bishop points to her attempts—made deliberately autobiographical through the use of "I" in these moments—to extricate herself from the terrible reality of her mother's illness and from her own anxiety and fear:

> A door slams.
> A door opens. The voices begin again.
> I am struggling to free myself.
> Wait. Wait. No one is going to
> scream.
>
> (270)

The narrative makes the discontinuous, unpredictable flow of events a present tense—an ongoing process of dealing with absence. Bishop does not give us a "finished" product of memory, some crystallization of events, but instead shows the subjective re-creation of the past (a method to be addressed more fully in Chapter 5). The child wants to absent herself from the overwhelming grief, but Bishop's rendering of conditions in the present tense, as they are in the process of being pieced together, subverts such a desire.

As the "mortal" scream remains with the "slp" of the river, its "unexpected gurgle," Bishop realizes that she cannot be free from the knowledge of loss or the slipping of time. Words, time-laden, themselves embody displacement, so that when adults speak of "mourning," the child hears them saying "morning." Language becomes both the awakening to the experience of disruption and loss and the only way of managing it, of ushering in the new, from the basket of a recollected "sponge cake" (256), one of her mother's vestigial objects, handed between her grandmother and aunt, to the mental refrain and punctuational adjustments in another kind of cake, perversely humorous, sent to the asylum:

> Fruit, cake, Jordan almonds, a handkerchief with a tatted edge.
> Fruit. Cake. Wild-strawberry jam. A New Testament.
> A little bottle of scent from Hills' store, with a purple silk tassel fastened to the stopper.
> Fruit. Cake. "Selections from Tennyson." (272)

Bishop does not try to shut out the world through words, but allows them to bear the essential loss they in fact denote, a loss that, for Bishop, is always both personal and what we are all subject to in existing. "Five Flights Up" (*CP*, 181) will also illustrate how she alludes to loss but never fully particularizes it, ending rather weightily: "—Yesterday brought to today so lightly! / (A yesterday I find almost impossible to lift)." Loss appears not only as indications of her identifiable biographical traumas, but extends to "something" ever she has felt, an incommensurable loss that emerges in excess of any nameable lack.

Although Bishop tells us that her mother's almost material scream "hangs there forever" in the village and "unheard, in memory—in the past, in the present, and those years between," she suggests that the beatific sound of a blacksmith's hammer intercedes, almost as symbol and invitation to the craft of writing, to overlie her mother's horrific scream threatening to blot out or swallow up the child's identity. It is as if the blacksmith's "clang" permits her moments of recovery so she may forge ahead, but only intermittently, for the "pure note" seems itself to introduce or allow the scream:

> *Clang.*
> The pure note: pure and angelic.
> The dress was all wrong. She screamed.
> The child vanishes.
>
> (253)

The lines of this prose section are arranged as a poem's; without connectives, the events narrated become a series of dissociated events where the teller becomes distanced into third person, whose existence appears contingent upon an arbitrary and uncontrollable environment. Bishop's shifting in this story from first person to a vanishing third further underlines the way she must confess a decentered self, especially as it becomes shaped through language.

In interpreting the genre of the elegy, Peter Sacks reminds us that for mourners the successful acceptance of loss "requires a withdrawal of affection from the lost object and a subsequent reattachment of affection to some substitute for that object."[12] Perhaps the blacksmith's "note" can be read as a kind of substitution—but only if it is one that prefigures and marks further transmutation rather than any solid or static "object." The "pure note" cannot sustain her purely, free from the memory or anxious anticipation of the intrusive scream that so dominates Bishop's vision of the landscape that it becomes identified as "the pitch of [her] village"; what remains is space opened up by the scream: all her "notes" must refer and circle back to it as she instructs us to join her in the introductory paragraph: "Flick the lighting rod on top of the church steeple with your fingernail and you will hear it" (251). The rod divines how the past continues to live within Bishop's work; she reenacts her losses so that they can be endured: language is both the wound and the only way it can be addressed. In writing this breathtaking memoir, she turns to language for consolation but, immersed in human situation and desire, can never be fully satisfied with it. At least she cannot smugly pretend that language will stave off our frailties or make a fortress for the self; while her language mourns, it also reveals an identity less rigidly bounded—no antidote for grief, nevertheless a process for accommodating the existence of loss.

Bishop's vision and language, then, are molded by the events of loss. Children who experience the death of either parent at an early age suffer severely and carry the trauma of their loss into their adult lives. John Bowlby's notable three-volume study of the processes of attachment and loss support this claim and offer insight into Bishop's childhood scenario and her coming to terms with it.[13] According to Bowlby in his lecture "Childhood Mourning and its Implications," the premature loss of maternal care has, not surprisingly, an enormous unsettling impact upon the child even when the mother is substituted by another caretaker; often, as in the case of Bishop, the caretaker figure becomes a multiple and discontinuous one.[14] The child in such a situation is left with a less secure or unified sense of self.

What aggravates the loss of a parent is the child's inability to mourn fully. "Healthy" mourning generally divides into four necessary phases, even as they overlap or become repeated: the mourner first enters a state of numbness with some outbursts of distress or anger; then a phase of yearning and searching for the lost figure as if believing the deceased must still exist; next, a period of disorganization and despair; and then finally, a condition of acceptance and restructuring (89). Bowlby explains that the process of mourning for children is most likely to take a course that for adults is deemed pathological where "development of defensive processes is accelerated" (54) so that yearning for and reprimand of the lost one, both integral to the complete grieving process, are short-circuited and become unconscious; what will appear as acceptance is really numb detachment. The child, lacking the sense or illusion of a fully developed identity, appears unable to face directly the death of a figure she has been entirely dependent upon; for as Chodorow puts it in *The Reproduction of Mothering*, any separation from the mother at an early age "threatens not only anxiety at possible loss, but the infant's very sense of existence" (60).

Mourning, specifically childhood mourning, is relevant here not to construct a pathology out of Bishop's life, but to connect her process of writing with the process of confession and grieving. It makes sense that her fiction and life are pervious because hers is a language of enmeshment and loss. "In the Village" is one of Bishop's attempts to come to terms with her early losses; such losses shape a particular way of seeing the world, and as we have seen, the sign of loss becomes indivisible with the landscape. She puzzles, for example, over whether the horizon darkening is external or actually a coloring of "the rims of the eye." Such boundaries between biography and art, self and other, inside and outside (as between a child and its mother's body in the pre-Oedipal stage) interpenetrate, or are restlessly inverted, successively, as if in some improbable view-finder:

> Outside, along the matted eaves, painstakingly, sweetly, wasps go over and over a honeysuckle vine.
> Inside, the bellows creak. (253)

Grief is matted, must be gone over and over, and inside, life goes creaking on, "awful but cheerful" ("The Bight," *CP*, 60).

Painstakingly, "In the Village" depicts the numbness of grief and its vivification—the child's visual turning-aside from the drama of her mother's return and episodic outbursts toward the details of village life—from cow flops that are "fine dark-green and lacy and watery at the edges" (263) to candy, "humbugs," that "are brown, like brook water, but hard, and shaped like little twisted pillows" (267)—as if in looking she could make a series of miniatures or postcards, carefully rendered so as to hold back recognitions of loss that might overwhelm their serrated edges. Yet Bishop seems to remake a portrait of the artist, committed not to Eliotic distance and impersonality, but to the struggle and survival of consciousness with the loss that denotes it. The shadow of what is ignored—the scream and its absence—is cast upon everything the child perseverates upon with, paradoxically, an averted gaze. The central anguish invades and seeps into the peripheral. Her mother, not even named, though Miss Gurley the seamstress and Nate the blacksmith are, becomes metonymic with the scream. A minimal and conventional interaction with her mother further foregrounds the unreality and transitoriness of their relationship, while acknowledging that its very absence ensures its centrality:

> My two aunts come into the kitchen. She is with them, wearing the white cotton dress with black polka dots and the flat black velvet

bow at the neck. She comes and feeds me the rest of the porridge herself, smiling at me.

"Stand up now and let's see how tall you are," she tells me.

"Almost to your elbow," they say. "See how much she's grown."

"Almost."

"It's her hair."

Hands are on my head, pushing me down; I slide out from under them. Nelly is waiting for me in the yard, holding her nose just under in the watering trough. My stick waits against the door frame, clad in bark. (260–61)

The awaiting stick saves her from drowning as the mother becomes a suffo-cating figure to be escaped: the child's cow Nelly, "her nose just under," even possesses more reality, probably because with the animal the child can exert some control. Stunningly, Bishop makes no overt reference to her mother in published material before "In the Village," evading her both in life and in writing. Though she had been wrestling with autobiographical fragments for years and continues to struggle with the personal in her art, it is not until she finds herself in a relatively secure relationship with Lota that she can let her-self write explicitly and for publication about her loss, and it is only after her lover's death that she can write about all the other losses it resurrects. Simi-larly, if almost more striking, little mention is made of her dead father, the eternally-mourned-for by her mother, except as a memory called up and then immediately repressed: "A silver-framed photograph, quickly turned over" (255). Poignantly, among Bishop's papers investigating her genealogy lies a copy of a page from *Worcester Magazine*, with a column obituary for her father, "one of the ablest men among the contractors and builders who have made Worcester famous," "known throughout the trade as one of the most capable estimators in the structural world," who left Classical High School "to become time keeper in the business founded by his father."[15] Bishop must have felt the painful irony in her father's architectural expertise and job as timekeeper: her mother's and her own loss placing the idea of home and time, forever, in crisis.

After the encounters recorded in the story, Bishop never saw her mother again. And Bishop's story was published only after her mother had died. (For us, she remains shrouded as well in the asylum, her psyche mysteriously dis-missed as permanently insane, and her experience of loss undocumented ex-cept as it appears bound up in Bishop's writing.) Undoubtedly, "In the Village" allows an enormous release for Bishop, a space where she may confess her shame (she attempts to conceal the address of the parcels being sent by her grandmother to her mother in the asylum) and her longing for a more solid world (as represented by the blacksmith and his makings) along with the recognition and acceptance of impermanence and frailty. Of the address at the sanatorium she says "It will never come off," while almost everything else in the village, including the post office, which "sits on the side of the road like a package once delivered" (272), and "tilts a little, like Mealy's shop, and inside it looks as chewed as a horse's manger," is ready to be sent away or crumble. Assuredly, then, "In the Village" is cathartic, but language, the story discovers, also heightens her sense of painful loss through an articulation of it.

I agree with Patricia Yaeger in *Honey-Mad Women* that too much emphasis has been placed on the limitations imposed upon women in a language predominantly authored by males rather than upon the ways women may use language for their own pleasures and needs.[16] She alerts us to those "seriously playful, emancipatory strategies that women writers have invented to challenge and change the tradition" (20) and holds up "In the Village" as an example of one "way of theorizing woman's ability to unlimit her language" (123); for her, the story allegorizes the writer's coming into her own through a struggle with maternal and paternal poles. She schematizes: "'In the Village' tells the story of a pensive child who, to preserve herself and become a writer, turns from the uncontrolled, frightening, animal sounds made by her mother's body to the controllable articulations of a symbolic father. The heroine—who is Bishop herself as a little girl—finds solace in the craft of the paternal blacksmith whose laborious music resonates through the village of Bishop's childhood" (135).

As I have discussed, however, the blacksmith offers no real "solace," and if we too firmly connect Nate with "art" rescuing us from "life," we miss Bishop's purposeful depiction of him as Vulcan, a raw and uncivilized nature in a passage like the following: "Nate was there—Nate, wearing a long black leather apron over his trousers and bare chest, sweating hard, a black leather cap on top of dry, thick, black-and-gray curls, a black sooty face; iron filings, whiskers, and gold teeth, all together, and a smell of red-hot metal and horses' hoofs" (252–53). The child, it is true, takes pleasure in seeing discrete elements as "all together," a reality of intense interconnection and enmeshment, but such a vision does not erect a "symbolic father." Yaeger is herself dissatisfied with perceiving the paternal as saving the child from the immediacy and pain of the maternal as she writes: "'In the Village' is also a story about the hope of the paternal name. While Bishop seems to take refuge in the patronym, she actually uses the 'name of the father' to hold open the 'name of the mother' in a new way" (137). Yet Yaeger never clarifies what is meant by "a new way" so her earlier interpretation of the story, as discovery of relief through the paternal, appears to hold final sway. Finally, however, she argues that the maternal and paternal vocabularies intersect, allowing for the invocation—"Oh, beautiful sound, strike again!"—which closes the story to refer to both clang and scream, as "an impassioned apostrophe to the mother's voice which is gathered and cherished by language itself" (144). But even while "In the Village" savors language, such exultation in no way emancipates language from pain and loss, nor from the elements—air, water, fire, earth—invoked at the last page by both the elemental clang and scream, not to be severed (274).

If Yaeger sagely refuses to accept only negative readings of woman's power within discourse, too much emphasis can be placed likewise upon the liberation afforded women through their unique relation to language. The tendency among critics to read Chodorow's model of female psychological development, for instance, only in terms of its benefits, obfuscates the detriments that Chodorow also points to: the difficulty in maintaining autonomy and the terror of feeling too much fusion or connectivity with the world. While Bishop does celebrate boundary motility and permeability, she can only do so because she has been able to relive and encode her losses through a mourning process. Such a process does not demand that the paternal protect the maternal and allow it speech, as Yaeger might suggest. Instead, the feminine offers Bishop more ready access to the reexperiencing of an elemental or archaic loss through language.

What permits art and forging ahead is not erasure or transcendence but an acceptance of the "unexpected gurgle," of the permeating scream and the insistent frailty of all objects. We should not understate the role of Miss Gurley as a major figure for the writer's craft; the seamstress remains—more, I think, than the blacksmith—an alternate poet. Her work is a grammar of pleasurable integration and painful binding, "vegetation" and invention:

> Her house is littered with scraps of cloth and tissue-paper patterns, yellow, pinked, with holes in the shapes of A, B, C, and D in them, and numbers; and threads everywhere like a fine vegetation. She has a bosom full of needles with threads ready to pull out and make nests with. She sleeps in her thimble. A gray kitten once lay on the treadle of her sewing machine, where she rocked it as she

sewed, like a baby in a cradle, but it got hanged on the belt. Or did she make that up? But another gray-and-white one lies now by the arm of the machine, in imminent danger of being sewn into a turban. There is a table covered with laces and braids, embroidery silks, and cards of buttons of all colors—big ones for winter coats, small pearls, little glass ones delicious to suck. (258).

Embellishment insists that we return to all our resources, dangerous and delicious. When the child swallows a coin Miss Gurley gives her, she recognizes the alchemical necessity of "original" loss—it does not disappear but operates as source for further change and growth; preservation is just not possible and nothing safe from metamorphosis, as when she reflects: "I put my five-cent piece in my mouth for greater safety on the way home, and swallowed it. Months later, as far as I know, it is still in me, transmuting all its precious metal into my growing teeth and hair" (259). And so when the child "absconds" with one of her mother's embroidery tools and buries it "under the bleeding heart by the crab-apple tree," she celebrates the "stich-work" that will become her own, and recognizes the foreclosure of her mother's creativity, her "beautiful work" of a tablecloth left unfinished (257).

This theme of appearance and disappearance, or burial and resurrection circulates through "In the Village" (and will recur in my discussion of Freud's "fort-da," the main motif of the last section of this chapter). The process of recovering (a word that suggests both presence and absence) lost objects and reusing them—a process Sacks might refer to as substitution—dictates much of Bishop's poetic practice. She speaks for the changing and not the changeless, for the "old sunken fender of Malcolm McNeil's Ford . . . supposed to be a disgrace to us all" (273), drowning and transmuting; for "the clothes, crumbling postcards, broken china, things damaged and lost, sickened or destroyed, even the frail almost-lost scream" (247): these things she does not want mended; she wants them to speak their imperfection, their connection to those who loved them and to mortality, their exciting and dangerous immersion within the elements.

Mourning comes late, just as what we write will always be transmuted and follow behind what we experience—sometimes moments after, sometimes decades after. "In the Village" could only be written after her mother died, after an absence "alive forever." One can mourn a loss for as long as time lasts. Yet even as Bishop writes to enact loss, she can only do so by displacing what has been lost; language, for her, does not permit escape from loss but foregrounds it.

II

Through research into notebooks and letters unavailable before, David Kal-stone in *Becoming A Poet* braids the poet's life with her art, and goes beyond his earlier position in *Five Temperaments* where he ranked Bishop as nearly confessional: "What I have felt most moving about her work is the slowly emerging, careful acknowledgement of the autobiographical strength of her poems"; like Lowell and Merrill, she relies on "the most energetically op-posed uses of the resources of the past—and particularly of childhood."[17] Of all her commentators, Kalstone seems most aware of the almost indistin-guishable reciprocity of life and art in her poetics, of the way her work is above all else an expression of her temperament. He singles out "the sense of personal loss so often implied behind Bishop's observations" as an explana-tion of her passion for details and hawk's eye:

> Bishop lets us know that every detail is a boundary, not a Blakean mi-crocosm. Because of the limits they suggest, details vibrate with a meaning beyond mere physical presence. Landscapes meant to sound detached are really inner landscapes. They show an effort at reconsti-tuting the world as if it were in danger of being continually lost.(22)

But while this reading is sensitive to Bishop's spirit and her almost excessive awareness of boundaries, it nevertheless reflects an impulse like Jerome Mazzaro's to regard her writings as "stays against confusion."[18] Her "effort at reconstituting the world" does indicate, as Kalstone suggests, a fear that it will be lost, but not therefore, a desire for permanence or stasis; it celebrates an oscillation between constitution and deconstitution, form and formless-ness, gain and loss. A profound sense of death in life, the interplay between these forces, informs her vision—which prefers, therefore, those things that show boundaries as they quiver and waver, that show the mark and threat of death and dissolution forthrightly, even as they threaten the integrity of the self. This heterogeneity is a feminist and postmodern gesture; as Hélène Cixous's manifesto, "The Laugh of the Medusa," puts forth, women may write woman through an economy of openness and giving, a trespassing of

oppositional "couples," the Derridian third term of hymen or threshold unsettling binary oppositions, rejecting stasis and resolution.[19]

Perceiving the intertwining of Bishop's life and her writing, Thomas
Travisano contends that a traumatic childhood has led her "to seek out tenuous islands of sanity and permanence" in her work.[20] Apparently he also
seems to have taken up the "stay against confusion" argument as he connects
Bishop with Stevens—only to mistakenly distinguish them when he writes:
"Significantly, Bishop's emblem of art is motionless and hermetic—it is a fatal point of terminus, as Stevens's emblems of imagination rarely or never
are" (39). Travisano is thinking, in particular, of "The Imaginary Iceberg"
from North & South where the speaker protests, "We'd rather have the iceberg than the ship, / although it meant the end of travel." He sees the iceberg
as an artist figure who crafts cold solid shapes, who "cuts its facets from
within," but what makes the iceberg an attractive symbol for Bishop is not its
immobility or permanence but rather its dangerousness, movement, and
mystery—as an imperiled entity split between the visible and the immersed.

When Elizabeth Bishop published her translation in 1957 of The Diary of
Helena Morley, she confirmed an interest in a personal mode of writing (following as it does "In the Village") that acknowledges displacement and necessitates writing loss. Her poetry had by then been widely acclaimed, but she
found the diary significant and riveting enough to spend three years at work
upon it. As Robert Giroux notes in his introduction to The Collected Prose,
"she would offer her next book of poems only to the publisher of the diary"
(vii–viii). As a poet who lived and wrote as exile, Bishop translates the marginal: a half-child woman, a nonliterary figure, a Brazilian; she discovered
the diary as a traveler might the records of another traveler with, one imagines, an inevitably mixed sense of kinship and alienation; most likely, however, she saw in Helena's relatively secluded life reflections of her own
deprived Nova Scotia childhood. Helena Morley's diary rises up as testimony
to the art of losing, the work of mourning. A diary most vigorously documents an awareness of unavoidable loss: dating her pages, the diarist can
never forget that her writing and her self exist within time. A diary also seems
to be an especially feminine genre.[21] These attributes of diary writing are
closely allied since to be a woman writer in a patriarchal culture means to
feel loss keenly. Conditioned and excluded by a masculine discourse,
women turn to private and subjective mediums that give importance to those
domestic or common inspirations of daily life, locate the self as it is implicated in quotidian affairs, not as it fulfills some larger public or heroic ethos.
The diary appeals to Bishop as a "found object," a homemade artifact that

proffers a particularly feminine writing of self and loss. As inaugurating Bishop's serious work in translation, it also has special attractions—in highlighting the making of experience in memory as a kind of translation itself. Translation, where identity or preserving likeness is at stake with the inevitable difference that results from reading one word as another, seems the medium par excellence of inevitable metamorphosis, of recovery and loss.

Fifty-three years after Helena Morley concluded her diary, it is a sense of self as constituted by its delicate and inexorable relationships with others that leads her to reflect in the preface Bishop includes: "Happiness does not consist in worldly goods but in a peaceful home, in family affections, in a simple life without ambition—things that fortune cannot bring and often takes away" (x). These homely and lucid lines catalogue all those "things" Bishop either felt deprived of or purposely evaded through literal and imaginative travel. Tellingly, Bishop's next volume after the translation would be *Questions of Travel* (1965), which includes poems more obviously autobiographical than her previous work and "In the Village," the story written a decade earlier.

Helena Morley's world attracts Bishop through its simplicity and domesticity, yet it does not offer an escape into a more Edenic realm, into "the obverse of her own childhood" as Helen McNeil proposes.[22] Instead, it represents "a world of bitter poverty and isolation" (*Diary*, xxiv). The pristine Nova Scotia landscape evoked by "In the Village" startles with its "too dark, too blue skies" (251) and though it shimmers, in it the child must confront "an immense, sibilant, glistening isolation" (265). Helena's diary seems similarly inspired by a landscape of loss, and through it, Bishop mourns the losses of her own childhood. Helena may inhabit a close-knit community, but her private world is also intensely fragile and threatened. A pivotal moment in the diary is the death of Helena's grandmother, her central loved one throughout. Bishop's early losses made her bonding with her own grandmother (who died in 1931) both particularly frightening and significant. She frankly relates some of these details of her initiation to loss in "Primer Class" (a prose piece charting a primary encounter with language and geography):

> My grandmother had a glass eye, blue, almost like her other one, and this made her especially vulnerable and precious to me. My father was dead and my mother was away in a sanatorium. Until I was teased out of it, I used to ask Grandmother, when I said goodbye, to promise me not to die before I came home. (*CPr*, 6)

The glass eye alerts the virtually orphaned proto-poet to the cultured fragility of all things, and her grandmother becomes both fine artifact and fracturable being. (This self-mirroring image appears as she proposes again and again the never-to-be-used title *Grandmother's Glass Eye* for a volume of poetry).[23]

Helena's passion for confession recognizes loss and writing as inextricably connected, just as Bishop's prose works implicate the act of writing in self-revelation and an awareness of dissolution. Helena feels safe confiding her "weaknesses" to print "because only the paper is going to know" (56); Bishop's like admission of such imperfection imbues much of her work as when Lucy, an early character from "The Baptism" (1937) records diarylike her guilts and losses along with the flights of her imagination, as for instance:

> *'January 25th*: I felt very badly last night and cried a great deal. I thought how Mother always used to give me the best of everything because I was the smallest and I took it not thinking of my sisters. The lamp began to smoke. The smoke went right up to the ceiling and smelled very strong and sweet, like rose geranium.' (166–67)

Lucy is hauntingly akin to Helena, who craves her "castles in the air" (*Diary*, 78), and whose writing becomes a means of confessing outside a religious context and a way of coming to terms with, not an effort to terminate, insecure experience.

Helena's account conveys an intense awareness of death and of endearing idiosyncrasy and eccentric survival in the face of it. The character portraits in *The Diary* emerge, as Bishop suggests in her preface, as reminiscently Wordsworthian—figures made somehow grotesque by their losses and their commitment to thrive in spite of them. Conscious of her contribution as retrospective, Helena examines the present with the nostalgic sense of its already being past:

> Because I'm never too lazy to write, I'm going to write down here a story of the old days, for the future, as papa says. Who knows if in the future there won't be many more inventions than there are today? José Rabelo spends his time weighing vultures on the scales, in order to invent a flying-machine. Wouldn't that be wonderful! Sometimes I feel envious when I see the vultures soaring up so high. How would it be if I could turn into a vulture? It would be awfully funny. But it would be better to discover something so that people wouldn't die. (78)

Flights from death occupy Helena. As do flights into self-destructiveness and both have personal relevance for Bishop. Helena speaks of "a very funny drunken relative" who whenever he has any money spends it on drink but vainly protests, "If I had enough will-power not to drink, I'd look after you and him and everyone else" (215). Plagued by alcoholism herself, Bishop often thinks about her Uncle Arthur in a way that resembles Helena's perspective on her relative; she writes to Lowell, for instance, when she is contemplating her story on Artie: "He became the best fly fisherman in the country but also the village drunk."[24] Ultimately, writing becomes, increasingly, a way to mourn losses; to recognize "the old days" is not to evade but to raise the ongoing fact of mortality.

Another striking Wordsworthian or prototypical Bishopian figure in the diary is Parentinho: "Ever since I've known him he's been skinny, with such an old, greenish frock-coat, his head lost under a hard hat much too big for him, enormous shoes that would each hold two feet, walking twirling his cane down the capistrana in the afternoons" (229). He appears to cope with his destitution by devotion to a sister "whom no one's ever seen, who never leaves the house" (220). (Claustrophobic women demand Bishop's interest, as we shall see.) They give each other the same unspent silver piece as an interchangeable birthday present wrapped up with a verse:

> Accept the little
> Love can offer.
> If I had more,
> More I'd proffer.
> (*Diary*, 229–30)

This sounds strikingly in tone like Bishop's "Poem," which asks only "the little that we get for free," that requires less to be more, deficiency to become sufficiency. Love, or what we have of it, along with our perishable writings, must suffice to cope with impinging time and loss. The death of Helena's grandmother comes as the climactic low-point in her narrative; religious faith withers in the presence of an irredeemable loss: "I don't know why God let me know grandma! I might have been so happy, because my parents are both strong and healthy, if I'd never known her. If only she'd died when I was little the way the other one did!" (224). Helena ends the diary feeling that her grandmother, though dead, still somehow actively influences, through memory, her family's fortune; she watches over them: only the human and its relationships mourned, not the godly, survives, and it does so through her writing.

"Memories of Uncle Neddy" (1977), the most recent piece in *The Collected Prose* (a memoir that reveals, like her translation of the diary, the personal tenor of her work), continues to make sense of her "imaginary iceberg," those aesthetic priorities that dismantle oppositions and show life as it is shot through and scripted with death. The story recalls her uncle's fascination (and her own) with navigations and divagations, and in this piece, with the sinking of the *Titanic* in particular. The fascination seems, in part, due to some family facts: in an autobiographical sketch written in 1961, she records that her "great-grandfather, was master-owner of a bark in the West Indies trade. He also wrote a small text book on navigation. He was lost at sea, with all hands, off Sable Island in a famous storm in which many ships went down." Such a paradoxical combination of telling life history—the text book and the sinking, the authorial control and the loss: these elements infuse all her autobiographic excursions. She herself had visited Sable Island in 1943.[25] Along with *"Inglesby's [sic] Legends, Home Medicine,* Emerson's *Essays,"* her uncle, she tells us, possessed "three different books about [the *Titanic*], and in the dining room, facing his place at the table, hung a chromograph of the ship going down: the iceberg, the rising steam, people struggling in the water, everything, in full color" (245–46). This chromograph approximates Bishop's sense of art—life at its most intense pitch, when it is about to be lost. She half-guiltily confesses her excitement while surveying the *Titanic* volumes: "I could scarcely wait to take [them] out— one very big and heavy, red, with gilt trimmings—and look at the terrifying pictures one more time" (246). "Actual photographs" (246) and imagined delineations need not be too finely divided under the spell of the child's own vision, which prefers the instability of adventuring to a Sable Island, and the potential failures in navigation, to the uneventful movement in a ship's confinement.

Bishop's poetics make visible and palpable the presence of mortality and the self as inextricably bound up in the soot and mould of living, the loss her books and writing denote:

> Except for the fact that they give me asthma, I am very fond of molds and mildews. I love the dry-looking, gray-green dust, like bloom on fruit, to begin with, that suddenly appears here on the soles of shoes in the closet, on the backs of all the black books, or the darkest ones, in the bookcase. And I love the black shadow, like the finest soot, that sud-

denly shows up, slyly, on white bread, or white walls. The molds on food go wild in just a day or two, and in a hot, wet spell like this, a tiny jungle, green, chartreuse, and magenta, may start up in a corner of the bathroom. That gray-green bloom or that shadow of fine soot, is just enough to serve as a hint of morbidity, attractive morbidity— although perhaps mortality is a better word. The gray-green suggests life, the sooty shadow—although living, too—death and dying. (228)

These reflections and the story itself are occasioned by the recent arrival in her Rio home of pictures of her Uncle Neddy, and of his sister, Bishop's mother. She speaks of his reproduction as if it were a present animated embodiment of him:

> And Uncle Neddy, that is, my Uncle Edward, is *here*. Into this wildly foreign and, to him, exotic setting, Uncle Neddy has just come back, from the framer's. He leans slightly, silently backwards against the damp-stained pale-yellow wall, looking quite cheerfully into the eyes of whoever happens to look at him—including the cat's, who investigated him just now. (228)

The story concludes with a transgression of time and space; not without pleasure, she will have to "watch out for the mildew that inevitably forms on old canvases in the rainy season" (250), while her uncle will cross into geography he could not enter while in the flesh. Even as this story seems primarily concerned with Bishop's relationship to a male figure, it offers a vision of transgression and the possibility of crossing boundaries akin to those "more permeable ego boundaries" assigned to feminine identity; such a vision proposes an unsettled subjectivity, springing from her topographical displacements between Nova Scotia and Brazil, along with their essential interconnection in an expansive, exfoliating self.

For Bishop, art and the experiencing consciousness cannot be separated. Art is a dynamic process, a concourse. We do not move into the object, finding rest for our consciousness within permanent forms or objects, but negotiate our way within the blurring of these two arenas. An impulse kindred to her translation of Helena Morley's voice can be seen in her attention to artifacts generally overlooked or frowned upon as homey or of "low quality." Robert Dale Parker dismisses, unfairly I think, "Large Bad Picture" with the weak assumption that it lacks a real poetic subject.[26] Bishop does not write about her uncle's paintings because she thinks them flawless masterpieces, but takes them up as would a collagist: they are the "found objects" that refer to the life lived and being lived and are not set up as reified or perfected forms.

The later "Poem" in *Geography III* (*CP*, 176 – 77) takes another of her uncle's paintings as its subject and places it on a par with her own present activity of writing. As she watches the painting she is transported to her uncle's imagined landscape, which intersects with her own memory of that Nova Scotian world, until the two become indistinguishable. Her "union" with her uncle transgresses "mortality" as much as it is constituted by it:

> Our visions coincided—"visions" is
> too serious a word—our looks, two looks:
> art "copying from life" and life itself,
> life and the memory of it so compressed
> they've turned into each other. Which is
>   which?
> Life and the memory of it so cramped,
> dim, on a piece of Bristol board,
> dim, but how live, how touching in detail
> —the little that we get for free,
> the little of our earthly trust. Not much.
> About the size of our abidance
> along with theirs: the munching cows,
> the iris, crisp and shivering, the water
> still standing from spring freshets,
> the yet-to-be-dismantled elms, the geese.

What abides is the live details of our memories—the extra funding allowed by "our earthly trust." With the present progressives of continued activity, the painting is moving and living but not in the same way Keats's Grecian urn is: "the yet-to-be-dismantled" will not crystallize upon the Bristol but participates with the viewer in memory and time. What coincides, ultimately, is her experience of death where "life and the memory of it so cramped," as if coffined, come into sudden lucid view. In mourning her uncle and the world he inhabited, she identifies with the process of dying and recognizes her own artistic mortality.

"Gwendolyn" (1953) predates much of the prose work (including Helena's diary) I have been alluding to but underlines this way of reading Bishop's poetics as hinging upon the active experience of loss, which does not disappear with the writing of it. A heightened consciousness of death allows her to

write that she had always "of course" been "particularly interested in children's graves" (222). Bishop confronts mortality, not as a purely individual
plot, but as an invitation to record family history and relations, our "earthly
trust" or restitution for the loss of a transcendental account. The story, which
focuses upon the death of a childhood friend, begins with the poet as a child,
ill and confined to bed yet amused by her grandmother's "crazy quilt," as the
child of "In the Village" is drawn to Miss Gurley's house of scraps and patterns. Encoded in the quilt's heterogeneous "irregularly shaped pieces" is the
passage of time, and those relationships that make it up:

> My grandmother had made it long before, when such quilts had been
> a fad in the little Nova Scotian village where we lived. She had col-
> lected small, irregularly shaped pieces of silk or velvet of all colors
> and got all her lady and gentleman friends to write their names on
> them in pencil—their names, and sometimes a date or word or two
> as well. Then she had gone over the writing in chain stitch with silks
> of different colors, and then put the whole thing together on maroon
> flannel, with feather-stitching joining the pieces. I could read well
> enough to make out the names of people I knew, and then my grand-
> mother would sometimes tell me that that particular piece of silk
> came from Mrs. So-and-So's "going away" dress, forty years ago, or
> that that was from a necktie of one of her brothers, since dead and
> buried in London, or that that was from India, brought back by an-
> other brother, who was a missionary. (214–15)

The quilt conjures up the homemade yet dark character of Bishop's art—
made up of the very losses or "cut pieces" it holds together. The "'going away'
dress" reminds us of her mother's irremovable mourning dress; the seamstress of that story inevitably sews everything together with her chain-stitch
machine, including a kitten, we recall. Binding and discontinuous, legible
and "crazy," the quilt accommodates loss without denying or refuting it, and
inscribes the self only as it exists in the irregular patchwork of relationship
and temporality, as did Helena Morley's diary.

The self in this story finds coincident the knowledge of dying with gender
identity, pointing as does "In the Waiting Room," to female sexuality as simultaneously repulsive and alluring. The narrator of "Gwendolyn," presumably the young Bishop, is to spend the night in bed with the dying child and
confesses: "I was so overwrought with the novelty of this that it took me a
long time to get ready for bed" (220). Hesitation, anxiety, and excitement

about intimacy involve an awareness of impending death, Bishop wants us to know; instead of getting into bed, the narrator picks up and examines the sick girl's dirty underclothes, which "shocked [her] so deeply" (220); the lace drawers are apparently evidence of Gwendolyn's gender and her imperfection.

One of Bishop's earliest prose efforts, "The Baptism" (1937), further binds loss with ambivalence over gender and unstable identity. As with Helena's diary, this story foregrounds those difficulties connected with a particularly feminine self, with the struggle for both relationship and autonomy. It depicts a community comparable to the Nova Scotia of "In the Village" or the Diamantina of Morley's diary—brittle and ephemeral. Three orphaned sisters live a minimal and imperiled existence. Confined by "snow which grew too deep," those women's lives are claustrophobic, overwhelmed by their own dependence upon one another. As the opening paragraph so perfectly and simply exposes, they are held together as if in fluid, vulnerably, on a mobile rock:

> It was November. They bent in the twilight like sea plants, around their little dark center table hung with a cloth like a seaweed-covered rock. It seemed as if a draft might sway them all, perceptibly. (159)

Later the snow will rise so high, it will seem "as if they inhabited a sinking ship" (163). The absence of parents goes unexplained, but intrusive: Lucy records in her diary—in language much like Helena Morley's—of her lost mother: "I felt very badly last night and cried a great deal. I thought how Mother always used to give me the best of everything" (166); the absence of any prominent male figure is also quite visible. A father appears only through his traces: the travel books, including *Wonders of the World*, he left behind. As do the other books the sisters read and reread—*David Copperfield* and *The Deerslayer*, texts about the orphaned and the pioneering, about the need to make do and deal with rough inclement circumstances—the travelogues take them, especially Lucy, imaginatively outside their enclosed world.

Through Lucy, Bishop confronts her own multiple anxieties: her mother's madness, potentially her own, and her fear that bonding means either bondage or abandonment. Lucy, like the child Bishop, peruses the wonders of exotic lands, dreams of escape, while Flora and Emma fear she will leave them. Complex and mixed, Lucy not only adumbrates Bishop's impulse to travel and rebel; she also embodies what Bishop ultimately must leave behind, the Baptist religion, her mother, and the Nova Scotia village. The story, then, in part deals with genealogical pressures and endowments. Noted in the earlier autobiographical sketch already cited are her mother's family's "taste for wandering" as well as this bit of relevant history: "Two great-uncles were Baptist missionaries in India and one of them wrote the first novel to be written in Telegu—besides other works. A third, at the age of fourteen, started painting portraits of sailing ships for the ship-builders then flourishing in Nova Scotia." The appearance in the story of a missionary from India, Miss Gillespie, harkens back to those wandering uncles. Lucy's interest in the woman and her subsequent conversion to the Baptist faith cause her Presbyterian sisters great alarm, and reveal Bishop's own ambivalence toward this character. In her conversion, Lucy attempts to move outside the entrapping domesticity of her sisters, but in the process becomes more unbalanced, subject to a vertigo that will possess not a few of Bishop's figures who discover—in their wandering—the slipperiness of their identity, the frailty of their autonomy.

> Once when Lucy went out to get wood from the woodshed she didn't come back for fifteen minutes. Emma, suddenly realizing how long it had been, ran outside. Lucy, with no coat or shawl, stood holding on to the side of the house. She was staring at the blinding dazzle the sun made on the ice glaze over the next field. (164)

No houses are stable in Bishop's world, and it is intentionally not clear here whether Lucy is holding on to the house because she fears that it will drift away or because she feels that she might. The sun and ice conspire for this protovisionary bent within an unsteady landscape.

In her struggle for continuity and stability, Lucy keeps "a record of her spiritual progress" in a *Jumbo Scribbler* (another endearing conflation of the "high" and "low"); through her entries, written as a kind of survival digest, we watch her become more and more overtaken by vague guilt and by hallucinations of some menacing "face moving towards [her]" (165). Lucy's conversion, with the feeling of sinfulness that comes with it for her, ultimately kills her because it requires "the use of total immersion" (166). After her baptism, Lucy comes down with a fever and hallucinates the face of God coming "into the kitchen," and she ends up running toward the stove screaming (169). Kitchens and stoves, associated with domestic safety, turn dangerous as they do in the highly personal "Sestina" of *Questions* where "small hard tears / dance like mad on the hot black stove" (123). In that poem the very act of writing a sestina is implicated in disclosing the experience of loss, not to be separated from the losing and reusing of the same six nouns, a method heightened in the villanelle, "One Art" (to be discussed in detail in the closing section of this chapter).

No middle ground exists in this story: Lucy appears to have choices, but they turn out to be the same one. Her sisters represent a stifling dependency, but retreat from them signals immersion, suffocation within her own delusions. Once so enchanted by travel, Lucy will say to Flora near the end, "What does it matter where the road goes?" (167). Flora and Emma potentially stand in for the two maternal aunts in whose care Bishop was partly placed in Nova Scotia. As Bishop was much more exposed to the feminine than the masculine in her upbringing, Nancy Chodorow's paradigm of mother-daughter relationship in this context becomes evocative.

> The patterns of fusion, projection, narcissistic extension, and denial of separateness . . . are more likely to happen in early mother-daughter relationships than in those of mothers and sons. . . . [T]he mother does not recognize or denies the existence of the daughter as a separate person, and the daughter herself then comes not to recognize, or to have difficulty recognizing, herself as a separate person. She experiences herself, rather, as a continuation or extension of . . . her mother in particular, and later of the world in general. (*Reproduction of Mothering*, 103)

Because of the fusion of identities that can occur in the mother-daughter relationship, "there is a tendency in women toward boundary confusion and a lack of sense of separateness from the world." Though most women, ultimately, gain "ego boundaries," Chodorow argues, "separation and individuation remain particularly female developmental issues" (110). While Chodorow does not think that children necessarily suffer from being parented by multiple figures, the lack of a primary caretaker as a result of a crisis of death or institutionalization destabilizes the child's development, and escalates the "boundary confusion" already present. Bishop's displacement among different caretakers and homes along with the lack of a father promotes senses of self and gender less rigidly bounded.

"The Baptism" is early in Bishop's career, and she has not seen, I think, any of the advantages of immersion or enmeshment and of a more fluid, multiple self. Later, in the poem "At the Fishhouses," Bishop will call herself "a believer in total immersion"; she, like her Lucy, will sing as a favorite militant hymn, "A Mighty Fortress," but with more irony. Homelessness and expatriation have their bonuses. "The House founded on the Rock" is as unrealistic as it is entrapping ("The Baptism," 165). While an exile in Brazil, Bishop asserts a poetic independence, sets up a provisional self positioned "outside" her homeland, but also "inside" a community, one she has fashioned for herself. Throughout her writings, Bishop experiments with her sense of self split by the need to be connected and dependent and the desire to be isolated and independent; both the urgency within her to travel, to keep moving, and the desire to plant stakes, stay in one place, make an environment suitable for an alterable self. The child of "In the Village," Helena Morley, Gwendolyn, Lucy—all seem deliberately gendered figures. Bishop connects the feminine and her early experience of loss through them and is able to write a self-in-process, not tied to either pole of home or travel, male or female, artifice or nature.

III

Though personal loss is often not explicitly confronted in Bishop's poems, it pervades them. Readers of Bishop frequently turn to "One Art" in *Geography III* as distinctively Bishopian in its restraint, formality, classicism. Yet this poem deals openly with loss and has been rightly called by J. D. McClatchy "painfully autobiographical."[27] The formal demands of the villanelle keep "squads of undisciplined emotion" from overwhelming the poem, while James Merrill has spoken of "One Art" as resuscitating the villanelle in that its "key lines seem merely to approximate themselves, and the form, awakened by a kiss, simply toddles off to a new stage in its life, under the proud eye of Mother, or the Muse."[28] Personal expression makes the form looser, more pliant and intimate. In fact, Bishop uses form frequently, and especially here, to show its arbitrariness, its attractive flimsiness. Bishop claims that she had not been able to write a villanelle before but that "One Art," possessing a somewhat diaristic dating through its metrics and tone, "was like writing a letter."[29] It is a form tellingly imitative of the obsessional behavior of mourners with their need for repetition and ritual as resistance to "moving on" and their inevitable search for substitutions.

We are ultimately left not with control but with the unresolved tension between mastery and a world that refuses to be mastered; we are left with language. Restraint is tense hilarity here:

—Even losing you (the joking voice, a gesture
I love) I shan't have lied. It's evident
the art of losing's not too hard to master
though it may look like (*Write* it!) like disaster.

The imperative self-prompt "(*Write* it!)" conveys the immense energy needed
to utter the last word of "disaster." From the beginning, Bishop presents "the
art of losing" as perverse rejection of the desire to win. In the poem's alternating rhyme of "master" with "disaster," disaster has the last word. "The art of
losing isn't hard to master" is true because losing is all we do. The poem reveals a struggle for mastery that will never be gained. We can only make loss
into therapeutic play. One does try to master loss, but Bishop recommends
that we recognize our powerlessness and play with the conditions of loss: the
blurring and splitting of presence and absence, being and nonbeing.

Bishop's "art of losing" resembles what Freud in *Beyond the Pleasure Principle* calls the rule of "fort-da" (gone / there), after a game his grandson constructed in his mother's absence:

> The child had a wooden reel with a piece of string tied round it. It
> never occurred to him to pull it along the floor behind him, for in-
> stance, and play at its being a carriage. What he did was to hold the
> reel by the string and very skillfully throw it over the edge of his cur-
> tained cot, so that it disappeared into it, at the same time uttering the
> expressive "o-o-o-o." He then pulled the reel out of the cot again by
> the string and hailed its reappearance with a joyful "da" ("there").
> This, then, was the complete game—disappearance and return.[30]

At first perplexed by an impulse seemingly opposed to the pleasure principle,
by a symbolic repetition of the distressing experience of the mother's departure, Freud offers two explanations for the child's apparent gratification in
this loss game.

> At the outset he was in a passive situation—he was overpowered by
> the experience; but, by repeating it, unpleasurable though it was, as
> a game, he took on an active part. These efforts might be put down to
> an instinct for mastery acting independently of whether the (repeated)
> memory were in itself pleasurable or not. But still another interpreta-
> tion may be attempted. Throwing away the object so that it was
> "gone" might satisfy an impulse of the child's, which was suppressed

> in his actual life, to revenge himself on his mother for going away
> from him. In that case it would have a defiant meaning: "All right,
> then, go away! I don't need you. I'm sending you away myself." (10)

Freud finally hands over to a "system of aesthetics" (17) the consideration of
how pleasure can come from repeating traumatic moments of dissatisfaction.
The child's rendering of loss in symbolic terms with the accompanying ver-
balization "fort-da" suggests that loss marks entry into language, as language
marks entry into the awareness of the presence of absence. The shifting between such appearance and disappearance, as we have seen, becomes quite
vivid through abruptly sequential sentences of "In the Village":

> First, she had come home, with her child. Then she had gone away
> again, alone, and left the child. Then she had come home. Then she
> had gone away again, with her sister; and now she was home again.

In a sense, Bishop practices the "instinctual renunciation" Freud points to in
her poem not only by making loss an intention and active practice (as she
does by swallowing the coins and burying the needles in the story) but by losing and recuperating words in rhyme. Poetry can imitate through refrain the
experience of "fort-da."

The poet's "one art" handles plural loss; but the expansion of this phrase
to include so much validates such activity as the one and only one possible—
with death as the ultimate project to be undertaken even as it is postponed
within language. The middle line endings weave together to spell ultimate
"evident" loss—"intent" / "spent," "meant" / "went": the other side of will and
choice must always be loss of control, abandon, renunciation. Bishop instructs us: "Lose something every day," and in the third stanza, "Then practice losing farther, losing faster." The tercets logically build up from small
(keys) to big (continent) with demonic precision and momentum. We are re-
assured by the second stanza that mastery will come to the novice in time,
that we will develop the ability to "[a]ccept the fluster." Yet the items lost
become increasingly personal with her "mother's watch" at the center, deliberately at the beginning of a line as if to skip over it with a distracting excla-
mation, one that further heightens the way the poem presents a consciousness in process:

> I lost my mother's watch. And look! my last, or
> next-to-last, of three loved houses went.
> The art of losing isn't hard to master.

Still a potentially "last" or "yet-to-be-dismantled" house remains for us to see slip away from the poet, but there will always, one senses, be a further house, the never-to-be-secure home of her childhood that must be continually re-figured, the child of "Sestina" drawing yet "another inscrutable house." As we move forward, we also step backwards. The watch stands in for her mother's absence and loss—a timekeeper that reflects its inability to "keep" time. Embedded in the loss of the watch is also the loss of her mother's care-taking and vigilance, as well as her father's position as timekeeper.

In the penultimate stanza, she leaps from the moment of initial loss:

> I lost two cities, lovely ones. And, vaster,
> some realms I owned, two rivers, a continent.
> I miss them, but it wasn't a disaster.

She can afford to let go of these "realms" because her imagination can pro-vide new ones. She travels from one tercet to the next, pushing the poem in opposing directions with rhyme. Crisis occurs just when we might expect "mastery." Even within lines there emerges the desire for mastery along with its inevitable breakdown. Enjambed lines in all stanzas but the next to last in-dicate slippage. A complete sentence occupies only part of a line in stanzas 2, 4, and 5 and so disintegrates any effect of finality or surety. Movement in time—"losing farther, losing faster"—is loss, and Bishop reinforces her theme of displacement with "farther" liminally haunted by "father."

Bishop's characteristic dash emphasizes breakage and propels us forward into the last enjambed four lines:

> —Even losing you (the joking voice, a gesture
> I love) I shan't have lied. It's evident
> the art of losing's not too hard to master
> though it may look like (*Write* it!) like disaster.

Loss and love are significantly enjambed with the first two lines of this final stanza, but they not only confess how loss and love are bound, but give con-tinuing evidence of "I love)," risked with a solitary parenthesis in the line. The most intimate words are not deemphasized by being parenthesized but blaze out as a temporary withholding, as her most prominent resistance to and acceptance of losing. We no longer have an object such as the timepiece standing in for a person but an evanescent voice and gesture, silhouette and trace. There appears a breakdown also in the certainty of the declaration

"The art of losing isn't hard to master" by the addition of "not too hard" and
an admission of strain with the fiercely whispered "(*Write* it!)" between the
stuttered double "like." Her "write it" is another way of saying "don't lose it."
But disaster exceeds troping. Writing reveals a doubleness: Bishop wants language to gain mastery, but writing brings us back to the recognition of displacement and loss. Rhyming, dashing, parenthesizing, joking—all these
are activities meant to contain but in emphatic practice remind only how
such strategies finally fail. They can lead to renunciation not by making "disaster" into reified form but by accepting it as process and reenactment.

The "work of mourning," explains Freud, involves a gradual withdrawal of
investment from a loved and lost object but against such a necessity "a struggle of course arises—as may be universally observed that man never willingly
abandons a libido position, not even when a substitute is already beckoning
to him."[31] Bishop's art is one that gives up fixed positions. We can now
understand, perhaps, how "One Art" is only seemingly far removed from *The
Diary* or "In the Village": these texts demonstrate as well, as we have seen,
Bishop's concern with absence as it participates in writing. Language insists
upon presence but always keeps loss in sight through its movement; ultimately it cannot hold back the fluid self and reminds us of the space left between us and our words.

Elaborating upon Freud's "fort-da," which brings language and loss together, Jacques Lacan asserts that the experience of primal loss and the
emergence of identity coincide in language. An originary unrelocatable moment, removing us from a state of undifferentiated wholeness with our
mothers, commits us to continuous desire and translates us into the symbolic
order of language and law. We become bound up in the paradoxical condition that "is neither the appetite for satisfaction, nor the demand for love, but
the difference that results from the subtraction of the first from the second,
the phenomenon of their splitting"; our "demand for love," the articulation
of it, then, puts us forever out of love's reach.[32] Coming to see and say ourselves outside of the maternal body, we call ourselves others and feel the loss
that this entails.

Since our identity, our assertion of "I," can only be constituted through
language, according to Lacan, we see ourselves as whole or unified subjectivities only through the "function of méconnaissance" most notable in the mirror stage when the child sees its fragmented drives and motor impulses
duplicated as a whole—but a whole that rests on the split or chasm necessi-
tated by mirroring; the "méconnaissance" occurs as "form situates the agency
of the ego, before its social determination, in a fictional direction" and offers

a gestalt, or "an exteriority in which this form . . . is certainly more constitu-
ent than constituted" and that "symbolizes the mental permanence of the I,
at the same time as it prefigures its alienating destination."[33] Language, thus,
aids us in believing the false vision of wholeness even as it shows such a vision to be an oversight. Consciousness attempts to veil over the power of the
signifier over the signified, "the incessant sliding of the signified under the
signifier" that represents the operation of the unconscious.[34] Poems that reflect such ontological uneasiness will appear from Bishop's first volume on,
with its "Gentleman of Shalott" presenting a character divided by a shifting,
unstable mirror, living within the breach "of constant re-adjustment," within
perpetual yet "exhilarating" uncertainty and halfness (CP, 9). Such a poem
almost literalizes the Lacanian fracturing of the self.

Lacan, as does Bishop, always points us back to our language. Dreams rely
upon the functions in language of metonymy and metaphor, covered over in
waking consciousness to conceal fissure. Both metaphor and metonymy reveal that we cannot escape an endless chain of signifiers. Metaphor corresponds to "condensation," the superimposition of one signifier upon another:
"*One word for another*, that is the formula for metaphor"; metonymy, on the
other hand, reflects "displacement," the continual "veering off of signification," the "eternally stretching forth towards the *desire for something else*"
("Agency," 156), much like the tireless and timely parataxis another early
poem "Over 2,000 Illustrations and a Complete Concordance" discovers in
its own text and the childhood book it describes with "Everything only connected by 'and' and 'and'" (58).

According to Lacan's psycholinguistic model, we are constituted by a language that deconstitutes us, where "no signification can be sustained other
than by reference to another signification" (150): subjectivity is always then,
at risk, so precarious that it becomes appropriate to say: "I think where I am
not, therefore I am where I do not think" (166). The entry into the symbolic
through the Oedipal event inaugurates a gendered subject while the desire
for wholeness exists in excess of possible satisfaction: this desire for completion will be thwarted by the subject's fragmentation within language. The
phallus comes to stand for that moment of rupture from the imaginary dy-
adic relation with the mother, where one does not feel desire for the Other,
because the Other is yet the self, or not other, without limit or demarcation.
Lacan's definition of demand is relevant in showing the gap that persists between the subject's need and demand; this gap constitutes desire, so that
"[d]emand constitutes the Other as already possessing the *privilege* of satisfying needs, that is to say, the power of depriving them of that alone by

which they are satisfied"; this explains the "unconditional element of the demand," which must look beyond itself to some fictive "'absolute' condition,"
and it is from such an absence, "the residue of an obliteration" that "the
power of pure loss emerges," which cannot, in any last analysis, be singu-
larized or pinpointed ("Signification," 287).

Such an understanding of language and identity as grounded in loss is central to Bishop's feminist attempt to undo fixed or unitary identity. Jacqueline
Rose's introduction to Lacan's essays makes clear his acknowledgment that
the phallus is made only to *figure* by anatomy and signals its own "pretence
to meaning," and the impossibility of satisfying desire; sexual identity is only
"enjoined" upon the individual through entrance into language.[35] Because of
the arbitrary element in gender division, Rose sees implicit in Lacan's argument the possibility that "anyone can cross over and inscribe themselves on
the opposite side from that which they are anatomically destined" (49). Lacan's project, in this light, encourages boundary transgression, especially if
we consider his belief that analysis should not allow an individual to mask
over the precariousness of her or his identity.

In the Lacanian economy, woman becomes, however, "other." As Rose
exposes, the phallus is by no means unproblematically privileged, for it is
"from the Other that the phallus seeks authority and is refused," but even as
woman is subversive Other, Rose does not think females have "access to a
different strata of language" (as does Yaeger, for example, in her discussion of
"In the Village"): there is no escape from the Law of the Father (55). However, as Lacan does not differentiate enough the breakage of mother-child
dyad in terms of the child's gender, he misses the distinct relationship that
persists between mother and daughter. The female may indeed, come to the
symbolic via an alternate route—her language a different relation to loss.
For the girl child, the ruptured primordial relationship may appear less final,
and her gender role less reified than the boy's in his identification with his
father, as Chodorow has described. Rose objects to Chodorow's apparent assumption of a unified identity (37), yet Chodorow acknowledges gender position as social construction that makes intrasubjective shifting more available
to women; in his emphasis on lack and loss, Lacan does not acknowledge *relation* (as do both Chodorow and Bishop), primarily because his androcen-
tric perspective posits woman as the eternal Other.

If language is joined inseparably with the recognition of loss, females
come to that language doubly exiled from the dominant sign system. Nevertheless, identification with the mother makes for a potentially more pluralis-
tic and multiple self. Julia Kristeva, for instance, rereads Lacan and posits a

"questionable subject in process"[36] that exists through the fluctuation between the poles of the semiotic (associated with the unconscious, the maternal, the disruptive) and the symbolic (responsible for the rational, the
paternal, the systematic). She considers such movement "poetic language,"
which through its "signifying operations, is an unsettling process—when not
an outright destruction—of the identity of meaning and the speaking subject," and links the feminine with poetry, or more precisely, with the disruption it produces. While she does not explicitly catalogue her writing as
feminist or, for the most part, treat women writers, Kristeva tellingly con-
cedes: "It is probably necessary to be a woman . . . not to renounce theoretical reason but to compel it to increase its power by giving it an object beyond
its limits" (146).

Bishop's poems subvert the very forms—not in themselves radical or
"avant-garde"—they employ. "One Art," specifically, casts itself either forward or backward: testing the limits of rational control, revealing the subject
unsettled within flux; it literalizes displacement through its calling up of and
discarding of objects. While "One Art" appears almost hyperrational, it remains consistent with Bishop's earlier more explicit surrealism—the Paris
poems "Sleeping on the Ceiling," "Sleeping Standing Up," and "Paris, 7
A.M.," to name the most striking—which openly affronts reason and logic,
manipulating dream symbols in incongruously neat stanzas, to disorient and
to trouble. We come upon form, yet cannot locate or settle into a "subject."
Bishop wrote at least seventeen drafts of "One Art" before she considered it
written.[37] Not surprisingly, the act of writing is a focal concern of the poem,
as becoming an artist is in the story "In the Village." Earlier drafts of the
poem show her struggling with the crucial final stanza where phrases such as
"Say it," "Oh, go on, write it!" recur as she tries to allow herself to articulate
"disaster." Draft 2 even has the tentative entitlement: "(Why not just write
'disaster'?)," protected within a parenthesis. The stilted archaism of "shan't"
reveals the essential feebleness involved in the final version's assertion "I
shan't have lied." In some of the telling drafts, she simply admits "all that I
write is false. I'm writing lies now. It's quite evident"—with false crossed off.
Writing may tempt us into lies, but it also shows us up. It is only in the process of "writing it" that Bishop can face the catastrophic losing of a love,
though the drafts do not foresee surviving such an event: the first one trails
off with the impossible maxim, "He who loseth his life, etc.—but he who /
loses his love—never, no never never never never again—" (draft 1).

As Lorrie Goldensohn acutely reminds us in her study on Bishop, written
with biography as guide to the poetry, we cannot read the poems in *Geogra-*

phy III, and especially "One Art," underestimating the impact Lota's death
had upon Bishop or without appreciating the topographical loss Bishop felt
in repatriating to the States from Brazil: loss of person, home, family, country can hardly be disengaged (126). The seventeen drafts Bishop wrote present a series of "mislayings," a word Bishop uses in her first version, and the
published poem continues to confess its inevitable lying. "I really / want to
introduce *myself*," says draft 1: identity is predicated upon mislaying, so that
like the more lavishly described loved one who disappears into a flickering
"you," the "I" completely goes under. The "you" is at first an "average-sized"
"dazzlingly intelligent person" with blue eyes that "*were* exceptionally beautiful" (draft 1), and does not, by the way, seem necessarily identifiable with
Lota, but with all those whom she has lost or could lose. What becomes "eyes
of the small wild aster" in draft 2 evaporates in the remaining trials. "One
Art," with all its drafts, represents an archaeology of the struggle with losing,
a process that is always with us, so that every loss comes to be all losses, retro-
gressive and prospective, shuttling through villanelle. As a love poem, "One
Art," as Goldensohn points out, does not necessarily signpost a same-sex relationship. Yet it must; for we know what we know. It is stitched together
through a lineage of female loss, with the mother's watch in the centrifugal
position, with all other love relationships with women timed by it.

Throughout her work, Bishop will test and question the boundaries imposed by "theoretical reason" with the awareness that we must resort to them;
if we continue to use Kristeva's model, language and sense emerge only in
the spaces created through severance from the semiotic. Retrieval through
rhyme in "One Art" again serves as a way of pointing up the passage of language from the semiotic through the symbolic; form becomes a net through
which identity and all its belongings slip. In spite of Bishop's reliance on
form, her poem disturbs through its attention to arbitrary and frangible
boundaries. Ultimately, Bishop practices forfeiture, a recognition of human
limits and imperfection, and therefore, also a potentially freeing activity.
When Adrienne Rich writes "It's true, these last few years I've lived / watching myself in the act of loss," she pointedly addresses Bishop's "One Art."[38]
Instead of sanctifying art, Rich insists upon imperfection, and says that "the
art of losing" is "for [her] no art / only badly-done exercises." Rich's poem insists on the primacy of loss and refuses to accept "acts of parting." She concludes inconclusively:

> trying to let go
> without giving up   yes   Elizabeth

a village there   a sister, comrade, cat
and more   no art to this but anger

Celebrating attachment to earthly things, Rich calls for a vitriolic response, not the pained submission that might be read in Bishop. Yet Rich's poem presents itself as both homage and umbrage in mirroring what "One Art" unsays by its terminal "disaster." Bishop does indeed feel her "heart forced to question its presumption in this world" (Rich, "Contradiction," *Your Native Land*, 98) because she does not see any reason to presume. Still "One Art" admits that—tied to the villanelle in a ritual exercise and exorcism of loss— she cannot but be *caught up* in desire and attachment. Bishop's poem suggests that she would like to write off artfully what she realizes always eludes inscription—those spaces marking the losses of a "questionable subject"; the form of poems becomes, again and again, expressive of the unruly processes of consciousness they denote.

Since so much of Bishop's work takes up the sense of loss in the shaping or deforming of identity and her own "questionable" sexuality as a lesbian, a post-Lacanian perspective seems in order. An investigation of her work as a whole from this perspective is overdue but, of course, cannot be accommodated in this chapter alone. From her first volume with her "Gentleman of Shalott," a poem confessing a fractured self, to her later Crusoe, nostalgic for his "island industries" and the "pretty body" of Friday, desired as it is absent, dead "seventeen years" (about the number of years she claimed to have enjoyed relative happiness in Brazil with Lota), she explores figures of uncertain identity and inconsolable loss. Ultimately, Bishop promotes the ability to operate in terms of division, to cross over gender categories without making them equivalent. She thinks back, for example, to the Lacanian moment of fissure and arbitrary positing of gender in "Exchanging Hats" (*CP*, 200), when she celebrates cross-dressing, "the transvestite twist": "Costume and custom are complex. / The headgear of the other sex / inspires us to experiment." Her experiment is in part to expose binary oppositions, to show them as they intersect rather than as they antagonize each other; she embraces doubleness, everywhere—she has to. This becomes literalized in her observation of a "conflux of two great rivers" in "Santarém"—binary oppositions—"life / death, right / wrong, male / female"—seem suddenly "resolved, dissolved, straight off / in that watery, dazzling dialectic" (*CP*, 185). Dissolving and resolving into one, such an experience occurs only in fleeting moments, and it doesn't do to ask for otherwise.

Loss situates us in language and serves us divisions and oppositions not readily overcome. Bishop's necessary repetitions of moments of loss, as in "One Art," testify to a mourning that includes the mourning for an unspeakable state. And whether or not she has closer access to the maternal by being female or whether such proximity in fact makes the dissolution of fixed categories as appealing as it might appear, we should, I think, call her vision of loss gendered. Bishop seems both attracted and repelled by what looks like a more feminine readiness to dissolve and erase boundary markers. Her biography insists that she make her experience of loss—as trauma and advantage—central to her art, and her poems demand that we look again at our assumptions about identity and gender. To be biographical, as I suggested earlier on, is not a project Bishop undertakes in order to present a fixed or static self but instead as a way of recording the loss of one. To write from personal experience is to legitimize the reuses of what is available, to resort to the homey, found objects of daily life. And these objects do not close the chasm between being and the world but draw our attention to the touching yet irreparable frailty that marks our lives in time: our only art becomes the writing of loss.

Here I have considered both early and late Bishop, poems and prose, as inscribed with a sense of personal loss as it shapes the poet's vision. A hierarchically developing canon does not really exist with Bishop, except as a narrative imposed with difficulty; instead, there is a metonymic linking among her volumes with her prose and translations as amazingly revealing glosses. Perhaps this alinear quality reflects her cultivated uncertainty and circularity as positive and inescapable forces in our dealings with the world. The interrogation of identity in North & South (1946) surfaces again in Geography III (1976): the questions posed and tuned differently because still unresolved, still living in time with the writer. A conversation goes on between her works, and if one misses the drift of it, old questions reappear at another interstice. Appearance and disappearance. Fort, da. We always return to the consciousness that all our language, all our systems of mapping emerge out of loss, and if we are like Bishop, they are homemade. Bishop's figures are those of displacement and paradox. The further she travels the map, the more she stands still, and "North's as near as West" ("The Map," CP, 3). As cartographer, she lacks depth. This is to say she does not ascend toward some theoretical plateau above experience. If she moves in a particular direction, it is further toward an aesthetics of loss, sufficiency, survival. But, of course, locomotion is endless; and she continues to back into the moment of departure from home turf. We begin with loss.

2

Artifices of Independence

We may ignore our own dependence, or refuse to
acknowledge that others depend upon us in more respects
than the payment of weekly wages; but the thing must be,
nevertheless. Neither you nor any other master can help
yourselves. The most proudly independent man depends on
those around him for their insensible influence on his
character—his life.
　　　　　　　　—Elizabeth Gaskell, *North and South*

　　　The ties were too close together
　　　or maybe too far apart.
　　　　　　　　—Elizabeth Bishop, "Chemin de Fer"

The title of Elizabeth Bishop's first volume of poetry could very well have
found inspiration in Elizabeth Gaskell's novel *North and South*, which
weaves together the opposing northern industrialist and southern ruralist and
proclaims an ultimate interdependency, exceeding materiality and social
hierarchy. *North & South* (with its visualization of connection through the
replacement of an ampersand for "and") explicitly resists solipsism and respects connection. Dependency, one thing upon another, one word upon
another, one self upon another, is an indisputable fact of our existence. At
the same time, such dependency leads Bishop to a homemade art that indicates not a comfortable domesticity but a creating and imagining of the independent self. It is not, then, possession or security that sustains the
homemade; for her, it is the lack of a permanent home—not only personally
but culturally—a lack, in other words, of a wholly satisfactory literary tradition to join.

Comprising thirty poems, most written before World War II over an extended period of time, and many relying on traditional forms of rhyme and meter, North & South, published in 1946, is Bishop's lengthiest volume. Unique and difficult in its *apparent* obliviousness to a poetic tradition it quietly but insistently reflects upon and revises, it appears, perhaps, her most unwieldy, and consequently, most frequently neglected. While the influences upon Bishop are numerous and diverse—George Herbert, Gerard Manley Hopkins, William Wordsworth, Marianne Moore, Wallace Stevens, Arthur Rimbaud, and Pablo Neruda, to name figures she refers to—her works make few explicit allusions to these writers or extensive imitation or adoption of their techniques. Her relationship to such figures is admiring and incorporating, yet questioning and independent. Primarily because questions of her role as an artist take the forefront in this volume, North & South is, to a great degree, Bishop's effort to define aesthetic priorities. What I described in more psychological terms in Chapter 1 appears here in terms of artistry: the confrontation with the paradoxical desire to be connected and to be also apart, to negotiate the essentially irreconcilable demands evinced by the "complaint": "The ties are too close together / or maybe too far apart." She seeks to be within poetic tradition, and at the same time, to be separate from it. In her self-definition as an artist throughout these debut poems, she must inhabit this ultimately undecidable, paradoxical position, and it is from such self-placement that she generates alternative poetic measures within the forms she has inherited.

Most of her modernist predecessors wrote theoretical pieces as companion to their poetry, feeling obliged to provide provisional maps so that readers— and even themselves—might begin to enter their unfamiliar and new terrain. Eliot's reviews and essays between the years 1916–25, numbering over a hundred, glossed the practices of "The Waste Land" and other intractable monuments; Pound's Guide to Kulchur (1938) supplemented and in part discovered the method of the Cantos; and William's Spring and All (1923), in more organic fashion, interspersed the pieces of his critical thought to make reading the poetic text both more and less possible. Even Marianne Moore, extolled by male modernists as exceptional and by Williams as their "saint," wrote numerous reviews of poetry and art during her years as editor with the Dial (1926–29), contributing to the current definitions of modernism. Since these figures represent the earliest and most influential guides as to what constitutes the modern, they obscure other visions and explain, in part, why a poet such as Elizabeth Bishop has not been considered more seriously as ground-breaking and as a shaper of poetic tradition. She never wrote a formal poetics. Yet *North & South*, I think, articulates how one might write and read poetry anew and throws in sharp relief the critical views of her predecessors and contemporaries.

As others have noted, modernism, in its rejection of Romanticism, emerged as a gender-biased force that valorized the masculine. T. E. Hulme's famous and influential manifesto "Romanticism and Classicism" described the former as "feminine," "damp," "vague," "emotional," "about to fly away into the circumambient gas" and the latter as "dry," "hard," "restrained," and by implication, masculine.[1] (Pound made his poetic metaphors even more overtly masculinist, comparing the mind to "an up-spurt of sperm" and imagination or originality to "the phallus or spermatozoid charging, head-on, the female chaos.")[2] Especially in the early stages of Pound's fashioning of imagism, any poet who could not abide by his stringent rules or who modified them to her own purposes was banished from current critical acclaim (which for some figures, such as Amy Lowell, became almost permanently damaging). Such models of "high" art as virile ghettoize the woman writer, aligning her with all that must be shunned—the so-called sentimental or emotional. The projects of women writers such as Marianne Moore and H.D. who attempted to "fit in" by rejecting their foremothers or sisters—Sara Teasdale, Edna St. Vincent Millay, and Elinor Wylie, for example—are seen only as they fulfill masculinist credos, and not by their subversion of values of domination, ego, and violence associated with the masculine. Marianne Moore's well-known decorum and propriety along with her technical extravagances disguise the feminist impulses in her work; Bishop, seeming to obediently follow the ethics of impersonality and restraint handed down to her from Moore, could be accepted only upon such limited terms. Bishop's refusal to be anthologized in women's anthologies reflects her discomfort with the lyrical feminine tradition the modernists rejected, but also suggests her ongoing dislike of restrictive labels and categories: "separating the sexes" seemed to her "a lot of nonsense"; such an attitude she considers "feminist," and belongs finally to both her independence from movements and her urgent desire to unsettle separating boundaries.[3] Instead of implying that gender is neutral, she resists, in postmodern fashion, the impulse to universalize. Similarly *North & South* can function as a metapoetic text without laying claim to hard-and-fast assertions of what constitutes poetic worth. Instead, Bishop meditates upon poetic activity to reveal the oppression of the woman writer within the binary structure encoded in modernism, her independence from it, and the paradoxical impulse to create an unsolitary tradition of her own.

The poems of this volume reflect her experiences in the different landscapes of New York, Paris, Florida, Cape Breton, but are not organized by
them. Since these poems are not naturalistic, she cannot see a place without
knowing how her mind mostly creates it, as in "Florida," where she finds it
perturbingly "all black specks / too far apart, and ugly whites; the poorest /
post-card of itself" (CP, 32–33). I see them, then, not in terms of physical
landscape but, primarily, as forwarding her own personal aesthetic and
voice. The volume will maintain tight, formal structures, while it will stretch
their borders, loosen their seams, let them exhale. "Florida," a relatively late
poem in this volume, holds together the life and decay of "The state with the
prettiest name, / the state that floats in brackish water" without end rhyme or
apparent stanzaic structure; the poem, with its mostly long lines with inter-
rupting shorter ones, is itself "a sagging coast-line," and resurrects a voice,
oppressed and distant out of a landscape inscribed with loss, patience, and
endurance:

> Job's Tear, the Chinese Alphabet, the scarce Junonia,
> parti-colored pectins and Ladies' Ears,
> arranged as on a gray rag of rotted calico,
> the buried Indian Princess's skirt;
> with these the monotonous, endless, sagging coast-line
> is delicately ornamented.

The poem ends with the alligator who "whimpers and speaks in the throat /
of the Indian Princess," a ventriloquist for an unexpressed sorrow of usurpa-
tion and displacement, a condition that describes the position of the woman
poet who must survive through absence and silence.

The first section of this chapter will show Bishop testing the limits of the
existing modernist aesthetics to offer an alternate poem, one that cannot affirm objects and artists as sacred or autotelic. While she asserts an independence, if cautious, from previous poetic models, her proto-postmodern
poems are rooted in an exploration of the connections between artifacts and
artists, artists and the world, the world and its artifacts—to overturn any strict
boundaries between them and to foreground the processes of language in the
construction of such categories. In the process she criticizes a poetry of impersonality, autonomy, and hierarchy; she questions the uses of tradition, the
impulse to privilege and quote from only "high" culture at the expense of the
personal, the ordinary, the homemade.

Even as it evidences a belief in necessary interdependence, certainly much of Bishop's first volume reflects a sense of isolation and a fear of solipsism, as the work of an artist just making her way into the literary world. The second part of this chapter, then, considers both the artist's need and fear of solitude, the hermit's predicament in "Chemin de Fer." What complicates Bishop's struggle between independence and connection are the particular difficulties involved in being a homosexual woman writer in the post–World War II period. Thus the third section of this chapter, concerned with her self-definitions as an artist, addresses not just the division she must negotiate between self and world, but a division within the self, partially the result of the obligation to be silent and secretive over sexual preferences in order to "fit in." Many of her artist figures are male—and split. I shall discuss the implications of this gendering and splitting in terms of her forging a poetics grounded in rupture, division, and ambivalence. Finally, this chapter on her early formed aesthetic "principles," if they can be termed as such, suggests that her relationship to tradition is a particularly feminist one, which I describe as a kind of affiliating bricolage, inspired, to some extent, by her interest in surrealism. Her re-version of the artist as homemade is both untied to and subversive of traditional poetics, yet inextricably bound up with the fabrics of other writers, other sources.

I

"The Map" (CP, 3), the opening poem of North & South and reprinted from Trial Balances,[4] Bishop's first public entry in print, establishes mapping, an observation often noted, as emblematic of her poetic activity; it will inaugurate a series of poems that propose new models for the artist and her artwork. It also reproduces her oscillation between poles of loss and return, disjunction and connection, and her discovery that North, furthest from South, also lies ultimately closest. The title suggests that the volume might be ordered in terms of her extensive travels in northern and southern climes during this period, but North & South also initials her childhood village in Nova Scotia: movement, thus, demands return and repetition. All of Bishop's refigurations of the poet and her craft valorize the indeterminate, the unstable, the subjective, the self-reflexive, as does "The Map." Even while she sets herself up as independent from tradition, she also recognizes her limitations and ties. Art objects must be mapped in relation and not set apart from the mind and world.

A finely poised sentence, the first line of "The Map" gives the impression of curt precision: "Land lies in water; it is shadowed green." But she works "lies," a word that appears frequently in this volume, in its double directions: it primarily signifies a prone, static posture but also duplicity, a meaning that intensifies our suspicion of land that is "shadowed." All locations, in a sense, turn into lies because their identities are always impositions and constructions. The stanza questions the stability of boundaries and of how we perceive them:

> Land lies in water, it is shadowed green.
> Shadows, or are they shallows, at its edges
> showing the line of long sea-weeded ledges
> where weeds hang to the simple blue from green.
> Or does the land lean down to lift the sea from under,
> drawing it unperturbed around itself?
> Along the fine tan sandy shelf
> is the land tugging at the sea from under?

Is the land "unperturbed" or "tugging"? Located in the midst of a visual and linguistic quandary, "shadows" could be "shallows." The relationship between land and sea depends upon both mapmaker and perceiver. Rudolf Arnheim, in an astute essay "The Perception of Maps," describes how the map artist can give either illusion of "the land lean[ing] down to lift the sea from under" or "the land tugging the sea from under," scoring their nagging relativity:

> On maps the oceans normally appear to recede beneath the land. The land is seen as figure, monopolizing the coastline, which is seen as belonging to the land, not to the water. This, however, is the case only when the proper perceptual conditions are met. The blue of the water, being a short-wave color, helps make it recede. Texture greatly enhances the substantiality of the land. On sea charts, which give texture to the waters and leave the land empty, the land tends to become ground and to yield the contour of the coastline to the water.[5]

Perceptual tricks must be played to show the relative substantiality of either land or sea. But these deceptions and the abandonment of absolute valuations also involve another definition of relativity as kinship, community, and connectedness. Both considerations underpin Bishop's awareness of the constant need for creating and sustaining relationships, drawing lines that can connect any one point to any other.

A map has no center, and in fact, paradoxically, no borders: "In an iconic image, such as a map, no detail is ever hermetically closed off from its context. Maps discourage the isolation of single terms. They preserve the community of the real world. They show things in their surroundings and therefore call for more active discernment on the part of the user, who is offered *more than he came for*" (Arnheim 195, emphasis mine). A field for unlimited reflection, subjective concourse of departure and arrival: the map attracts Bishop as artifact, rather than say urn or vase, objects that potentially exclude or fend off the world even as they lend possible order to it, because it is centerless, interrelational and viewer-dependent.

The poem's middle stanza, no longer relying on a rhyme scheme, releases the speaker and viewer from the poem's tight grip. Its first five lines endow relationship between Labrador and Alaska, and our interaction with "these lovely bays" with a glacial delicacy:

> The shadow of Newfoundland lies flat and still.
> Labrador's yellow, where the moony Eskimo
> has oiled it. We can stroke these lovely bays,
> under a glass as if they were expected to blossom,
> or as if to provide a clean cage for invisible fish.

"The moony Eskimo" provocatively "oils" Labrador (which acts as both region and hunting dog), and we can magically transform the estuaries by caressing them "under a glass." With these sensuous opportunities, she proposes a glass barrier between us and the map: we can only "stroke" the bays "as if they were expected to blossom / or as if to provide a clean cage for invisible fish." The hypothetical construction "as if" along with a pair of alternatives declare that flowers or fish are only possibilities and that, in fact, there can only be a hypothetical "clean cage," those translucent bars upon our imaginings. The barrier between us and the map is only a permeable, fissured one. Her fish, because they are invisible, may slip through glass.

This map (as with a catalogue of other unlikely but humble artifacts), then, gets a life of its own. It is through the imagination that we know things and we cannot otherwise. Names given to towns and cities slip from the printer and his rational control, and in ecstatic trespassing, disregard textural and tonal borders:

> The names of seashore towns run out to sea,
> the names of cities cross the neighboring mountains
> —the printer here experiencing the same excitement
> as when emotion too far exceeds its cause.
> These peninsulas take the water between thumb and finger
> like women feeling for the smoothness of yard-goods.

A dash for Bishop often signals some critical shift or juncture, here high-lighting what could well be a response to what Eliot considers the need for an "objective correlative" in poetic practice. He says, we recall, in "Hamlet and His Problems":

> The only way of expressing emotion in the form of art is by finding an objective correlative; in other words, a set of objects, a situation, a chain of events which shall be the formula of that particular emotion; such that when the external facts, which must terminate in sensory experience, are given, the emotion is immediately evoked.[6]

But the search for immediate "objective equivalents" to emotional states too sharply divides these areas. The aesthetic value of the map, Bishop suggests, resides in the printer's "excitement," in his "excessiveness." But there can be no ultimate equivalence between the tactile, "feeling" women and the peninsulas in their intimate, homey relationship with the sea (or between either and the map itself), and there can be none between Bishop's sense of loss and dislodgment, and her temporary recoveries of place or situation. Emotion in her, however, can sometimes seem to recede far from its cause. "The Map" is not an emotionally overwrought poem, but neither is it emotionally flat or anemic; the map "lies" as subjective engagement and colorful inequivalence: "external facts" presented by the map are ineluctably immersed, dipped within the unformulated, uncharted emotional milieu of the map maker.

Identity depends on difference. In the last stanza, she returns to the same-nesses of the first stanza's rhyme scheme (abba)—not to a stability but to an acknowledgment of how we ceaselessly create limits, arbitrary and shifting:

> Mapped waters are more quiet than the land is,
> lending the land their waves' own conformation:
> and Norway's hare runs south in agitation,
> profiles investigate the sea, where land is.

That "Norway's hare runs south in agitation" reflects a dissociation between the shape given the country by the cartographer and synecdochic displacement of the hare for Norway; the hare, agitated and curious, also anticipates the sandpiper in a much later poem who "runs to the south, finical, awkward, / in a state of controlled panic" (*CP*, 131): both these beings mirror Bishop's sense of herself, her frenetic wish to investigate and reflect rather than to delineate or pin down.

The last lines of "The Map" refute any absolute order or privileged position in a topography that "displays no favorites." The colors given to countries are as apparently random as direction and typography—"North's as near as West." "More delicate than the historians' are the map-makers' colors" because hierarchy and chronology must blur within Bishop's visionary yet surface temperament. "Are they assigned, or can the countries pick their colors?" she asks, urging us to wonder with her, if she cannot pick her own, or if she must use those forms assigned by tradition, retinting them differently?

Early on critics recognized Bishop's work as innovative and fresh without being able to be too specific or definite, praising her expert descriptive powers, at the expense of all else. Marianne Moore, introducing her in the anthology *Trial Balances*, circumscribes Bishop within the artistic parameters established by her own work, and by those of her contemporaries. While Moore might have been Bishop's "most important model," as Robert Lowell has suggested, she also served as a figure whom Bishop needed to resist and about whom she felt increasingly ambivalent, as her memoir of Moore in "Efforts of Affection" demonstrates.[7] She met Moore, it must be remembered, in 1934, the year she would graduate from Vassar and, much more traumatically, the year her mother died. Moore most certainly represented a kind of mother-substitution for her, the Kore figure who might lead her to an upper-world poetic blossoming. As Betsy Erkkila in *Wicked Sisters* makes us aware, the relationship between Moore and Bishop was laced with difficulty and vulnerability.[8] Erkkila refutes the common assessment of their connection as primarily nurturing and empowering: as champion of and maternal chaperone for Bishop's early work, Moore's artistic values, in fact, often worked to suppress and delimit the younger poet's evolving differences. Elegantly summing up their underlying conflict in terms of Bishop's rejection of modernism, Erkkila writes: "Moore's poems state, affirm, moralize, and assume all things as part of a spiritual scheme. Bishop's poems question, challenge, doubt, and destabilize in ways that undermine the modernist and humanist faith in the coherence of self and world and the very possibility of meaning, value, and the imagination itself. In Bishop's poems the sordid facts of modern existence remain unrecuperated and unredeemed" (120). Bishop's famous unheeding of Moore's advice to delete the use of "water-closet" in her anti-war poem "Roosters" exemplifies Moore's, finally unacceptable, prudery. Such an apparently small and innocuous disagreement signalled a vaster split between the two poets, and as Erkkila insightfully suggests, "Roosters" also can represent a "veiled 'coming out' poem" of "personal protest against the 'senseless order' of marriage and heterosexuality" (126). Presumably Moore was no more able to openly confront her friend's lesbianism than she could tolerate "vulgar" expressions.

To use one of Moore's succinct proverbings from her defense of modern poetry, "we / do not admire what / we cannot understand."[9] We could also add: we like what we see reflected of ourselves. Moore would ignore some of those evidences of Bishop's transgressive self, unamenable to modernist dictum and unfamiliar to her own sensibility. Moore recognizes both invention and imitation in her 1935 review "Archaically New" but makes much of what she calls Bishop's "rational considering quality" and "avowed humility":

> One would rather disguise than travesty emotion; give away a nice thing than sell it; dismember a garment of rich aesthetic construction than degrade it to the utilitarian offices of the boneyard. One notices the deferences and vigilances in Miss Bishop's writing, and the debt to Donne and Gerard Hopkins. We look at imitation askance; but like the shell which the hermit-crab selects for itself, it has value—the avowed humility, and the protection.[10]

Like Eliot in "Tradition and the Individual Talent," she commends the eclipse of the self and reverence for the past. But Moore hits the mark more closely, I think, perhaps without knowing it, when she suggests that Bishop, with her debt to Donne and Hopkins remaining, would rather dismember, take apart, than confirm past fabrics and constructions. Moore appreciates that Bishop's "direct description is neat, never loose" and raves that "sensation, yet more difficult to capture than appearance, is objectified mysteriously well." *North & South*, seen through Moore lenses, is a "small-large book of beautifully formulated aesthetic-moral mathematics" (408). Deference, rationality, objectivity, accuracy—characteristics privileged by Moore's reviews—determine how Bishop has usually been read. These are, however, gestures her poems question or refute. Lowell has rightly distinguished Bishop from Moore as "usually present in her poems; they happen to her."[11] She "centers them on herself" (188): this is a primary activity of her poems even as they occlude her explicit presence. Restraint is not simply aesthetic propriety; with her, it will test, as I showed with "One Art," the limits of silence and distance.

Direct expression of emotion and self is anathema in the strictly modernist and male-centered credo. Perhaps if each individual self gave up her own personal longings and desires in the poem as a transcendent object, external chaos might be overcome. Famously, Eliot articulates his "impersonal theory of poetry": "Poetry is not a turning loose of emotion, but an escape from emotion; it is not the expression of personality, but an escape from personality."[12] The artist is only the "finely perfected medium" receiving and converting materials of the tradition into "new combinations." Bishop's poems do not exult in emotionality, but they pivot upon the intensive reflection upon the processes of her own consciousness: the multiple, even dismembered, self as it comes up against the world and its dismemberings.

In *North & South*, Bishop most often chooses to write about an already mediated reality, as in "The Map," and draws attention to the impossibility of doing anything else; yet her artifacts never attempt to transcend the world they are a part of. Costello aptly calls Moore a "kleptomaniac of the mind" whose poetic creations spring from museums and overlapping sources—advertisements, pamphlets, photographs, clippings, postcards, reproductions.[13] Even as Bishop allegorizes or even, at times, in Moore-like fashion, moralizes through animals and landscape, she remains distinctively present in her approach. In her thorough and illuminating examination of the debts to Moore and her departures from her, Keller reminds us, with Costello, that Moore's subjects are mostly "secondhand," and that "Bishop's landscapes, by contrast, tend to be places where she has lived or at least visited, and her personal relation to them and to the creatures living there is apparent" (98–99). This sense of immediacy and experience, I think, makes all the difference, even as it aggravates the tension between the subjective and personal and the things described within Bishop's more postmodern work. While she will also highlight the fact that the reality she opens up is an already processed and filtered one, she does not rest within self-consciousness, behind artificial barricades; she recognizes that it is her own perception, even personality, that emerges and becomes in her writings. As has been discussed in Chapter 1, how the genre of autobiography—without the traditional self at center—might be adapted to poetry was of great interest to Bishop.

Like Moore, Bishop is precise in her culled descriptions, which need not have identifiable referent, yet she is so for dramatically different ends. In

the service of a much more impersonal voice, Moore's every aesthetic principle has a moral or ethical correlative; her depictions often enclose us (even
as her forms seem so much more experimental than Bishop's) in a world of
balance and repose. In "Frigate Pelican," for example, she is intent upon
classifying the bird, fit it to abstract categories or "proper" nominations:

> Rapidly cruising or lying on the air there is a bird
>   that realizes Rasselas's friend's project
> of wings uniting levity with strength. This
>   hell-diver, frigate-bird, hurricane-
> bird; unless swift is the proper word
>   for him, the storm omen when
> he flies close to the waves, should be seen
>   fishing, although oftener
>   he appears to prefer
>
> to take, on the wing, from industrious crude-winged
>   species,
> the fish they have caught, and is seldom successless.
>   (Moore, CP, 25–26)

This bird does not know illiterate air, but to "[realize] Rasselas's friend's project" is to fail. This could be a quite poignant confession of personal trauma,
as Moore's father, a failed inventor, went mad, but the poet cloaks her vulnerability and the bird's through masterly and restraining syllabics; the pelican triumphs and takes flight, in spite of obstacles and elaborate
circumlocutions. Later, as in many of Moore's poems, the animal described
reveals her own characteristics as poet, as "the unconfiding frigate-bird
hides / in the height and in the majestic / display of his art." But humility,
self-sufficiency, camouflage—these qualities always receive the highest
praise, each admired characteristic sheltered within some emblematic creature. As when point-blank, "To a Snail" analogizes the "natural" involuted
shell of a snail with the self-effacing artifice of composition and its moral
equivalent: "Contractility is a virtue / as modesty is a virtue" (Moore, CP,
85). Bishop's later prose poem "Giant Snail" similarly posits a figure for psychic survival, but it contrasts tellingly as she takes on the persona of the snail;
the ending turns particularly revealing:

> But O! I am too big. I feel it. Pity me.
> If and when I reach the rock, I shall go into a certain crack there

for the night. The waterfall below will vibrate through my shell and body all night long. In that steady pulsing I can rest. All night I shall be like a sleeping ear. (*CP*, 141–42)

At home with self-pity, her subjective identification underlines inadequacy and limitation; sensory particulars, furthermore, override the creature as metaphor for withdrawal and rhetorical restraint.

Of Moore's "descriptive poems," Costello alerts us to their distance and awareness of the world at large:

> These poems are set apart, but are cognizant of the wider world which they cannot monitor. Their specificity, paradoxically, increases their abstraction, for while we are not drawn into the world of jerboas and pelicans, it is in the context of that world brought into the imaginary field of the poem that our orderings are accomplished. And since these orders are not pressured in the emotionally weighted realm of human situations, they provide a satisfaction. (*Marianne Moore*, 61)

Abstract and removed, Moore's poems permit us, temporarily, to escape emotion and personality. While Bishop's map, delicately colored, allows a similar "field" for an order apart from an unruly world, her object becomes subjected to disclosing interrogation. Her "Sandpiper" (*CP*, 131) offers a self-portrait vividly distinct from Moore's: her bird is "in a state of controlled panic," not possessing majestic, "seldom successless" control. Bishop would rather parody escape from the groundswells of disorder and panic than escape them.

As Bishop continues to forge her model of artist and art object, "Imaginary Iceberg," an early poem of *North & South*, will further show her connection with other poets distinctly, including Moore; at the same time, however, she cuts her ties with them. The title itself resonates with a Moore-like attraction for the imagined and outlandish, and would seem to invoke an abstract world apart from human conflict. Her diction and catachresis, too, take from a more metaphysical register as when she apostrophizes (a mode she will use less and less):

> O solemn, floating field,
> are you aware an iceberg takes repose
> with you, and when it wakes may pasture on your snows?

Snow and field conflate, and iceberg becomes torpid cow. The opening belies a desire for stasis and permanence at the cost of all movement, at the cost
of even death:

> We'd rather have the iceberg than the ship,
> although it meant the end of travel.
> Although it stood stock-still like cloudy rock
> and all the sea were moving marble.
> We'd rather have the iceberg than the ship;
> we'd rather own this breathing plain of snow
> though the ship's sails were laid upon the sea
> as the snow lies undissolved upon the water.

Why must we choose? The vessel suggests security, utility, even survival. All
Bishop's visions of ocean travel are overshadowed by danger—and excitement, as we have seen. While the tourist apparently prefers the immobile to
the dynamic, we discover that the iceberg attracts because its stillness por-
tends upheaval, its moment of rest implicates an end to repose. It offers a
moment of grandeur and gathers all attention to the viewer's performance:

> This is a scene a sailor'd give his eyes for.
> The ship's ignored. The iceberg rises
> and sinks again; its glassy pinnacles
> correct elliptics in the sky.

The pinnacles adjust for symmetry, correct for constancy, whimsically and
arbitrarily. Yet this aspect of the iceberg brings out its artificiality. A sailor
would die for the vision of its elusive magnificence as an artist might.

> This is a scene where he who treads the boards
> is artlessly rhetorical. The curtain
> is light enough to rise on finest ropes
> that airy twists of snow provide.
> The wits of these white peaks
> spar with the sun. Its weight the iceberg dares
> upon a shifting stage and stands and stares.

The iceberg needs to "dare" the overpowering forces of nature. To be "artlessly rhetorical," in Bishop's view, is to be aware of the contrivances of lan-

guage and rhetoric; nature metamorphoses into a "scene," ephemeral and contrived: really, the iceberg is imagined; its allegorical genius and courage—"The wits of these white peaks / spar with the sun"—are enjoined by insistent alliteration.

As in many of Bishop's poems, the vehicle of her metaphor fluidly shifts. So that where the iceberg seemed to represent some ideal artifact in the first two stanzas, in the last one, it turns into the artist herself, or a model for one. "This iceberg" could be read as a form of self-identification.

> This iceberg cuts its facets from within.
> Like jewelry from a grave
> it saves itself perpetually and adorns
> only itself, perhaps the snows
> which so surprise us lying on the sea.

Powerful, self-sufficient, bishopic, the iceberg appears to exist beyond mere appearance and change; Moore would like these lines for their delineation of self-containment and exogenous, synthetic exoticness. And Stevens, whose 1931 edition of *Harmonium* Bishop claims to have known by heart, would have appreciated her rendering of such a nonreferential, symbolist scape.

Yet does Bishop fully identify herself with this "object"? While the first lines of the poem shock a bit with their dismissal of travel, they reveal the tension and anxiety she associates with displacement. The iceberg's stillness is, however, a matter of perspective. It has its own internal movement, multiplying facets and perspective, themselves "like jewelry from a grave." And we ourselves, in flux, must move on and recognize the current we live in: "Good-bye, we say, good-bye, the ship steers off / where waves give in to one another's waves," looking forward to the valedictions in "The Moose," "Goodbye to the elms, / to the farm, to the dog" (*CP*, 169–73). The iceberg then, is double, with its vast properties in process. And Bishop's craft reflects upon itself, both as something staged independently and part of a climate, "a warmer sky," with territories already staked out. The artist figure evoked by the last three lines reflects this doubleness:

> Icebergs behoove the soul
> (both being self-made from elements least visible)
> to see them so: fleshed, fair, erected indivisible.

"Self-made," the iceberg is both substantial, material, and immaterial, spiritual. "Behoove" and "soul" obtrude incongruously (as "shan't" does in "One Art," self-mockingly, to alert us to stiltedness and artifice), the iceberg also described as "fleshed" and "erected." If the iceberg is "indivisible," it has unity and cohesion only as an illusion. Everything of this poem reveals as it conceals; as the iceberg sinks and rises, we never have the whole. The sailor can substitute for the artist, even as he doesn't: the iceberg can "stare" at us, force its enigmatic power upon our imagination, but we will always be divided from the scene, if only by an invisible curtain; we may even have an aesthetic quasi-spiritual experience but paradoxically we must give up our eyes in the looking. Similarly, her "Casabianca" (CP, 5) shows how we use language to declare our identities and passions: "Love's the boy stood on the burning deck / trying to recite 'The boy stood on / the burning deck'"; but it is as afterthought, paradoxically through sinking and burning, that these emerge if at all, or so the poem ends: "And love's the burning boy." Bishop's imagination does not allow for escape, but exults in being caught in the fray, the moment where loss defines the perishable present.

"Large Bad Picture" (CP, 11–12) further defines Bishop's early artistic priorities in its rejection of unity, perfection and permanence, and it can be read as a kind of response to Keats's "Ode to a Grecian Urn." Its subject, chosen from among the humble wreckage of her family memorial, does not evidence a lack of grander themes but a redistribution of contemplation, a refutation of old hierarchies. Not only does she select an object of admittedly reduced quality but she increases its scale—no elegant and delicate artifact or ornament, microcosm of some ordered universe, here.

Reading and watching the canvas, she connects with her great-uncle's artistic ambitions "before he became a schoolteacher." Characteristically indeterminate, the poem opens, dense with "er" and "or" sounds, delaying the subject of the present participle:

> Remembering the Strait of Belle Isle or
> some northerly harbor of Labrador,
> before he became a schoolteacher
> a great-uncle painted a big picture.

He aspires through painting to transcend mortality. And he provisionally succeeds (through the straits of this poem); while Bishop also presents the *limits* of his ability and her own, of all art. Yet she joins her uncle in a fantasy of this almost limitless landscape, "[r]eceding for miles on either side," with its cliffs "hundreds of feet high." We rapidly discover that this is not a scene of serenity and perfection: the bases of the cliffs are "fretted," the bay is "masked by perfect waves," and as Bishop makes the place her own, it becomes both present and conflicted. At the center of the poem we have all she can manage of stillness, a moment in the midst of potential destruction:

> On the middle of that quiet floor
> sits a fleet of small black ships,
> square-rigged, sails furled, motionless,
> their spars like burnt match-sticks.

This suspended "middle" of the poem breaks down as she returns the "semi-translucent ranks," the multiple vital birds "hanging" from the sky as letters, as *ns*, to a continuous present, universally overheard:

> One can hear their crying, crying,
> the only sound there is
> except for occasional sighing
> as a large aquatic animal breathes.

Crying and "occasional sighing," the off-rhyme of "is" with "breathes," all indicate emotions of desperation, and support a reading of the enigmatic last stanzas as dismissal of consolation:

> In the pink light
> the small red sun goes rolling, rolling,
> round and round and round at the same height
> in perpetual sunset, comprehensive, consoling,
>
> while the ships consider it.
> Apparently they have reached their destination.
> It would be hard to say what brought them there,
> commerce or contemplation.

She mocks what seems to be the painting's Romantic wishfulness, for a kind of consistently eternal moment, a Keatsian "perpetual sunset." The "small red sun" spins around "at the same height" and it is "comprehensive, consoling" because it holds everything in a false unity. But the closing three lines undercut this image as has the picture, evoking embattlement and struggle, all along. "Apparently [the ships] have reached their destination," as we have in the poem. But only "apparently." And there is no way of knowing or discovering exactly where we've arrived. Bishop cannot say what her relative wanted to achieve, "commerce or contemplation," and she can't deliver one or the other without rift. Her uncle's painting, a found object, like the map, cannot be decontextualized, but depends upon a commerce with the viewer experiencing it within time. Bishop's reclaiming of a painting otherwise neglected or inconsequential transfers the value of the object to the mental processes of the finder. "Large Bad Picture" centers not upon the deficiencies of the painting but more upon the poetic choice of the familial, and the making of it an almost hallucinatory event. The use of a regular rhyme scheme, with occasional deviations, counterpoints the disturbances and dismembering in the poem.

Poems of this volume are formal, but deceptively: form—as with the other objects or artifacts discussed so far—does not indicate closure or stasis, nor offer a reprieve from a troubling internal or external world. So artful, so prosodically marvelous, her poems yet question form and the value of art. The map, the iceberg, the painting: all icons for an aesthetics of personality, subjectivity, flux and interaction. Her metapoetic contemplation of the "appropriate" subjects for art culminate in "The Monument," a poem that works against the modernist rage for accuracy and exactitude in description. T. E. Hulme, for example, in the essay cited above, assumes the relationship between things and words proportionate. In spite of Bishop's fondness for formal devices, her poetics valorizes the disproportionate and inequivalent. Hulme assumes that only a "properly aesthetic emotion" is needed "in order to get the exact curve of the thing." Though Hulme encourages zestful seeing to revitalize worn-out language and the purging of old modes of description, he nevertheless attaches inordinate value to finding the appropriate vocabulary that will limit a thing's curve, or stop it in its flight; words from this perspective still adjoin with determinate referents, the *ns* cannot cry overhead.

In one of her rare academic commentaries on poetics, an unpublished article about W. H. Auden called "Mechanics of Pretence" (1934), Bishop adumbrates a theory of poetry that responds to a disjunction between the world and language:

> One of the causes of poetry must be, we suppose, the feeling that the contemporary language is not equivalent to the contemporary fact; there is something out of proportion between them, and what is being said in words is not at all what is being said in "things."[14]

Yet she also indicates that we must "pretend" that no space exists between the two, and our sense of "things" through poetry becomes inseparable from words, from poems.

> But as the imaginary language is elaborated and is understood by more people, it begins to work two ways at once. "Things" gave use to the language; now the language assumes an independent life in the "things," first dimly perceived in them only by the poet. To the initiate, the world actually manages to look like so-and-so's poems. The play becomes a play on a stage dissolving to loose the ground underneath.

In language that could come from "The Imaginary Iceberg," she suggests that, ultimately, words take us away from any firm ground, or away from the illusions that any such ground exists, and this is the groundlessness she treads.

A rather longish poem for *North & South*, "The Monument," inspired by Max Ernst's frottage, *Histoire Naturel*, is not only emblematic of the kind of art Bishop wants to create, but one imagined almost entirely without external referent; she does in language what Ernst does in another medium. Stevens has aptly said: "A poet's words are of things that do not exist without the words."[15] The monument memorializes imperfection, incompletion, whimsicality, and stands as an epistemological crossroads. André Breton quotes Ernst in "Situation of the Object" extensively (probably because Ernst traces his inspiration back to the surrealist's manifesto). In this document, Ernst describes the origin of the frottage technique in brilliant detail:

> Taking as my point of departure a childhood memory in which a mahogany veneer panel opposite my bed had played the role of optical stimulus for a vision while I was half asleep, and finding myself in an inn at the seashore on a rainy day, I was struck by the way that my eyes were obsessively irritated by the ceiling, whose cracks had been accentuated by many cleanings. I then decided to question the symbolism of this obsession, and to aid my reflective and hallucinatory faculties, I got a series of designs out of the boards by randomly covering them with sheets of paper that I began rubbing with a lead pencil. I emphasize the fact that the designs thus obtained progressively lose—through a series of suggestions and transmutations that occur spontaneously, as happens with hypnagogic visions—the character of

the material (wood) being questioned and take on the appearance of
images of an unexpected preciseness. . . . My curiosity being aroused
and struck with amazement, I came to use the same method to question
all sorts of materials that happened to enter my visual field.[16]

As found objects come into their own, they leave behind their materiality.
Language itself emerges in the interrogation of its own substantiality. Bishop
will explore, like Ernst, what can be discerned in between states, half asleep,
as poems such as "Paris 7 A.M." (CP, 26–27), "Sleeping on the Ceiling" (CP,
29), and "Sleeping Standing Up" (CP, 30) most dramatically demonstrate,
and finds imaginative freedom through violating those necessities imposed
by environment by never forgetting they exist, like the language we use to
provisionally fix or mark our worlds.

"The Monument" (CP, 23–25) provides an aesthetics of uncertainty; and
like so many of the other artifacts in her world, it undermines itself, sheds a
stable appearance. A monument usually suggests solidity and endurance, but
Bishop exposes an underlying timeliness and frailty that radiates out of and
looks back from all creations and artifacts.

The poet takes us on an investigation of this thing that in spite of her "unexpected preciseness" dissolves or evades exact definition, complicated by the
inclusion in the poem of another voice—perhaps a peevish critic's—who de-
rides the monument. Though the poem's opening piles up descriptive
phrases, it does not diminish our uncertainty; it takes us toward the monument without bringing to it any settled or uniform perspective:

> Now can you see the monument? It is of wood
> built somewhat like a box. No. Built
> like several boxes in descending sizes
> one above the other.
> Each is turned half-way round so that
> its corners point toward the sides
> of the one below and the angles alternate.

This is language of approximation and continual modification. Even the
cautious assertion that it is "somewhat like a box" is immediately refuted,
subjected to question. A minimal surety is that "it is of wood." But of wood
that can be put to multiple, accidental purpose. Just as the "angles alternate,"
each boxlike structure rises to the top; our view must always partake of
partiality, incompletion. "A sort of fleur-de-lys" unexpectedly and approxi-

mately emerges out of the topmost cube, "lys" a homoscopic "lies," underlining the monument's artificiality. The flower presides with puritanical
rigor and ridiculousness, (if both are not the same), with its "long petals of
board, pierced with odd holes, / four-sided, stiff, ecclesiastical." This four-
fold symmetry is doubled and displaced by another incongruous image of
"four thin, warped poles" rising out of the dogged iris that, uncertainly and
ambiguously as her eye, is precariously "(slanted like fishing-poles or flag-
poles)." Bishop's is a language of alteration, emendation, metamorphoses
(more accountable to a postmodern perspective), not of reduction, singularity, unicity. "Or" poses many alternate angles, introduces perspectives; her
favoring the preposition "from" allows things to turn from one thing to another without signaling any single originary point.

   The poem takes us around the monument and shows the surrounding to
be as much a part of the object as the questions posed to it by the viewer and
critic. Again exactitude and measurement characterize the description, yet
none of her assertions or measurements let us grasp or hold on to the thing
delineated:

> The monument is one-third set against
> a sea; two-thirds against a sky.
> The view is geared
> (that is, the view's perspective)
> so low there is no "far away,"
> and we are far away within the view.

"The view is geared," arranged by some unknown architect, aggravating our
relation to the "view's perspective," which forever moves out of our reach, as
the "boards" of the sea stretch backwards, "its long grains alternating right
and left / like floor boards—spotted, swarming-still, / and motionless." The
humpbacked inverting "swarming-still" suggests furtive movement and the
following adjective "motionless" draws more attention to the second word of
the compound. In this construed world, things alternate, suspend between
two opposing poles but can also accommodate both. No rigid "either / or"
propositions damage covertibility.

   In this landscape where analogy and description break down, the sea "is
like floor-boards," put together along with the sky with its "palings, coarser
than the sea's / splintery sunlight and long-fibred clouds" by palpable wood
that perhaps the artist has found. In another world here, not impaled by
sharp referents, our conventional conceptions of sea and sky vanish into
grain. No map exists for this fictive scape that frustrates the critic posing anx-

ious questions (that look forward to those of the primer prefacing *Geography III*), and trying to fix reasonable limits to the space the monument occupies:

> "Why does that strange sea make no sound?
> Is it because we're far away?
> Where are we? Are we in Asia Minor,
> or in Mongolia?"

Each art object generates a new map of arbitrary relations and placements.

The poet reveals the double-edged nature of monumentalizing—monuments are marks that divide the living from the dead, the past from the present.

> An ancient promontory,
> an ancient principality whose artist-prince
> might have wanted to build a monument
> to mark a tomb or boundary, or make
> a melancholy or romantic scene of it . . .

Origins are uncertain; we only have traces and a "scene" without definite boundaries. The interrogative voice continues to complain about the artificiality of the object, about being made to detect it as nonrepresentational:

> It's like a stage-set; it is all so flat!
> Those clouds are full of glistening splinters!
> What is that?"
>   It is the monument.

The monument is always evading vision, always in movement, only momentarily stopped as the poet, after blank space, flatly identifies it. Subjected to chance and "nature," "all the conditions of its existence," material is renewable and recreational; art can be homemade, it can be homey; in fact, we learn from Bishop, it must be. The last stanza elaborates upon the monument's homeliness that both partakes of and transcends "real" nature, which exists by interdependency and interaction, no one element surviving on its own:

> It is an artifact
> of wood. Wood holds together better
> than sea or cloud or sand could by itself,
> much better than real sea or sand or cloud.
> It chose that way to grow and not to move.
> The monument's an object, yet those decorations,

carelessly nailed, looking like nothing at all,
give it away as having life, and wishing;
wanting to be a monument, to cherish something.
The crudest scroll-work says "commemorate,"
while once each day the light goes around it
like a prowling animal,
or the rain falls on it, or the wind blows into it.
It may be solid, may be hollow.

The bones of the artist-prince may be inside
or far away on even drier soil.
But roughly but adequately it can shelter
what is within (which after all
cannot have been intended to be seen).
It is the beginning of a painting,
a piece of sculpture, or poem, or monument,
and all of wood. Watch it closely.

Though the monument seems to make a strange place of its own—abstract and ethereal, as the landscape resembles nothing better than itself—it nevertheless gives itself away, stamped unmistakably human, its "decorations / carelessly nailed." What makes it so is its transparency as a fabrication of desire and "wishing."

"The Monument," then, essentially deals with the impossibility of having monuments, of shoring fragments up against our ruins. The commemorative impulse circulates Bishop's poems about paintings (as in "Large Bad Picture") and objects, as Costello has pointed out. We want to commemorate, put on record, commit to memory, know by heart. But the poem testifies to erasure and forgetfulness: the best we can do in our "crudest scroll-work" is to write in our homeliness and frailty, give ourselves up to time and chance.

By now we might be asking, like the critic of "The Monument": "A temple of crates in cramped and crated scenery / what can it prove?" This is not the melancholy or Romantic scene we're familiar with. The object evades delimitation and it does not deify its artist-prince whose bones are dislocated. Bishop anticipates "the death of the author," a postmodern predilection of Bishop's, adumbrated in Michel Foucault's "What is an Author?" Foucault compares writing to a game "that invariably goes beyond its own rules and transgresses its limits, and says of this "interplay of signs": "In writing, the point is not to manifest or exalt the act of writing, nor is it to pin a subject within language; it is rather a question of creating a space into which the writing subject constantly disappears."[17] Foucault says writing is no longer "something designed to ward off death":

> Writing has become linked to sacrifice, even to the sacrifice of life: it is now a voluntary effacement which does not need to be represented in books, since it is brought about in the writer's very existence. . . . Using all the contrivances that he sets up between himself and what he writes, the writing subject cancels out the signs of his particular individuality. As a result, the mark of the writer is reduced to nothing more than the singularity of his absence; he must assume the role of the dead man in the game of writing. (141–42)

And as it turns out, this disappearance of the "artist-prince," ruler of the representational realm also dissipates any sense of fixed gender or genre, and writing extends into painting, music, sculpture, architecture. With "Large Bad Picture," Bishop uses the personal to investigate the fluidity of selves in commerce, continuing in her dismissal of a conventionally bounded ego. Here as the explicitly personal disappears almost entirely, we are left, boards shifting beneath our feet, with another monument signaling loss.

Bishop casts out the mythical "artist-prince" (which includes Ernst and herself); instead we are given a marker of the ongoing process of creating from remains. It is just barely—"But roughly but adequately"—a shelter "for what is within." And the poem informs us that all creations are provisional, and the monument is "like nothing at all" and at the same time "is the beginning of a painting, a piece of sculpture, or poem, or monument / and all of wood." Such an abandonment of unilateral aesthetic categories, such crossing out and over, implies that Bishop expects us to do the like and requires our absorption and participation in the continuation of this piece. "Watch it closely," she says. "The Monument" stands and falters as a leading away from an art that esteems "direct presentation" and instead considers what might be seen and created through the shifting about of words and pieces, those signs of our impermanence and vulnerability.

II

It should be apparent, at this point, how strongly *North & South* comments upon its own practices, and through seemingly abstract or impersonal poems, explores the possibility of creating alternative models for creativity and for artifacts of the imagination, implicated in the world they inhabit and the processes of consciousness that describe them. But this volume, by no means, presents a settled or fully calculated poetics; much here, as I have implied, displays the struggles of an emerging poet, whose sense of isolation is quite intense. Her personal loneliness translates into a cultural one. (Bishop's correspondence with Moore greatly assisted her, if only to direct her to another path, as later would her personal and professional relationship with Robert Lowell. Such literary connections were rare, however; Moore, whose influence is most felt in *North & South*, maintains a comparatively distant, though sympathetic, relationship with Bishop's innovations and explorations.)[18] And as I have suggested, it becomes increasingly necessary for Bishop to set herself apart from Moore, to feel a radical isolation.

"The Sea & Its Shore" (1937), with strong postmodern predilections in its foregrounding writing as inseparable from the world it creates, argues the permeability of boundaries, ampersand making sea and shore enmesh. Allegorical and fable-like, it generates a figure for the isolated modern artist. Edwin Boomer seems to emerge arbitrarily, by chance, without past:

> Once, on one of our large public beaches, a man was appointed to keep the sand free from papers. For this purpose he was given a stick, or staff, with a long, polished wire nail set in the end.
>
> Since he worked only at night, when the beach was deserted, he was also given a lantern to carry.
>
> The rest of his equipment consisted of a big wire basket to burn the papers in, a box of matches for setting fire to them, and a house. (*CPr*, 171)

She emphasizes the bare aspect of his house, which "was more like an idea of a house than a real one" (171), simplified so much in Thoreau fashion that "everything that makes most houses nuisances had been done away with" (172). All that exists for Boomer, who "lived the most literary life possible" (172), are the letters he must incinerate; no piece of writing is sacrosanct or more valuable than another, and one creates not by erecting or entirely respecting tradition, but by, perhaps, looking for the "parti-colored pectins" and "the rag of rotted calico" ("Florida," 32).

Before he burns his evening's find, Boomer categorizes it with his own arbitrary system and makes "no distinction between the bewilderments of prose and those of poetry" (178). His first classification is telling: "everything that seemed to be about himself, his occupation in life, and any instructions or warnings that referred to it" (174). One snippet of this type recommends the life he pursues, the solitude he almost religiously exercises: "The Excercitant will benefit all the more, the more he secludes himself from all friends and acquaintances and from all earthly solicitude, . . . he comes to use his natural faculties more freely in diligently searching for that he so much desires" (175–76). Such a view of the artist as purely independent Bishop does not fully validate, and as in other poems constructing male artists, she approaches Boomer with a divided mind. (And, after all, as with all of Bishop's "artistic" statements, this story devolves upon the personal, Edwin Boomer's initials mirroring her own; and almost too transparently, this beach visionary and mad isolate is also sonically connected to her mother, whose maiden name was Bulmer.)

Boomer's making of his career a monastic pursuit, Bishop places in ironic light, as she does her own aspirations for transcendence in "Seascape," a poem that plays upon Bishop's longtime desire for the solitary life of a lighthouse keeper.[19] Even if one were to get over the fake and gaudy versions of nature transformed into the "celestial, its white herons got up as angels," its vision of heaven inclusive of "bright green leaves edged neatly with birddroppings / like illumination in silver," the transcendent state eludes articulation:

> But a skeletal lighthouse standing there
> in black and white clerical dress,
> who lives on his nerves, thinks he knows better.
> He thinks that hell rages below his iron feet,
> that that is why the shallow water is so warm,
> and he knows that heaven is not like this.
> Heaven is not like flying or swimming,
> but has something to do with blackness and a strong glare
> and when it gets dark he will remember something
> strongly worded to say on the subject.

Will what the lighthouse remembers not be lost, once again, in metaphor? He thinks he knows what hell is, even if he can't describe heaven positively; even as she assumes the clerical austerity of the "skeletal lighthouse," Bishop, who lives on her controlled nerves, warns us against any such surety. Her Boomer continues to comment on the uncertainty involved in his metatextual employment.

The pieces Boomer collects reflect upon Boomer's activity, and one in particular seems to glibly dismiss his raison d'être: "The habit of perusing periodical works may properly be added to Averrhoe's catalogue of ANTI-MNEMONICS, or weakeners of the memory" (176). The surrealists speak of "l'art d'oubli," the destabilization of old conceptions, an exciting but also terrifying prospect—the individual consciousness left with itself in the discrete and discontinuous moment. Is this the literary experience alternative to Eliot's shoring up the tradition, the bulwark preventing the sea from too much overtaking the shore? Or, is this all we have, Bishop's Crusoe picking up bits and pieces, choosing the colors that will sustain her temporarily? Every literary declaration seems, in Bishop, to carry with it a personal one. The desire to forget must certainly reflect her need not only to separate herself from tradition, but also the need to repress the disturbing inheritances of a traumatic past. Every fragment, however, it would appear, reminds us of our histories, and our being in time. Her "Quai d'Orléans" (*CP*, 28), a poem written in 1937, the year she wrote her Boomer story, and dedicated to Margaret Miller (her friend who lost an arm in an auto accident she was involved in the same year),[20] poignantly underlines such a knowledge: the poem describes "a mighty wake" of leaves trailing behind barges on the river and then disappearing "down the sea's / dissolving halls." What can be read inscribed in such a process of dissolution is our timeliness and mortality; she mourns that unconscious nature reflects us, not in numinous transcendent correspondence, but ironically to preserve our dismemberment and decay:

> "If what we see could forget us half as easily,"
>   I want to tell you,
> "as it does itself—but for life we'll not be rid
>   of the leaves' fossils."

We are remembered in such fossils and remains, testimony to loss.

Boomer picks among the fragments, his fossils, on the beach: they all refer him to his intractable instability. Among these fragments he finds an advertisement for "JOKE SPECS WITH SHIFTING EYES," alluding to the decentering of the self, of the "I," and the impossibility of lining up vision. In "U.S.A. School of Writing," (1966), Bishop will describe *her* "transvestite twist," her temporary job during the Great Depression working under the pseudonym of Mr. Margolies for a correspondence school; a fragment from one of the correspondents appears on Boomer's shore and in this way Bishop's self becomes intertextual and the two Bs come closer, as "he felt that the question posed was one having something to do with his own way of life":

> "I wasn't feeling well over my teeth, and I had three large ones taken out. For they made me nervous and sick sometime, and this is the reason I couldn't send in my lesson although I am thinking of being able to write like all the Authors, for I believe that is more in my mind than any other kind of work, for I am concentrating on the lessons, frequently, many times.
>
> "Mr. Margolies, I am thinking of how those Authors write such long stories of 60,000 or 100,000 words in those magazines, and where do they get their imagination and the material." (177)

Yes, where do writers get their material, and where does it end up? At this point, Bishop anticipates what Williams does in *Paterson*, as he gathers and interweaves bits and pieces from newspaper clips and from personal letters. Yet she will object to Williams's use of Marcia Nardi's letters as she does later of Lowell's use of Elizabeth Hardwick's in their practices partly because both appropriate women's voices that cannot be heard on their own terms. Her objection to what Williams does to Nardi turns back to a personal identification, and Bishop's ever-carefulness regarding human suffering; she writes Lowell in 1948, "And then maybe I've felt a little too much the way the woman did at certain more hysterical moments—people who haven't experienced absolute loneliness for long stretches of time can never sympathize."[21] Bishop's quoting from her own correspondents always consists of a sympathetic identification, on some level, with them. Even in Boomer's claims that "the best part of the long studious nights was when he had cleared up the allotted area and was ready to set fire to paper jammed in the wire basket," it is in the burning that imagination finds release, that he "noticed eagerly each detail of the incineration" (179). Such "irreverence" toward texts in this story is directed, I think, at the maintenance of a hierarchically established literary canon that contains unbearably heavy or overshadowing models, legitimated by those who might appropriate other silenced voices, like that of her Indian princess in "Florida," for self-serving ends.

Bishop's own silence about her sexuality, for instance, reflects her protective attitude toward her personal history, and also her sense that she must mysteriously encode her transgressions. Her new forms will be ephemeral, multiple, and disconnected from the mainstream, as are Boomer's: the writing he burns takes, as the paper "fell twisting into shapes that sometimes resembled beautiful wrought-iron work, but afterwards they dropped apart at a breath," and the ashes become "as white as the original paper, and soft to the touch, or a bundle of gray feathers like a guinea hen's" (179). The imagination works best when it is unburdened of past monuments and can experience the bare, ascetic moment, makes up its own course, sees in what remains only fragments to be perused and rearranged as in a collage but then obliterated, not shored against our ruins. But if Boomer is a figure for the artist, must Bishop, occupying such a role, assume the almost complete solitude and independence of her paper collector?

Bishop's early work frequently addresses her sense of isolation as a homosexual poet, set apart from tradition. She appears to vacillate between upholding a belief in the ultimate solitude of the artist and questioning the necessity of such a condition, searching for a model of art as assemblage or quilt, that attests to connection. As we shall see later in this chapter, such piecing, however, rests on ruptures, breakages, pieces cut away from their usual surroundings, yet the pieces need not be burned to nothing, and can be salvaged, reconstructed in new relationships.

For a five-stanza ballad written in trimeter lines, "Chemin de Fer" is a complex multivalent poem about the desire and fear involved in relation and connection. It is, as well, about the limitations imposed by the past. Can we, if we wanted to, burn it up as Boomer does? We learn from the poem that it is as hard—if not harder—to break ties as it is to make them. The railroad divides the landscape, but binds it with its grid. The first word of the poem is "Alone," yet it is immediately tested and made uncertain.

> Alone on the railroad track
> I walked with pounding heart.
> The ties were too close together
> or maybe too far apart.

That her heart is "pounding" suggests that she might be familiar with what lies in this landscape that does not invite. We feel familiar too, if oddly, with the elements of her description reminiscent of Walden; yet here the pristine isolation and grandeur of nature is dismantled. With its own surrounding pine and oak woods, Thoreau's pond is beatific and transparent, "remarkable for its depth and purity."[22] "Without any visible inlet or outlet," his pond appears austerely self-sustaining. The pond looks back at Thoreau at times with "the colour of iris" (156) as corresponding to his own being, not with a blank unmirroring stare. There can be no absolute aloneness when in communion

with a nature where "Every little pine needle expanded and swelled with
sympathy, and befriended [him]" (116). With the "perennial spring," such
immanence and color Bishop drains from her more degraded, hybrid setting:

> The scenery was impoverished:
>   scrub-pine and oak; beyond
> its mingled gray-green foliage
>   I saw the little pond
>
> where the dirty hermit lives,
>   lie like an old tear
> holding onto its injuries
>   lucidly year after year.

Isolation has lost its attraction and glory; the pond reflects "lucidly" not the
expansive enlarged soul but the "dirty hermit" with his petty, small grudges
and "injuries." The hermit and the pond become almost indistinguishable:
is it the hermit or the pond that "lie[s] like an old tear." Both, seemingly.
Words, spare and scrubbed, work against each other here: "dirty" tugs away
from "lucidly," and joined phrases "scrub-pine" and "gray-green" pull apart.

Could "the ties be too close together" because the speaker identifies with
the hermit? After all, she is alone; but she is walking through the stagnant
landscape along the tracks that both connect her with him and allow her to
disconnect from him, and to make the ties—lines of alternating lengths—
that construct the poem. The hermit takes "action," disrupts her meditation,
and alerts us to his solitariness:

> The hermit shot off his shot-gun
>   and the tree by his cabin shook.
> Over the pond went a ripple.
>   The pet hen went chook-chook.

Repetition of "shot" in "shot-gun" and the homophonic correspondence of
"shook" and "chook-chook" reflect an inescapable circularity. The hermit's
only act barely disturbs the universe; his phallic emission is inconsequential,
dissolves in the landscape. His absurd cry cannot even return to him: it confirms only his alienation, not even his existence:

> "Love should be put into action!"
>   screamed the old hermit.

> Across the pond an echo
> tried and tried to confirm it.

For the hermit, the ties are certainly "too far apart": he has lost all connection. For the speaker / poet, they become "too close together." In fact, they are always already both: for in fearing identification with the hermit and his solitary life, she sets herself apart and confirms her own "Alone." At the same time, the poem itself is bound by a system of linguistic reverberations and ties.

"In Prison," written a couple years after "The Sea & Its Shore," continues to express this ambivalence toward solitude and connection, the apparent "fate" of the poet. It begins with what, to some, might seem a perverse claim: "I can scarcely wait for the day of my imprisonment" (*CPr*, 181). This story interrogates the boundaries the self erects, and assumes the extreme viewpoint of another solitary (and another male), like Boomer, who has found his life's fulfillment in being cut off, being confined and left to his own resources. It is the minimalism, the limitations of necessity that allow the imaginative powers to be most taxed and activated. His fantasy cell is forever interpretable, indeterminate and disfigured like those fragments on Boomer's shore:

> I should like a cell about twelve or fifteen feet long by six feet wide. The door would be at one end, the window, placed rather high, at the other, and the iron bed along the side—I see it on the left, but of course it could perfectly well be on the right. I might or might not have a small table, or shelf, let down by ropes from the wall just under the window, and by it a chair. I should like the ceiling to be fairly high. The walls I have in mind are interestingly stained, peeled, or otherwise disfigured; gray or whitewashed, bluish, yellowish, even green—but I only hope they are of no other color. The prospect of unpainted boards and their possibilities of various grains can sometimes please me, or stone in slabs or irregular shapes. (185)

He could live with the eccentric piece of "The Monument," apparently. But wherever he finally is "securely installed" (186), it will be "best decided, as of course it must be, by chance alone" (187). Chance and necessity—both provide the limits that turn the individual inward, to use what materials are available. When he claims that his "one desire is to be given one very dull book to read, the duller the better" (187) he is asking for a mental shore un-

crowded by the intricacies of other people's ideas and fancies, not unlike the
later Bishop who in "The End of March" (*CP*, 179–80) would like "to do
nothing, / or nothing much, forever, in two bare rooms: / look through binoculars, read boring books." His literary bent is like Edwin Boomer's, uncon-
cerned with hierarchy of taste or the weight of the tradition; he would rather
have the second volume of his ideally boring book, for then he "shall be able
to experience with a free conscience the pleasure, perverse, I suppose, of interpreting it not at all according to its intent" (188). One reads a book not to
plumb its depths, but to find what we have within us; this, he believes, is the
"lamentable but irremediable—state of affairs." His book's formal limitations
could induce endless quiltlike writing: "From my detached rock-like book I
shall be able to draw vast generalizations, abstractions of the grandest, most
illuminating sort, like allegories or poems, and by posing fragments of it
against the surroundings and conversations of my prison, I shall be able to
form my own examples of surrealist art!—something I should never know
how to do outside, where the sources are so bewildering" (188). While he has
read the significant prison literature, he disdains the bulk of source literature
about prisons, "determined to uphold [his] own point of view, and not wanting to introduce any elements of self-consciousness into [his] future behavior" (185).

Boundaries, then, only turn the self toward its "own point of view." Yet
Bishop knows that writing emerges from other writing, endlessly. This in-
mate's prison wall will become a pastiche he will contribute to; he will not
need to ascribe authority to any single writer:

> Writing on the Wall: I have formulated very definite ideas on this im-
> portant aspect of prison life, and have already composed sentences
> and paragraphs (which I cannot give here) I hope to be able to in-
> scribe on the walls of my cell. First, however, even before looking
> into the book mentioned above, I shall read very carefully (or try to
> read, since they may be partly obliterated, or in a foreign language)
> the inscriptions already there. Then I shall adapt my own composi-
> tions, in order that they may not conflict with those written by the
> prisoner before me. The voice of a new inmate will be noticeable,
> but there will be no contradictions or criticisms of what has already
> been laid down, rather a "commentary." (188)

This is neither a patriarch's nor a solipsist's voice. The prisoner's writing will
establish relations with those who came before him. He continues as a ven-

triloquist for subversion. Within form, the chance of deviation is more possible, noticeable, as he says he will find slight ways to alter his uniform: "I shall leave the top button of the shirt undone, or roll the long sleeves halfway between wrist and elbow" (189). He will serve his life sentence, like Bishop, with subtle but marked deviation: "It is entirely a different thing from being a 'rebel' outside the prison; it is to be unconventional, rebellious perhaps, but in shades and shadows" (190). Bishop will often appear to fit the bill, of say, the Eliotic tradition of formal and emotional restraint, but she carefully deviates, shading out of the typical or expected.

In spite of Bishop's identification with this would-be prisoner in his difference and isolation, she takes issue with him (as she did, somewhat, with Boomer), and maintains a distance from all those who would too readily erect boundaries, even those of the imagination. This narrator cannot tolerate the ambiguity Bishop thrives in as he claims that he "should bitterly object to any change or break in my way of life" (191). Bishop is well aware that to be so self-enclosed and land-locked—this prisoner, unlike Bishop, finds "something fundamentally uncongenial about the view of the sea" (191)—is as dangerous as being too reliant on communities, traditions, the past. Nevertheless, she does empathize with those who seek minimalist abodes; removal and solitude, however painful, sometimes seems the only recourse, as with the female narrator of Eudora Welty's "Why I Live At The P.O.," a story Bishop admired. Because of family conflicts, the character moves into the local post-office where she works, and makes a place for herself out of choice and necessity, through ingenuity and imagination:

> And that's the last I've laid eyes on any of my family or my family laid eyes on me for five solid days and nights. . . . As I tell everybody, I draw my own conclusions. But oh, I like it here. It's ideal, as I've been saying. You see, I've got everything cater-cornered, the way I like it. Hear the radio? All the war news. Radio, sewing machine, book ends, ironing board and that great big piano lamp—peace, that's what I like. Butter-bean vines planted all along the front where the strings are.[23]

We seem back in Thoreau's bean fields, and the life of the "Excercitant." Yet it is such inventiveness through hardship that Bishop endorses and incorporates in her portrait of the artist's craft that also, in the outcome, demonstrates a belief in connectivity, a theme I explore in the final part of this chapter. But further examination must first be made of the internal divisions within her artists, whether figured as cartographer, struggling with imagination and history ("The Map") or as Bunyan's pilgrim, suspended between faith and disbelief ("The Unbeliever," CP, 22). That her prototypic artists are usually male becomes part of the self-questioning of this volume. She seems to be asking not only how she might access independence and tradition, solitude and community, but also how might gender, the way we're split, affect vision and the way we create.

III

Wallace Stevens confesses that "the poetic process is psychologically an escapist process" and that the poet must evade the "pressure of reality," which he defines as "the pressure of an external event or events on the consciousness to the exclusion of any power of contemplation."[24] Contemplation he finds harder and harder to achieve in modern life since "for more than ten years, the consciousness of the world has concentrated on events which have made the ordinary movement of life seem to be the movement of people in the intervals of a storm" (20). Only in the imagination can one find or provide respite:

> The mind has added nothing to human nature. It is a violence from within that protects us from a violence without. It is the imagination pressing back against the pressure of reality. It seems, in the last analysis, to have something to do with our self-preservation; and that, no doubt, is why the expression of it, the sound of its words, helps us to live our lives.(36)

Bishop does not support this kind of "self-preservation," and her poems scrutinize the artist decomposing within the texture of reality, not pressing back against it. If poems like "The Monument" recommend an aesthetic process and subjects undeniably separate from tradition, other poems in this volume posit models of the artist as existing in the wake of a fragmented or dispersing identity. The figure of "Chemin de Fer" is not only isolated but internally split.

"Cirque d'Hiver" (CP, 31) takes up the sense of crisis and splitting that belongs to Bishop's artist figures. The poem orchestrates a division between horse and dancer as well as between nature and artifice—divisions that mirror the poet's sense of self—through five stanzas all with the tight-knit rhyme scheme of *abcbb*; most of the lines employ direct and unconvoluted syntax, making the artifice appear less artful than it is.

> Across the floor flits the mechanical toy,
> fit for a king of several centuries back.
> A little circus horse with real white hair.
> His eyes are glossy black.
> He bears a little dancer on his back.
>
> She stands upon her toes and turns and turns.
> A slanting spray of artificial roses
> is stitched across her skirt and tinsel bodice.
> Above her head she poses
> another spray of artificial roses.

It is not until the final stanza that we understand the poet's involvement with the circus toy and realize that the creative act can itself resemble a cirque d'hiver, encompassing both playfulness and interrelation along with the darker, more somber aspects of winter hibernation and isolation.

Clearly the speaker in this poem achieves an identification with the circus horse and, if only momentarily, transcends her isolation. But again, as in other poems of this volume, Bishop impassively faces bracing limitation and the possibility of failure. The first three stanzas make it obvious that the horse and dancer represent two opposing poles of artistic temperament, comparable to those of Prospero and Ariel; Bishop seemingly valorizes the former for his gravity and "formal, melancholy soul." But "[h]is mane and tail are straight from Chirico," suggesting that while we may be in a classical world, it is one tinted with the extravagancies and strangeness of the surreal, with the eeriness and heavily symbolistic quality of a Chirico landscape.

As the central enjambed portion of this poem recognizes a division between horse and dancer through a stanza break, it also shows them as painfully interdependent, some androgynous but always split, whole. We already know that he "bears" her, that though slight, she burdens.

> He feels her pink toes dangle toward his back
> along the little pole
> that pierces both her body and her soul

> and goes through his, and reappears below,
> under his belly, as a big tin key.
> He canters three steps, then he makes a bow,
> canters again, bows on one knee,
> canters, then clicks and stops, and looks at me.

Not only is the toy divided, so is the dancer herself in "her body and her soul": both pierced and dependent upon the speaker here for reactivation through the "big tin key." Is this toy an emblem of the poet's muse—always divided? Its mechanical, interrupted two-step canter is imitated by the poem's clicking into inevitable rhyme and metrical regularity. Yet the moment of confrontation with the horse waxes almost lugubrious: the horse—like her map—has been endowed consciousness.

The final stanza propels us into a crisis we feel has been encountered more than once, a moment available only as the dancer, the figure of artifice and play, turns temporarily away; it is this hazardous moment that could signal either the inception or demise of poetic inspiration:

> The dancer, by this time, has turned her back.
> He is the more intelligent by far.
> Facing each other rather desperately—
> his eye is like a star—
> we stare and say, "Well, we have come this far."

As Bishop can finally say "we," even as they face "each other rather desperately," she unites with the horse in his predicament. With the retrieval of the word "back" from the first stanza, the dancer "has turned her back," and we are left wondering whether having "come this far" really can mean progress or distance or if they have reached once again an unsurpassable boundary or limit to the imagination's power. In this light, "Cirque d'Hiver" is a Sisyphisian poem and Bishop becomes the horse bearing the weight of the absurd and of existential *Geworfenheit* (dereliction). Isn't this poem about finding out what might suffice, accepting that one must return to the eye, the "I" staring back at itself? Yet as we have come this far, it is not as a unified subjectivity, but as a fractured one.

The division between horse and dancer seems rigidly gender-based: the horse with his phallic key, the pink dancer in her tinsel. Yet because the horse is mechanical, the dancer's roses are artificial, and they appear interdependent, gender categories are themselves called into question. "The Gentleman of Shalott" (*CP*, 9) further elaborates upon this gender-questioning as it undermines any firm ontological status in several ways. Without an integrated stable self, this parable poem suggests, the artist must make the most of his predicament. Bishop, of course, takes her cue from Tennyson's poem "The Lady of Shalott," and in one of her rare direct allusions to another literary text, does so in order to subvert it. She substitutes the sexes, revealing the difficulty involved in gendering the artist female. Whenever a woman looks into the mirror of literary tradition, she finds herself split. Tennyson's poem confirms a phallocentric vision that validates the curtailing and limitation of women's mobility. Forbidden to look directly upon Camelot, Tennyson's lady may only participate in the world through reflection:

> And moving thro' a mirror clear
> That hangs before her all the year
> Shadows of the world appear.
>
> .   .   .   .
>
> The knights come riding two and
>   two:
> She hath no loyal knight and true,
>   The Lady of Shallott.
>   (part II, lines 10–12, 25–27)

Symmetry breaks as she trespasses and suspends her endless activity of gazing and weaving. Seeing Lancelot, "she left the web, she left the loom," and disaster follows: "Out flew the web and floated wide; / the mirror cracked from side to side." Before dying, she engraves her name on the prow of a boat— all that remains of her identity, unacknowledged by Lancelot who, smug and self-assured, can only say: "'She has a lovely face.'" By substituting gentleman for lady, she makes an identification between them.

Bishop's gentleman has none of Lancelot's smugness, because he feels no unified identity but in holding himself as "one," must feel his doubleness and the potential for dislocation and cracking. Ambiguously male, only a pronoun genders him—otherwise he cannot be fixed. The mirror divides the self, but keeps it only precariously reflexive:

> Which eye's his eye?
> Which limb lies
> next the mirror?
> For neither is clearer

> nor a different color
> than the other,
> nor meets a stranger
> in this arrangement
> of leg and leg and
> arm and so on.

The first line alerts us to virtual and ambivalent boundaries, and the confusion involved in knowing them. Reflection and self cannot be disentangled. With the constant potential for slippage and disintegration. For perhaps experiencing Dickinson's strange and altered state in Poem 937:

> I felt a Cleaving in my Mind—
> As if my Brain had split—
> I tried to match it—Seam by Seam—
> But could not make them fit.

Living in a phenomenologically soluble world where any false move could mean fatality is also a Dickinsonian obsession, but in Bishop's poem a more self-reflexive gesture is made in terms of the poet's craft and sex. The poet and poem, artist and object, cannot be separated and so the relations between them are not calculable. Inside, outside: there are no clear lines. The gentleman's thought becomes inseparable from his physical sense of limits. "But he's resigned / to such economical design," we learn, while Bishop refers to her own design, her own slender line, and her own fear, possibly, of poetic imbalance and precarious sexual identity. The terminal words keep us on the move, "slips" restrained by "fix," and "stays put" overruled by "run."

> If the glass slips
> he's in a fix—
> only one leg, etc. But
> while it stays put
> he can walk and run
> and his hands can clasp one
> another. The uncertainty
> he says he
> finds exhilarating. He loves
> that sense of constant re-adjustment.

>He wishes to be quoted as saying at present:
>"Half is enough."

Now "his hands can clasp one," and with them doubled and rhymed with "run," he can achieve a kind of symmetry; but the excitement lies in "that sense of constant re-adjustment" that requires the individual to live fully in the present with its half-certainties. The charming and pert construction, "he says he," is an echo chamber where "saying" only affirms our division. Self-knowledge begins and ends in the moment of enunciation, always a dangerous project. "Half is enough" because it has to be; we can never have the integral whole—minimalist portions and angles must do.

If Bishop tends to make her artist figures male, she does so not only to identify herself with the privileged gender, but to survive through what Luce Irigaray calls mimicry: the female, instead of remaining mute, speaks in the masculine mode, a complex textual process lucidly formulated by Toril Moi as the only way a woman "can rescue something of her own desire."[25] Open expression of lesbian desire would seem to be not only a dangerous prospect but a hindered one: how to find models to represent it? And, as with her gentleman, Bishop's figures are not indisputably or wholly male; at times, they seem to be not so much males as delineations of "what is possible" both for the artist and for sexual expression. (Bishop has not yet become fully aware of the possibility that she might make a "permanent" and stable life with another woman.)

Bishop, then, utilizes mimicry by posing both as one who tries to maintain symmetry and as one who deposes binary oppositions as ludicrous and phallocentric. But she is not simply rejecting the antifeminist stance of most modernism; she is also questioning its narrow limitations and heterosexist bias. In her "Gender Trouble," Butler points to the "false stabilization of gender in the interests of the heterosexual construction and regulation of sexuality" and shows a set of more complex relations, claiming "gender discontinuities that run rampant within heterosexual, bisexual, and gay and lesbian contexts in which gender does not necessarily follow from sex, and desire, or sexuality generally, does not seem to follow from gender."[26] Such a sensitivity to discontinuities and dissonance seems present in Bishop's subversion of stable, predictable, and masking categories. While Bishop's Gentleman is doubled in his aloneness, neither of the reflected organs "meets a stranger / in this arrangement"; at the same time, desire becomes problematized and unexpressed in the more overbearing need to keep identity in proximate place. Within a rigidly heterosexual model, or within an unquestioned binary system rather than a "postmodern" perspective, options and possibilities become radically reduced as Butler summarizes: "One either identifies with a sex or desires it, but only those two relations are possible" (333). Bishop's gentleman begins to show the narrowness of such models and the alternative of same-sex desire and identification.

Bishop feels herself, in spite of her immersion in it, marginal to literary tradition, and her artist figures, consequently, mirror an isolation and independence as well as a risk-taking disposition. There is an exhilaration in their uncertain sexual denomination and their ability to "mimic" the regular or conventional, both in sexual and textual terms. The artist figure in "The Man-Moth," like her Gentleman, furthers this strategy of ventriloquism and subversion. The Man-Moth is a fantastical double creature, only accidentally "man," as Bishop tells us that she derived his name from accident, a newspaper misprint for "mammoth." The Alice of the city, changing perspective and size, forever alterable, without reliable identity. We begin disoriented. Or with a false sense of orientation, which no one provides more exactly than Bishop: "Here, above, / cracks in the buildings are filled with battered moonlight." Where is "here"; where is "above"? What is "battered moonlight"? We are given details about the Man-Moth's setting but none of them help us decide how to place him:

> The whole shadow of Man is only as big as his hat.
> It lies at his feet like a circle for a doll to stand on,
> and he makes an inverted pin, the point magnetized to the
>   moon.
> He does not see the moon; he observes only her vast
>   properties,
> feeling the queer light on his hands, neither warm nor
>   cold,
> of a temperature impossible to record in thermometers.

Everything is upside-down; because of shifting perspectives, there exists no means of gaining leverage or steadied perspective. In this stanza, too close to the moon to see it, he can only "observe its vast properties," which are indeterminate anyhow. An "inverted pin," he hangs suspended, overpowered by the moon; later in the fourth stanza, when "he returns / to the pale subways of cement he calls his home," we understand that he "always seats himself facing the wrong way." Measurement always fails as "up above" he cannot gauge the temperature of the "queer light on his hands," and underground, "He cannot tell the rate at which he travels backwards."

The figure depicted here is not a Promethean, or divinely inspired, some Romantic version of the poet. Instead the artist emerges as fearful, perverse, queer, and homeless, yet aspiring and daring. He embraces movement, willful traveling: "He flits, / he flutters, and cannot get aboard the silent trains / fast enough to suit him." The second stanza has made it evident that he prefers living in extremes, above, adjacent the moon, or where he is most comfortable, below, riding the subways. Yet it is "his rare, although occasional, visits to the surface" that most identify him with the poet Bishop constructs in this volume. Her Man-Moth will aspire to heights he knows are unattainable, will seek transcendence in spite of the threat to his very existence and survival; he has a mystic's compulsion and faith, but knows his limitations and deficits in the face of the unknown:

> He emerges
> from an opening under the edge of one of the sidewalks
> and nervously begins to scale the faces of the buildings.
> He thinks the moon is a small hole at the top of the sky,
> proving the sky quite useless for protection.
> He trembles, but must investigate as high as he can climb.
>
> Up the facades,
> his shadow dragging like a photographer's cloth behind
>   him,
> he climbs fearfully, thinking that this time he will manage
> to push his small head through that round clean opening
> and be forced through, as from a tube, in black scrolls on
>   the light.
> (Man, standing below him, has no such illusions.)
> But what the Man-Moth fears most he must do, although
> he fails, of course, and falls back scared but quite unhurt.

It is a matter of course to Bishop that her Man-Moth fails. But he possesses the charm and resilience of someone who wavers on the brink, risks much for exhilaration. His dream is of a rebirth, to push through "that round clean opening" and end up scrollwork, written into the light.

Bishop's Man-Moth certainly believes in overcoming death through the imagination—temporarily, occasionally. He returns, he must, to the sub-

way—to the violence within and without. And as other poems have demonstrated, Bishop's figures embrace impending loss, feeling that only by doing
so can they fully and authentically exist. Perverse, her figure, tempted by
self-destruction, could let the mirror slip, by reaching "for the third rail, the
unbroken draught of poison." His is an urban transcendentalism: "Just as the
ties recur beneath his train, these underlie / his rushing brain." The universe
mirrors his mind, but the "ties" that bind his brain to the tracks are those that
also keep him alienated, in a state of outsiderhood. The poem becomes as
personal as it can when Bishop assesses his fear of derailing, breaking into the
poison of hereditary susceptibilities: "He regards it as a disease / he has inherited the susceptibility to. He has to keep / his hands in his pockets, as others
must wear mufflers." Her mother's madness certainly lurks here, and the fear
of one's own, never entirely accountable, self and sexuality. Is the "disease"
also a reflection of homophobic self-incrimination, or shame at being differently and therefore dangerously oriented?

The final stanza makes the Man-Moth into much more than just another
version of the poet. Mercurial, he is also the muse, the creative power that
flits away. Bishop requests our attention to see that what is valuable to the
Man-Moth is his emotional potential—both destructive and revitalizing.
The Man-Moth offers an antidote to those poisons he fears most tasting, an
invitation to taste the fruits of his pain; the hope lies in this sharing of what
is often, in Wordsworth's phrasing, "too deep for tears":

> If you catch him,
> hold up a flashlight to his eye. It's all dark pupil,
> an entire night itself, whose haired horizon tightens
> as he stares back, and closes up the eye. Then from the
>   lids
> one tear, his only possession, like the bee's sting, slips.
> Slyly he palms it, and if you're not paying attention
> he'll swallow it. However, if you watch, he'll hand it over

However, like the circus toy of "Cirque d'Hiver," "he stares back," but staring
also "closes up the eye." And, in a sense, if the tear, "his only possession," is
"like the bee's sting," our tasting of it will spell his destruction. This tear appears singular and only renews itself as the Man-Moth "palms it," reingests it
as if partaking of some secret, transgressive pleasure, marking, perhaps, the
privacy and reticence of Bishop's own lesbian identity and her possible fear
of public opinion. That he must "palm" or steal his own fluid suggests self-

division, rather than self-sufficiency. The poem, then, ends uncertainly, and again, the tear is only "as from underground springs."

IV

Bishop does not make overtly theoretical statements about the relations between art and life, language and reality (except for that uncharacteristic Auden passage), but the early poems of this volume almost all deal with the artist's anxiety about what writing can accomplish. Loss of ground and footing always threaten the artist, in her terms, who feels the shifting stage of reality acutely, and the self, either helplessly indistinguishable from the world it perceives or sharply separated from it, divided from within. Bishop also remains quiet about her feminism. That she is not pleased with a male-dominated culture appears obvious, nevertheless, in her iconoclastic "Roosters" (as in Moore's "Marriage," much admired by Bishop, which exposes "that men have power / and sometimes one is made to feel it") where "uncontrolled, traditional cries" of sexual power relations are mocked, with the males "dressed" in military garb:

> Deep from protruding chests
> in green-gold medals dressed,
> planned to command and terrorize the rest,
>
> the many wives
> who lead hens' lives
> of being courted and despised;
>
> deep from raw throats
> a senseless order floats
> all over town.

The alienation expressed in poems such as "The Man-Moth" evidences her sense of entrapment within the "senseless order" of a male tradition and her desire, if not to escape, at least to play with, its divisiveness and its binarism, rejecting the rigid lives of cock or hen. Her artist figures, as we have seen, are usually male, but uneasily and sardonically. The Gentleman of Shalott's body, divided and sutured by a mirror, is only dangerously aligned and whole. Isn't this another expression of her frustration and delight with what Chodorow calls the "permeable ego boundaries" incumbent upon women? (*Reproduction of Mothering*, 169). Isn't it also quite possibly a figuring forth of the difficulty of leading a lesbian existence in a heterosexist society, one that demands the lesbian lead a double life, a doubling both external and internal? Bishop can maintain an inconclusive disposition in poems such as "Gentleman of Shalott" and "The Man-Moth," write herself in as ostensibly male, in order to reveal at once the liberating and constraining aspects of this transembodiment.

Bishop often engenders her artist figures male, if only to upset their fixed identity; she does give us female voices, but these, however, appear, less fantastical than her males, more obviously oppressed by their "hens' lives." "Cootchie" (*CP*, 46) depicts two women—one dead servant and her recollecting mistress—impoverished, obscure, and walled-in. Self-abnegation characterized Cootchie's existence:

> Her life was spent
> in caring for Miss Lula, who is deaf,
> eating her dinner off the kitchen sink
> while Lula ate hers off the kitchen table.

Servant and mistress join through deprivation. Miss Lula will honor the lost servant through her homemade memorial:

> Tonight the moonlight will alleviate
> the melting of the pink wax roses
> planted in tin cans filled with sand
> placed in a line to mark Miss Lula's losses;
> but who will shout and make her understand?

The tin cans (as will the oil cans, to some extent, in "Filling Station" [*CP*, 127–28], a poem vibrating with the absence of a maternal presence) encode loss and isolation. Though the companion's life as black woman has been overtaken by "white marl," the poem commemorates her: she has not been "trivial," or replaceable.

"Songs for a Colored Singer" (fashioned with Billie Holiday—whose songs often camouflage lesbian themes—in mind, as the voice of the Indian princess from "Florida") mourns deprivation and displacement, complains about oppression and imprisonment in a masculine world. Yet Bishop reveals such figures, who may feel claustrophobic, as transformative. The second song presents a woman who—marginalized by her relationship to the dominant race and undermined by an unfaithful lover—can nevertheless assert an uncompromising identity:

> Go drink your wine and go get tight.
>   Let the piccolo play.
>   I'm sick of all your fussing anyway.
>   Now I'm pursuing my own way.
> I'm leaving on the bus tonight.
>   Far down the highway wet and black
>   I'll ride and ride and not come back.
>   I'm going to go and take the bus
>   and find someone monogamous.
>   (CP, 48)

By the end of the song she has moved from "[p]erhaps that occasion was my fault" to "[f]or this occasion's all his fault." Bishop's "songs" express a longing and an ability to transform limitations.

As many feminist writers over the past decade have argued, women writers often cannot participate in the "modern poetic tradition" as full members, but only as subsumed or subordinated by it; they are measured by and against standards set and enshrined by the male canon, or left solitary to winter without predecessor or heir. Yet marginalization and dislocation, it also appears, has led women writers to utilize resources untapped otherwise. Bishop, I believe, enacts a kind of reclaiming through a subversion of modernist claims and phallocentric poetics. In detecting an alternate modernist realm alongside that of Pound, Joyce, and Eliot, Hugh Kenner discovers "the homemade world" of writers whose impulse was "to make" and construct objects using their own resources.[27] Of the poets he considers—Williams, Stevens, and Moore—he says: "A poetic was hammered out, as American as the Kitty Hawk plane, not really in debt of the international example, austere and astringent. That was partly because, as if on some frontier, they could afford to disregard ways of being misunderstood" (xvi). (Kenner, however, does not specifically consider this enterprise in terms of the feminine, even as he includes Moore in his analysis.) Bishop operates in the "homemade" line, and makes the word more resonant, as she uses the expression in "Crusoe" when her exile exclaims: "Home-made, home-made! / But aren't we all?" Her lyrics emphasize their homeliness, her making them out of her experience, out of her necessity to rename a world with her own language. Perceiving poetry

as homemade implies a domesticity but not one that narrows or confines—
because the homemade necessitates homemaking, a process that for Bishop
entails the recognition of loss and alienation, and that demands that we consider the gender implications of a poetics of the homemade.

Because the canon of American literature is predominantly male, Judith
Fetterley believes that women are forced to read as males—which problem-
atizes writing as well. Since "our literature is frequently dedicated to defining
what is particularly American about experience and identity," she contends
that our literature conflates being American with being a male.[28] The damaging effects of such a pervasive view account for the woman reader and
writer's self-denial: "To be excluded from a literature that claims to define
one's identity is to experience a peculiar form of powerlessness—not simply
the powerlessness which derives from not seeing one's experience articulated, clarified, and legitimized in art, but more significantly the powerlessness which results from the endless division of self against self, the
consequence of the invocation to identify as male while being reminded that
to be male—to be universal, to be American—is to be not female. Not only
does powerlessness characterize woman's experience of reading, it also describes the content of what is read" (xiii). As women readers, we become, in
many textual contexts, either an absence or a split self. In a more recent essay, Patrocinio P. Schweickart elegantly and precisely terms the process of
being forced in our reading to identify with males as "immasculation."[29]
What complicates this notion is that "to be universal, to be American" is also
to be heterosexual. In gendering many of her artist figures male, Bishop
forces us to recognize her "immasculation," her difficulty in feminizing
the artist and also to reveal the struggle to read and write herself as lesbian;
her women figures, in turn, often emerge as confined, deprived, power-
less—as does the "sad seamstress" in "House Guest" (CP, 148–49) who
cannot provide a "straight" and potent mythology for women's
creativity:

> Can it be that we nourish
> one of the Fates in our bosoms?
> Clotho, sewing our lives
> with a bony little foot
> on a borrowed sewing machine,
> and our fates will be like hers,
> and our hems crooked forever?

Clotho is not a muse for the agonistic Bloomian poet, but one that invokes affiliation through pain and identification. Alice Walker stresses the necessity for women to find models and the difficulty in finding them in a conventional literary setting. Walker found an artist figure in her mother who better supplied a way to create than any literary text or writer could, but who yet had correlatives in texts featuring women struggling with and transforming their lives:

> Like Mem, a character in THE THIRD LIFE OF GRANGE COPELAND, my mother adorned with flowers whatever shabby house we were forced to live in. And not just your typical straggly country stand of zinnias, either. She planted ambitious gardens—and still does—with over fifty varieties of plants that bloom profusely from early March until late November. . . . Whatever she planted grew as if by magic, and her name as a grower of flowers spread over three counties. Because of her creativity with her flowers, even my memories of poverty are seen through a screen of blooms—sunflowers, petunia, roses, dahlias, forsythia, spirea, delphiniums, verbena . . . and on and on.[30]

While Walker draws her strength from such personal recollections of her mother's art, in some ways, she suggests that one's "mother" need not be blood as "so many of the stories that [she] write[s], that we all write, are [her] mother's stories." What one finds in our "mother's garden" is an artistic credo that calls upon a creative handling of unknown or unfavorable situations. This creativity she finds epitomized in "a quilt unlike any other in the world" hanging in the Smithsonian Institution in Washington that "follows no known pattern of quilt-making," and "is made of bits and pieces of worthless rags." Walker valorizes the quilt for being put together with a careful yet haphazard, makeshift design. She remarks: "If we could locate this 'anonymous' black woman from Alabama, she would turn out to be one of our grandmothers"; through it we can detect an artist who "left her mark in the only materials she could afford, and in the only medium her position in society allowed her to use." The artist Walker reaches back toward utilizes bits, pieces, and rags—the available. She does not seek to escape the materials of her life. Without conflating a black woman's experience with a white one's, such assembling methods appear, strikingly, in Bishop. The absence of Bishop's mother is, of course, significant, and we might think back, as well, to the crazy quilt her beloved grandmother made much of in the story "Gwendolyn."

The technique Walker describes closely resembles what Lévi-Strauss calls "bricolage," a strategy Bishop devises to handle a forbidding exclusive tradition as well as a past traumatized by the loss of her own mother. As one who uses what is available, Bishop can upset rigid gender categories and take a traditionally male activity such as map-making and transform it into a watercolorist's terrain. Lévi-Strauss delineates the bricoleur as one who uses personal resources to gain access to the past and to formulate the present:

> He has to turn back to an already existent set made up of tools and materials, to consider or reconsider what it contains and, finally and above all, to engage in a sort of dialogue with it and, before choosing between them, to index the possible answers which the whole set can offer to his problem. He interrogates all the heterogeneous objects . . . to discover what each of them could "signify" and so contribute to the definition of a set which has yet to materialize but which will ultimately differ from the instrumental set only in the internal disposition of its parts. A particular cube of oak could be a wedge to make up for the inadequate length of a plank of pine or it could be a pedestal—which would allow the grain and polish of the old wood to show to advantage. In one case it will serve as extension, in the other as material. [31]

While Lévi-Strauss's bricoleur is most likely the universal male we are familiar with, such use of past materials is very different from a Nietzschean monumentalist or an Eliotic New Critic, and seems much more descriptive of what a woman or anyone oppressed must do to connect herself with a tradition. The bricoleur's agility comes from a keen sense of constraint and limitation coupled with an excitement for transformation and adequacy, characteristics that appeared, as well, in Ernst's formulations. Lévi-Strauss impresses us with the bricoleur's distinction from scientist or engineer as we commonly know them: "the engineer is always trying to make his way out of and go beyond the constraints imposed by a particular state of civilization while the 'bricoleur' by inclination or necessity always remains within them." Significantly, he conjoins the bricoleur's project with the surrealist's, a matching that suits Bishop's work well:

> Once it materializes the project will therefore inevitably be at a remove from the initial aim (which was moreover a mere sketch), a phenomenon which the surrealists have felicitously called "objective

hazard." Further, the "bricoleur" also, and indeed principally, derives his poetry from the fact that he does not confine himself to accomplishment and execution; he "speaks" not only with things, as we have already seen, but also through the medium of things: giving an account of his personality, and by the choices he makes between the limited possibilities. The bricoleur may not ever complete his purpose but he always puts something of himself into it. (202)

A poetry of "hazard," process, personality, incompletion. Bishop's eye is always on the "frailty of human arrangements," and it is through her knowledge of this frailty that she celebrates the disarrangements that compose her poems.

Bishop's admiration of Joseph Cornell and his box art further supports my sense of Bishop as bricoleur. Cornell's boxes assemble apparently unrelated, found objects and place them in unexpected relations. Bishop herself made a box, referred to as "Infant Mortality," which shows the interpenetration of life and death through objects such as sandals, baby-doll heads, pacifiers recovered on a Rio beach. Her translation of Octavio Paz's "Objects and Apparitions" (CP, 275–76) commends Cornell's "Monuments to every moment," made up of odds and ends, all telling "tales of the time." Bishop's "Jerónimo's House" (34), a poem about making do, about ad hoc domesticity, continues to demonstrate Bishop's disposition as Cornellian bricoleur. Each stanza balances delicately on the minimal pivots of her short lines. A jubilant voice and personality pervades the neglected, even disparaged objects of his world:

> My house, my fairy
>   palace, is
> of perishable
>   clapboards with
> three rooms in all,
>   my gray wasps' nest
> of chewed-up paper
>   glued with spit.

This is an imagined "fairy" home held together by the most fragile, slipshod materials. Yet this "gray wasps' nest" is Jerónimo's "love-nest," and the poet's model for creativity. The next four enjambed stanzas blossom with detail counted out to assure us only of the present moment and the decorator's ingenuity and spontaneity:

My home, my love-nest
    is endowed
with a veranda
    of wooden lace,
adorned with ferns
    planted in sponges,
and the front room
    with red and green

left-over Christmas
    decorations
looped from the corners
    to the middle
above my little
    center table
of woven wicker
    painted blue,

and four blue chairs
    and an affair
for the smallest baby
    with a tray
with ten big beads.
    Then on the walls
two palm-leaf fans
    and a calendar

and on the table
    one fried fish
spattered with burning
    scarlet sauce,
a little dish
    of hominy grits
and four pink tissue-
    paper roses.

The last stanza's spread is sculptural even as entirely infused with an intense consciousness of temporality. A calendar waxes superfluous as "left-over Christmas / decorations" harmonize with "one fried fish / spattered with burning / scarlet sauce." The fish and sauce are part of the interior decoration too along with the "tissue- / paper roses," not durable but roughly but adequately. The "little dish / of hominy grits" returns us to the essential grit, to the making of a home. One imagines Jerónimo at his "little / center table / of woven wicker" constantly in the process of re-creating his unfinished home, knowing its fragility, its "perishable / clapboards."

But Jerónimo's home is light, portable for the maker because always renewable through found resurrected objects. The speaker tells us of "an old French horn" that, though "repainted with / aluminum paint" carries a certain dignity as it has survived all moves. The last two stanzas show him more than reconciled with impermanence because of his handiness; we are invited to "come closer" into his meditational matrix and sense the fissility of "the writing-paper / lines of light" that inscribe this apparently forsworn "fairy palace" with its delicate and chance existence:

> At night you'd think
>   my house abandoned.
> Come closer. You
>   can see and hear
> the writing-paper
>   lines of light
> and the voices of
>   my radio
>
> singing flamencos
>   in between
> the lottery numbers.
>   When I move
> I take these things,
>   not much more, from
> my shelter from
>   the hurricane.

"Not much more" is needed as "these things" can be transformed anew; what has been given up and discarded, what, in fact, has perhaps had to face and be reshaped by the inclemencies and lotteries of nature, takes on immense value. Thus Bishop's liking of Gregorio Valdes (see her essay "Gregorio Valdes" [1938], in *CPr*, 51–59) and his naive and surprising art. She describes one painting of his as possessing the homeliness of Jerónimo's world, blending, as it does, modern consumer artifacts with the intrusions of nature and time: "The picture leaned against a cardboard advertisement for Eagle Whiskey, among other window decorations of red-and-green crepe-paper rosettes and streamers left over from Christmas and the announcement of an operetta at the Cuban school—all covered with dust and fly spots and littered with termite's wings" (CPr, 51).

Bishop's homemade art, like Jerónimo's and like Valdes's, scavenges from among what has been left behind, and often from her own workings. Valdes's "rosettes" will reappear in "The Fish" as the wasps' nest of "Jerónimo's House" will surface again in a much later poem, "Santarém." As Walker says of the Smithsonian quilt, art of this kind looks high where it also looks low (as seen in "Large Bad Picture"), a postmodern impulse to displace the insular aestheticism of high modernism. Limitations can contribute to invention, a truism Bishop proves with the vigor of one who knows absence and loss, and their inextricable relation to fertile imaginings. Jerónimo's house comes into being because it fronts the possibility of its nonbeing so intently. Finally, she suggests a view of limitation as empowering and liberating. And I think it is because her poems investigate possibilities and potentialities, in an affiliating bricolage, that they discover an almost visionary interconnectedness, a poetics of interdependency.

Yet while Bishop embraces the powers of the bricoleur's "homemade" imagination, she also doubts its abilities to bring us in contact with the world. Language is not transparent; it divides us from the world it hopes to make immediate. Almost obsessively this volume worries about the dangers of solipsism and the independent, unencumbered self. And, as we have seen, this self, in its gender questions, divides against itself. In "The Weed" (20–21), the speaker, suspended in a liminal state, neither death nor life, neither sleep nor waking, rearticulates this rupture:

> I dreamed that dead, and meditating,
> I lay upon a grave, or bed,
> (at least, some cold and close-built bower).
> In the cold heart, its final thought
> stood frozen, drawn immense and clear,
> stiff and idle as I was there;
> and we remained unchanged together
> for a year, a minute, an hour.

In its surrealistic gravity, the poem shades into parable. The heart and the self, divided, are yet "unchanged together." The "final thought" is "frozen," yet "idle," ready to be stirred, and the weed, "prodding [her] from desperate sleep," divides her heart, which like language, inevitably shoots up as a split sign:

> It grew an inch like a blade of grass;
> next, one leaf shot out of its side
> a twisting, waving flag, and then
> two leaves moved like a semaphore.

When she finally asks the weed: "'What are you doing there?'" it pertly responds, "'I grow,' it said, / 'but to divide your heart again.'"

As Bishop remakes Thoreau's pond in "Chemin de Fer," she also replies (as do most of her poems that take up questions of faith) to one of her admired literary predecessors, George Herbert; here, she seems to be responding to at least one of his poems, "The Flower," and cannot share his optimistic rendering of rebirth and growth, but only his longing for them and his parabolic and symbolic presentation. He must praise the division that nature involves us in because it spells ultimate union with a higher world of spirit. In the beginning of his poem, he asks in wonder: "Who would have thought my shrivel'd heart / Could have recover'd greenesse? It was gone / Quite underground" (137). The restlessness that characterizes our temporal lives, however, makes it possible for a rejuvenation of poetic powers, for him to "relish versing"; once more he can say, "And now in age I bud again, / After so many deaths I live and write." Recording our mortality makes us know that "we are but flowers that glide." Bishop's weed, however, threatens to "stand" in the "two rivers," broken without gliding. What marks her heart is not a flower, but a weed, a plant that tends to overgrow and choke out other desirable growth, suggesting a claustrophobia with the ties "too close together."

A series of poems in *North & South*, however, answer this "cater-cornered" isolation with a rejection of the logical and rational in favor of a more surrealist vision that foregrounds the interpenetration of waking and sleep, conscious thought and unconscious dream, male and female, life and death. Her interest in liminal states is not confined to the dead and meditating speaker of "The Weed," but appears in poem after poem: "Love Lies Sleeping," "Sleeping on the Ceiling," "Sleeping Standing Up," and "Paris, 7 A.M.," to name a few. Her surrealism is related to her poetics of connection; after all, one of the defining elements in surrealist practices is the bringing together of the apparently unrelated into unexpected juxtaposition, an impulse inherent in collage, box art and even crazy quilts—all models for Bishop's poetic forms. While she did not meet any of the surrealists during her stay in Paris in the 1930s, she seems certainly to have been influenced by the movement, as already evidenced in her reworking of Ernst's frottage method in "The Monument" and the found objects of "Jerónimo's House." To discuss the details of the relationship between Bishop and surrealism in detail, important as it is, would take me too far off course here.[32] Yet it is helpful to see the essential intuition of surrealism articulated by André Breton as informing Bishop's sense that the binary oppositions underpinning the uni-verse could be dissolved, if for her only temporarily, in some altered vision:

> Everything tends to make us believe that there exists a certain point of the mind at which life and death, the real and the imagined, past and the future, the communicable and the incommunicable, high and low, cease to be perceived as contradictions. Now, search as one may one will never find any other motivating force in the activities of the Surrealists than the hope of finding and fixing this point.[33]

(Keller also cites this quotation to underscore Bishop's postmodern desire to overturn binarisms.)[34] In the famous and much-quoted "Darwin" letter addressed to Anne Stevenson, Bishop iterates an acknowledgment of such "a certain point of the mind," though one that she would never claim she could, or would ever want to, fix or pin down:

> Dreams, works of art (some) glimpses of the always-more-successful surrealism of everyday life, unexpected moment of empathy (what is it?), catch a peripheral vision of whatever it is one can never really see full-face but that seems enormously important.[35]

Tentative as her assertion of them is, moments, for her, do exist, torn off from the edges of our everyday life, where we are linked to something that appears large and significant, an empathy that crosses and meshes boundaries in a world we so often feel disjoined or alienated from. And it must be, for her, a "peripheral vision" that connects, split as we are like the Gentleman of Shalott, and there always persists the possibility of not seeing at all; her poems seek out the privileged yet fragile moment, as in "Love Lies Sleeping" (CP, 16–17):

for always to one, or several, morning comes,
whose head has fallen over the edge of his bed,
    whose face is turned
      so that the image of

the city grows down into his open eyes
inverted and distorted. No. I mean
    distorted and revealed,
      if he sees it at all.

The restlessness of these stanzas appears characteristic of Bishop's swerving and turning between possibilities, and the chiasmus of the second aligns "inverted" with "revealed," as if the two were topographical opposites made, potentially, one. Splitting and inversion become dynamic sparks to understanding "the enormously important" that remains forever out of reach; her apparent rejection of the larger themes, the monumental ones of, say, Pound's or Eliot's, in favor of homier and smaller ones, is a matter of perspective and relative positions: the Darwinian gathering of "facts and minute details," rational and humble, also appears to be "sinking or sliding giddily off into the unknown," to quote other phrases from her letter to Anne Stevenson. Bishop's surrealism becomes an inquiry into the prospects of connection available through art, prospects that never become reified in some established closed aesthetics.

"A Miracle for Breakfast" (CP, 18–19), with the repetitious incantatory form of the sestina, trespasses familiar boundaries and transports her through the repeated words, a chain of touchstones, to a moment of peripheral expansion where the homemade and resourcefulness are once more applauded. I consider this poem her "Sunday Morning" as it rejects orthodoxy and exults in the real of her own fictions and irrealities; those apparently mundane pleasures of the earth, the "complacencies of the peignoir" are hers: "Every day, in the sun, / at breakfast time I sit on my balcony / with my feet up, and drink gallons of coffee." She claims this to be her "Depression poem," and in it she scorns the "miracles" that do not really exist for the oppressed (a community she makes herself a part of through her use of "we") but merely taunt them.

At six o'clock we were waiting for coffee,
waiting for coffee and the charitable crumb
that was going to be served from a certain balcony,

> —like kings of old, or like a miracle.
> It was still dark. One foot of the sun
> steadied itself on a long ripple in the river.

She is bringing into being her own miracle, as it steadies itself foot by foot in the sestina. "The charitable crumb" will be only "like a miracle" we know from the beginning. What finally "arrives" for those waiting are only "the makings of a miracle":

> Each man received one rather hard crumb,
> which some flicked scornfully into the river,
> and, in a cup, one drop of the coffee.
> Some of us stood around, waiting for the miracle.

Her miracle, however, comes unexpectedly, achieved by imagination, out of these minimal materials, out of "one drop"; she discovers her dream home extended before her in space, within the microcosm of the hard crumb, signalled by dashes that break her off from ordinary perception:

> I can tell what I saw next; it was not a miracle.
> A beautiful villa stood in the sun
> and from its doors came the smell of hot coffee.
> In front, a baroque white plaster balcony
> added by birds, who nest along the river,
> —I saw it with one eye close to the crumb—
>
> and galleries and marble chambers. My crumb,
> my mansion, made for me by a miracle,
> through ages, by insects, birds, and the river
> working the stone.

Her miracle is not a miracle, and yet it is: one that blurs the barrier between what she makes for herself and what the world and its nesting birds bestow.

The final tercet reasserts Bishop's skepticism and makes us feel the temporariness of these leaps of the imagination:

> We licked up the crumb and swallowed the coffee.
> A window across the river caught the sun
> as if the miracle were working, on the wrong balcony.

We always miss the communal miracle, perhaps. While Bishop never discards, entirely, spiritual opportunity, these lines rivet us with the knowledge of those obstructions to a visionary life; similar ones appear in John Ashbery's "As You Came from the Holy Land" where he comico-bitter says, "it is finally as though that thing of monstrous interest were happening in the sky / but the sun is setting and it prevents you from seeing it." Moments of revelation will always be shadowed with uncertainty as the moment in "The Weed" when the speaker becomes allured by the chance of a totalizing, comprehensive vision:

> A few drops fell upon my face
> and in my eyes, so I could see
> (or, in that black place, thought I saw)
> that each drop contained a light,
> a small, illuminated scene;
> the weed-deflected stream was made
> itself of racing images.
> (As if a river should carry all
> the scenes that it had once reflected
> shut in its waters, and not floating
> on momentary surfaces.)

Nothing, however, can be absolutely "shut in," we learn from a restraining parenthesis that nevertheless permits amplification, and it remains only "as if"; we live within the flux of "momentary surfaces," continual reconstructions, each poem "a small illuminated scene" subject to rupture from some imagined larger set.

Bishop presents herself in *North & South* as far from artless; yet we realize when we read poems like "Miracle for Breakfast" she is trying for the "artlessly rhetorical," fishing for what will suffice in the acts of the mind, "the unexplained moment of empathy" and connection. Morris W. Croll's "The Baroque Style in Prose," an essay Bishop was familiar with, characterizes the baroque as trying to capture "the motions of souls, not their states of rest."[36] In Stevensian spirit he affirms that "an idea separated from the act of experiencing it is not the idea that was experienced," and he claims for the baroque "the moment in which truth is still imagined." In baroque design, "symmetry is first made and then broken. . . . There is a constant swift adaptation of form to the emergencies that arise in an energetic and unpremeditated forward movement" (221). Finally, Croll indicates that the baroque, with its sense of emergency or crisis, is a mode suited for a "dramatic sense of reality," even for visionary "mystical exaltation" as it moves outward, testing limits, discovering.

Certainly a poem like "The Weed" can be read in this manner—as it borders on belief to meander away from it. And Bishop's prototypic faithful iconoclast in "The Unbeliever," whose belief is founded on instability and dangerous balancing: "He sleeps on the top of the mast / with his eyes fast closed." To not see is to see with the homemade imagination, as in "Miracle for Breakfast," and not to rely on fictive permanences or systems of belief. It is less usual to read "The Fish" (CP, 42–44), so often praised for naturalistic detail and acute observation, in surreal or spiritual terms. Yet arranged in simple, declarative, "unsophisticated" articulations, it demonstrates Bishop's method of catching the mind in the process of discovery, unraveling an experience in unexpected ways until it almost reaches a visionary resonance.

> I caught a tremendous fish
> and held him beside the boat
> half out of water, with my hook
> fast in a corner of his mouth.

"Tremendous" means both large and awe-inspiring. Bishop tries for connection with her multiple fish, which is a "grunting weight, / battered and venerable / and homely." Alien yet familiar, the fish *becomes* through her intense scrutiny, with those delicate colors belonging to a map-maker, an art piece in its intricacies of texture and shade, in its quiltlike fabrication:

> Here and there
> his brown skin hung in strips
> like ancient wallpaper,
> and its pattern of darker brown
> was like wallpaper:
> shapes like full-blown roses
> stained and lost through age.
> He was speckled with barnacles,
> fine rosettes of lime,
> and infested
> with tiny white sea-lice,
> and underneath two or three
> rags of green weed hung down.

We are not, however, left with some static, if peculiar, ornament, but are drawn with the speaker into the intensity of the fish's life and death struggle:

> While his gills were breathing in
> the terrible oxygen
> —the frightening gills,
> fresh and crisp with blood,
> that can cut so badly—

She attempts an identification. She has gone the distance from "I caught" to "I thought" to "I looked."

> I looked into his eyes
> which were far larger than mine
> but shallower, and yellowed,
> the irises backed and packed
> with tarnished tinfoil
> seen through the lenses
> of old scratched isinglass.

What she discovers is not identity, but difference, the eyes impenetrable and layered—mediated and distanced by the speaker's language. That she describes his eyes as "seen through the lenses / of old scratched isinglass" implicates both her vision and that of the fish as blurred and imperfect. Isinglass, a transparent gelatin from the bladders of fish and used, ironically, as a clarifying agent, only diminishes and reduces her ability to see the fish, which entails an interaction and exchange. The eyes (unlike her horse's in "Cirque d'Hiver") "shifted a little, but not / to return [her] stare."

> —It was more like the tipping
> of an object toward the light.

The approximation involved in all metaphor becomes suddenly startlingly apparent; she is reduced to the bare, impersonal, to an nondescriptive "It," and makes of experience a coming into, but not quite, illumination.

Yet something saves her and allows her to do more than look—to see; acknowledging difference, contiguity establishes itself in the almost successful surrealism of everyday life: "I admired his sullen face, / the mechanism of his jaw, / and then I saw." The lines, "frayed and wavering," the fish has broken, transfigure the poet's world; she bursts out, having come this far, in a provisional visionary moment:

> I stared and stared
> and victory filled up
> the little rented boat,
> from the pool of bilge
> where oil had spread a rainbow
> around the rusted engine
> to the bailer rusted orange,
> the sun-cracked thwarts,
> the oarlocks on their strings,
> the gunnels—until everything
> was rainbow, rainbow, rainbow!
> And I let the fish go.

Only after seeing the fish can she see "the little rented boat," which, like the fish, becomes dynamized, its deficiencies metamorphosing to matter for exultation. The fish is only ugly or grotesque to the untrained or unempathic eye. As the small space of the boat expands, her multiple prepositions override "thwarts" and tie "everything" into relationship. The poem takes us two ways: into recognizing difference and into apprehending unity, into perceiving connection and its frailty. But to comprehend, to totalize would be to underrate. We recall that this is a poem about a visionary moment: it can't keep, but must be let go. This poem, looser than others in this volume and preferring internal rhymes until its final couplet, highlights how fragile and unpredictable are our joinings and communions; it looks forward to the freer thawing forms of A Cold Spring.

"The Map" suggested that one can only read a map because every item in it depends on every other assigned name, color, shape. In this way, dependency appeared artificial. But as her artifacts and artist figures reveal—independence is as much an artifice. Though she reflects her own marginalization as a lesbian poet through them, Bishop uses them to reveal how they cannot be separated from the world they inhabit, the critics they face, the contexts they themselves partly generate. She defines herself in opposition to those modernists who would elevate art and take away its homemade character, its dependency on the self and its fondness for found objects. Whatever the oppressive conditions of our existence, limitations can be readjusted and we discover, perhaps, illuminations finding their way through our barlike grids. Limits, then, from Bishop's perspective, are not strictly formal; those oppressed because of their gender, their sexual preference, their race, or their class, turn to an art for survival and transformation.

North & South reflects an effort to stay within form while revitalizing it— to use limits as a metaphor for the boundaries Bishop overruns, to acknowledge predecessors without entirely assenting to them; *A Cold Spring,* written almost a decade later, presents us with poems virtually free from the metaphysical and archaic, and though she continues to reflect upon the craft of her poems, it leaves her free to turn from form to feeling and address her personal relationship with the world and significant others, to show herself vulnerable in love, desire, and frustration in ways the artist of *North & South* often appeared unready to risk.

3

A Conspiring Root of Desire:
The Search for Love

And think
of all those cluttered instruments,
one to a fact,
canceling each other's experience;
how they were
like some hideous calendar
"Compliments of Never & Forever,
   Inc."
                —Elizabeth Bishop, "Argument"

I

If a sense of loss often permeates Bishop's work, the desire for connection and intimacy becomes increasingly prominent. An ability to experience loss measures an ability to feel love, or so it would seem. When Bishop writes in "The Shampoo" (CP, 84), the final poem of A Cold Spring, that time is "nothing if not amenable," she indicates not just the potential for "nothing" or just the indifference of "some hideous calendar" in human affairs, the ties of "never and forever" binding us to a sorrowful track, but also time's blessing or "amen"—an acceptance and responsiveness that means "everything" if one allows even provisional reciprocity with others.

We don't usually think of Bishop as a love poet.[1] And, as I have discussed, we rarely think of her poetry in terms of her lesbianism. Millier's biography of Bishop makes it more possible to chart Bishop's significant love relation-

ships and to explore their connection to the poetry. [2] Of the many intense female friendships and love affairs she had, the following are the major ones
Millier documents: she travels with Louise Crane, a friend from Vassar, and
in 1938, even buys a house with her in Key West, though the women often
live there at separate periods; in 1941, she meets Marjorie Carr Stevens and
moves in with her in 1942 and "stayed there longer than she had ever stayed
in one house or one place, until May 1944" (178); she lives with Lota in Brazil for a period of more than fourteen years; during a stressful period with
Lota in 1964 and 1965, Bishop has an affair with Lilli Correia de Araújo in
Ouro Prêto, and buys Casa Mariana, a house across the road from Lilli; after
Lota's death in 1967, she begins a tumultuous period living with Suzanne
Bowen in San Francisco, a relationship that terminates in Ouro Prêto in
1969; and finally, Bishop meets Alice Methfessel at Harvard in 1970, who
would become the poet's "saving grace" in her last years. Such an outline is
meant to summarize and point to the scope of Bishop's involvements, all
seemingly silenced within the poet's published works.

Aside from Lee Edelman's insightful article on female sexuality in the
poem "In the Waiting Room," where he discovers "a cry of the female refusal
of position in favor of disposition";[3] Adrienne Rich's forerunning essay "The
Eye of the Outsider,"[4] which reveals Bishop's sexuality as extremely relevant
to her writing; and Lloyd Schwartz's discussion of a quite explicit but unpublished love poem,[5] there had not been much critical investigation of the
erotic in Bishop until Lorrie Goldensohn's inspiring *Elizabeth Bishop: The
Biography of a Poetry* (1991), which thus far, offers the fullest discussion of
Bishop's homosexuality. Goldensohn explores a neglected side of Bishop, the
love poet, through her detailed explication, a love letter itself, of an unpublished poem, "It is marvellous to wake up together," a rare explicit celebration of an amorous relationship (most likely with Marjorie Carr Stevens);
throughout, however, Goldensohn must often point out where Bishop's writing conceals: the published love poems are "nongender-specific" and "avoid
explicit mention of sexuality" (31). At the end of her discussion of "It is marvellous," she concludes: "In this poet elsewhere so much noted for the bril-
liance and gaiety of her wit, that portion of her adulthood dealing with
experiences of love and erotic intimacy, when translated into subject for poetry, seems to have halted, or been blocked, in the rooted sadness of her
childhood" (52). There is little question in my mind that the scarcity of love
poetry, in a traditional sense, results from such "rooted sadness," from the
experiences of loss, especially the loss of her mother. There are, quite
bluntly, as Goldensohn reminds us, few poems that foreground intimate re-

lation—struggle *or* fulfillment. Loss of significant others, and the importance of these others, however, is the guiding impetus to her writing. We do
not have stark confession, but rather passions covert and implied—as those
requested in "My Last Poem," Manuel Bandeira's lyric translated by Bishop,
which asks that his final poem "be gentle saying the simplest and least intended things" and that it have "[t]he passion of suicides who kill themselves
without explanation"(*CP*, 231). Unexplained confidences emerge through
irony and understatement, innuendo, and reverberation—and even gain in
passion perhaps. While it would seem that Bishop writes about animals and
places more than about people, she cannot really be reduced to a naturalist;
the human appears most in her interrogation of what language can achieve,
its limits and possibilities; she handles, I think, issues of intimacy and love
through a re-created rhetoric that emphasizes connectivity and relationship.

Little has been done, furthermore, to see Bishop in the context of a feminine or lesbian tradition of women writers; if she is mentioned in essay col-
lections devoted to women poets or in books on feminine poetics, it is only
in passing, as if her feminism is only of slight degree.[6] While I would not dis-
pute that her sexuality (and her feminism) caused her uneasiness and led to
more concealing and reticence than we would perhaps care for, many of her
poems, especially those in A *Cold Spring*, reflect upon feminine desire and
identity and in the process look toward an alternative love poetry. While
Bishop is not, as we have observed, forthright or confessional about sexuality
in published poems, some I examine here effectively break down traditional
concepts of the self in amorous relation. In order to make this an apparent
aspect of Bishop's second volume, I first turn back to earlier poems that evidence a criticism of stereotypical heterosexual relationships. The remainder
of the chapter mainly focuses on A *Cold Spring*, which continues to parody
male / female relations and to propose new kinds, in a fashion resembling
Gertrude Stein in "Lifting Belly," a highly private and coded dialogue subverting patriarchal love standards.

"A Cold Spring" becomes a pivotal poem in showing Bishop's reworking
of the lover and the beloved, and the dismissal of the typical subject / object
split in nature or love poems. A set of poems including "Insomnia," The
Shampoo," and "Sonnet" (the last poem she wrote), are examples of her taking on the, for her apparently uncharacteristic, role of lover. Even as many
of the poems in this second volume appear to be simply, if eccentrically,
landscape poems, not confessions of love, I propose a reading of them as rec-
ommendations for a prospective approach to nature as lover—quite dissimi-
lar to either Romanticism or Transcendentalism, in their attempts to access

the natural world, and close the gap between the perceiving subject and the desired object. Feminists Hélène Cixous and Margaret Homans become especially useful in underlining Bishop's reappropriation of language as a female erotics. A discussion of Bishop's translation of a Clarice Lispector tale, as analogy for her rejection of a language of mastery, possession, and phallocentric loving, concludes the chapter.

Bishop's love poetry, as I shall call it in spite of the seeming oddness of such naming, deviates sharply from the masculinist tradition (perhaps this is why we have not seen it) in its effort to bring the female body into her writing. Cixous's utopian, ebullient manifesto "The Laugh of the Medusa" describes a writing she believes does not yet exist, a feminine writing that liberates woman's body from phallocentric discourse but does not divorce sexual economy from the textual.[7] Reading Cixous illumines the feminist challenge and antitraditional currents in Bishop. Because of her peripheral position, woman, in Cixous terms, is able to know love differently from man and to write of it differently:

> Her libido is cosmic, just as her unconscious is worldwide. Her writing can only keep going, without ever inscribing or discerning contours, daring to make these vertiginous crossings of the other(s) ephemeral and passionate sojourns in him, her, them, whom she inhabits long enough to look at from the point closest to their unconscious from the moment they awaken, to love them at the point closest to their drives; and then further, impregnated through and through with these brief, identificatory embraces, she goes and passes into infinity. She alone dares and wishes to know from within, where she, the outcast, has never ceased to hear the resonance of forelanguage. (256)

Few women, thinks Cixous, have yet been able to begin inscribing such femininity. Yet I think traces of the strategy "To love, to watch-think-seek the other in the other, to despecularize, to unhoard" ("Laugh," 259) appear within poems by Bishop and expose her movement away from the love poetry of opposition and hierarchy toward one of exchange and alterability, a movement consistent with her poems on art, travel, and memory.

If we can escape "the false theater of phallocentric representationalism," Cixous contends that we will discover a "vatic bisexuality" that allows for differences, "stirs them up, pursues them" (254). Woman is more likely to be bisexual in these terms, by Cixous's lights, because she is not "poised to keep glorious phallic monosexuality in view." Similarly, in the abundantly liberating essay, "Compulsory Heterosexuality and Lesbian Existence," Rich wants to liberate woman from institutionalized heterosexuality, proposing quite plainly that "if women are the earliest sources of emotional caring and physical nurture for both female and male children, it would seem logical, from a feminist perspective at least, to pose the following questions: whether the search for love and tenderness in both sexes does not originally lead toward women; *why in fact women would ever redirect that search.*"[8] With such pointed questions in mind, she introduces a "lesbian continuum" that postulates "a range—through each woman's life and throughout history—of woman-identified experience, not simply the fact that a woman has had or consciously desired genital sexual experience with another woman" (51). At the same time, Rich does not want to sterilize lesbianism; instead, she emphasizes how "erotic sensuality" has been "the most violently erased fact of female experience" (57), kept out of literature as well as its criticism. As does Cixous, Rich unlimits woman's eroticism, shows it to have a scope unaccounted for by phallocentric definitions of loving relations and pleasures of the body: "As the term *lesbian* has been held to limiting, clinical associations in its patriarchal definition, female friendship and comradeship have been set apart from the erotic, thus limiting the erotic itself. But as we deepen and broaden the range of what we define as lesbian existence, as we delineate a lesbian continuum, we begin to discover the erotic in female terms: as that which is unconfined to any single part of the body or solely to the body itself" (53). The "patriarchal definition" of the lesbian as deviant or pathological probably contributed to Bishop's own silence about her sexuality. Nevertheless, in spite of her reticence, "woman identification" (63) as Rich defines it and which Cixous celebrates becomes a main poetic source and undercurrent for Bishop, in spite of her frequent male impersonations and parodies, especially in this volume.

The poems of A *Cold Spring* represent days and distance well beyond those of *North & South*; because of their slimness, however, the two volumes were published jointly under the title of *Poems*, winning the Pulitzer Prize in 1956. Written during a period of about a decade and in diverse landscapes—Florida, Mexico, New York, and finally Brazil—A *Cold Spring* is quite openly written in response to women Bishop was intimately connected with from the time of *North & South* (which bears no dedication, excepting the internal significantly elegiac ones of "Anaphora," postinscribed "In memory of Marjorie Carr Stevens" in 1959, and of "Quai d'Orléans," inscribed "for Margaret Miller"). Personal relationships are now more markedly credited in her work, and the individual who retreated to an isolated farmhouse to read Rimbaud has passed from the urgency for solitude to the desire for connection. A *Cold Spring* is dedicated to Dr. Anny Baumann, who acted as both physician, therapist, and lifetime friend for Elizabeth Bishop; the title poem is for Jane Dewey, a friend who lived in Maryland, and there is a poem expressly written for Louise Crane and another for Marianne Moore. One feels other unpenned dedications as well: the volume is an offering and an "amen," a sighing dismissal of patriarchal modes of loving and possessing. The dedications set the personal tenor of the volume with the sense of the primacy of woman-to-woman relationships. Yet while the poems can be considered more personal, they do not provide or testify to a unified, enclosed subjectivity. Her frequent abandonment of the first person might lead us to see the poems as stringently objective and impersonal; instead, they show the "gift of alterability" ("Laugh," 260), the feminine capacity for and readiness to shift the boundaries inscribing identity, the subject receptive and in transit, "beneath" and "within" (to use the prepositions of "O Breath," the last in "Four Poems," *CP*, 79).

As notes from manuscripts indicate, Bishop read Roland Barthes's *A Lover's Discourse*, though too late—probably the year she died—to have it influence the composing of her second volume of poetry, published in 1955.[9] Yet she anticipates the Barthian lover. His "portrait" of the lover as a "discursive site: the site of someone speaking within himself, amorously confronting the other (the loved object), who does not speak" (3) resonates in her own. At the same time, she calls such an isolated lover in dialogue with himself into question even as she identifies with him. He recalls the hermit of "Chemin de Fer" who wants "to put love into action" but can only fire his phallic gun, its sound reverberating back to him. Barthes's lover, constructed through language, introjects the loved object into himself and performs theatrical encounters with the other as an object that does not include an other's subjectivity. The discourse of his lover, therefore, speaks "an extreme solitude." His purpose is to find *himself* unveiled through love: "It is my desire I desire, and the loved being is no more than its tool" (31). All the phases of love exist as if always already completed—the yearning, the engulfment, the fear of abandonment, the loss: "lover's anxiety" he defines as "the fear of a mourning which has already occurred, at the very origin of love" (30). The process of love exists independently of and even divorced from the beloved. The "unknowable" remains for the lover as the "inability to fathom how he is seen by the other" (8).

Some of the love poems in A *Cold Spring* conjure up Barthian scenarios of anxiety or loss but the lover is never conceived in absolute solitude. A poem such as "While Someone Telephones" (one of the "Four Poems") shows a lover in the act of waiting, desperately. The "scenography of waiting" Barthes claims "mimes the loss of the loved object and provokes all the effects of a mirror mourning": waiting becomes "enchantment" (enchainment) when the lover sits "keeping the telephone open" (39). He pronounces: "The lover's fatal identity is precisely: *I am the one who waits*" (40). Bishop certainly understands the predicament of waiting—and of generating a condition of mourning through her writing, but she reveals the solitude and yearning of the lover as a state enforced by dualistic thinking; she shows the desire to make the beloved an object to be possessed or internalized as inauthentic narcissism.

Alicia Suskin Ostriker's "The Imperative of Intimacy: Female Erotics, Female Poetics" complements and minimally anchors the more dizzying flight and insight of Cixous in its proposal of an alternative female love poetry, one that approximates Bishop's.[10] Critics have protested perhaps too much her reticence and restraint (qualities valorized in women poets and not in men, as Gilbert and Gubar astutely point out), and these descriptive tags silence what she voices of the feminine. Pain, desire, loss—these *A Cold Spring* expresses and embraces, even if it is through negative proposition and "coincident conundrum" (a phrase from "Faustina," *CP*, 76). In short, Bishop urges what in Ostriker's phrasing is "the imperative to intimacy," which demands honesty regarding the emotional with the erotic. As Ostriker notes, woman's poetry enacts what women do best: connect. The tactile and the contiguous become predominant channels of experience. Male love poetry traditionally enforces a subject / object distinction that women's writing attempts to break down, blurring boundaries to see the self as it is traversed by and through others. "The assumption of the self as a rigidly bounded entity is a fiction" (Ostriker, 178), a lie to our biochemistry and daily interactions, but one that rules the masculinist poetic of love.

II

Bishop had written about love prior to *A Cold Spring*, in poems more rigorously veiled and impersonal than any that would appear in even *North & South*, where love lies certainly sleeping, emitting artful signals to a dreaming unconscious. "Three Valentines" (1934; *CP*, 225–27), crafted while in college, possesses the high diction and catachresis of the Metaphysicals. Marianne Moore mourned the loss of these poems from *North & South* along with "The Reprimand" (1935; *CP*, 228), a poem printed in *Trial Balances*, and which humorously scolds the tongue that would taste tears and yet not speak its own grief, a commentary on Bishop's self-aware and vulnerable reticence. Yet the formality of these early pieces makes them appear more justly as exercises rather than as urgent discoveries. The valentines, nevertheless, are Bishop's first attempts to treat the theme of romantic love, so carefully skirted by her first volume. The poem is predictably divided into three portions. She uses stock love imagery: Cupid, sparrows, Venus. Yet close attention reveals an already iconoclastic and challenging perspective on amorous discourse. Her baroque configuration renders love a brutally lascivious affair:

> Love with his gilded bow and crystal arrows
>> Has slain us all,
> Has pierced the English sparrows
> Who languish for each other in the dust,
> While from their bosoms, puffed with hopeless lust,
>> The red drops fall.

A love poem penned by a woman might be expected to be more "sensitive" or idealistic, yet Bishop invokes stark physicality. The English sparrows must be slain if we are not to be slain by them and the tradition they represent. Her Cupid "pink and plump and snug in sashes" she dismisses with provocative innuendo: "Oh sweet, sweet Love—go kick your naughty self / Around a cloud, or prick thy naughty self / Upon a gilded pin." The second valentine complains that love and the loved one lose "Dissimilarity" because we make the beloved into our own image and erase "all disparity." To eliminate difference is not to be rid of binarism; in fact, it is the desire to see the self in opposition to the need to overcome difference that makes the speaker dread the fusion love potentially becomes. This lover designs the beloved until he no longer senses the other—but in making her the same, puts his own identity through hoops:

> Nor does an eyelash differ; nor a hair
>> But's shaped exactly
> To you I love, and warns me to beware
>> My dubious security,
> —Sure of my love, and Love; uncertain of identity.

Security is neither possible nor desirable in Bishop's realm—uncertainty, we remember, can provide exhilaration. The third valentine dismisses Love entirely and with it the notion of a unified subjectivity vanishes from these poems. She depicts love, no longer as mischievous Cupid but as carnivore:

> Claws he has like any hawk
>   To clutch and keep,
>   To clutch so he may sleep
> While round the red heart's perch his claws can lock
>   And fasten Love.

Through these three valentines, she dismantles traditional love tropes. Earlier, in the highly cerebral argument of Love dissolving difference and therefore also identity, she echoes Shakespeare's not entirely unironic Sonnet 116: "Let me not to the marriage of true minds / Admit impediments. Love is not love / Which alters when it alteration finds." Love as fixed and constant that will not confess struggle she refuses and looks instead to dis-ease and "Love's limitation":

> Such curious Love, in constant innocence
>   Though ill at ease
> Admits, between you and himself, no difference
>   And no degrees . . .

For love and connection to exist, there must be difference; without it, narcissism results. Her later poems more vividly express this in the desire to free her writing from the violence of a subject / object split and also from the homogenization of the self completely dissolved with "no degrees" in the other. She embraces difference as does Cixous, who envisions it as death-defying and nourishing: "Writing is precisely working (in) the in-between, inspecting the process of the same and of the other without which nothing can live, undoing the work of death . . . not fixed in sequences of struggle and expulsion or some other form of death but infinitely dynamized by an incessant process of exchange from one subject to another" (254). A Cold Spring, in particular, will accentuate the desire for connection, not only figured as artistic affiliation. As she becomes more aware of and accepting of loss, her poems turn more fluid, less strict and confining. Her last poem, "Sonnet" (1979; CP, 192), taken up later in this chapter, is revolutionary in its use of the

love form, and dramatically enacts the urge to let go and to valorize intimacy
and difference.

Perhaps the most out-of-place poems in *North & South* are the "Songs for
a Colored Singer" (*CP*, 47–51), which bridge Bishop's formal voice with the
more conversational and confidential tone of *A Cold Spring*. These dramatic
songs, written for Billie Holiday, attempt to empathize, through Bishop's
own experience of loss, with other figures lamenting thwarted love. Blues
music, a genre Bishop must have felt akin to, frequently revels in the physical and often unromantic details of love and in its oppression; traditional love
poetry may be mournful but it is so because it longs for an "other" romanti-
cized and distanced. These songs testify to lived struggles with heterosexual
intimacy and its hazards. The first song treats a woman's problems with a
man who cannot settle down: she craves a more permanent stable home, but
she continues to see his virtues with his faults (typical of a Bishop speaker,
able to take on more than one position):

> He's faithful and he's kind
>   but he sure has an inquiring mind.
> He's seen a lot; he's bound to see the rest,
>   and if I protest
>
> Le Roy answers with a frown

The next poem presents another kind of difficulty and entanglement—a
woman, also dissatisfied with heterosexual relations but stronger and more
independent than the previous speaker, who wants to take to the road and
leave behind an unfaithful lover:

> The time has come to call a halt.
> I've borrowed fifteen dollars fare
> and it will take me anywhere.
> For this occasion's all his fault.

The third poem, a lullaby, presents a foreboding comparison between the
sinking into sleep of adult and child and a ship sinking and dying "lead in its
breast." The domestic situation of mother and child appears imprisoning, a
likely characteristic, considering Bishop's difficult identification with her
mother: "The shadow of the crib makes an enormous cage." The cage in this
poem as well as in "It is marvellous to wake up together" and "Rain Towards

Morning" are explored in detail by Goldensohn as recurring emblems of "the constraints of her separateness, and the conflicts of her identity as both woman and poet" (45). The tensions within close relationships in these three poems culminate and shift in the final one, which recommends the transformative power of language along with the "conspiring root" of intimacy. One word changes into another for the sake of contiguity and closeness.

> What's that shining in the leaves,
> the shadowy leaves,
> like tears when somebody grieves,
> shining, shining in the leaves?

Leaves turn to tears turn to dew turn to seeds turn to flower or fruit turns to a face turns to faces, all adumbrating a hidden grief. Repetition of words in immediate succession gives the words tactility and substance. Each stanza of this poem takes the previous vehicle and changes it into another, a method that dissolves rigid distinction between vehicle and tenor, and with it the subjectivity proposing a comparison. Associations made through metonymy become more viable. The leaves that ultimately become an army of faces will not allow us to stay fixed in one place: "the conspiring root" in words keeps us plotting together. "War's over soon," she sings in the previous lullaby; here, she suggests a cooperation between words. As Ostriker maintains, feminine erotics and linguistic cooperation "become a figure . . . for every reunification needed by a divided humanity" (176) and so implicitly, if not always directly, reject racism, class oppression, imperialism.

III

Such root conspiracy between vehicle and tenor appears distinctly in another poem of *North & South*, "Casabianca" (*CP*, 5), which makes the very articulation of desire the conceit for love. It begins, quirkily, in convolution: "Love's the boy stood on the burning deck / trying to recite 'The boy stood on / the burning deck,'" and manages to finish "And love's the burning boy." Love, in linguistic gymnastics, burns through deck to boy. This arsenal and destructive image of love continues to operate in *A Cold Spring*, where Bishop both parodies traditional heterosexual relationships and refigures eroticism in her language. "Four Poems," often overlooked by critics, most

obviously deal with matters of love. They seem complementary in some
sense to "Songs for a Colored Singer," the songs of women trapped within a
patriarchy looking for "sorties," to use a Cixous word. The final and fourth
one abandons the speaking subject for a language that promotes fusion and
nurturance. It sings a utopian moment through a lullaby to open up a
threshold space of not waking, not sleeping. Dichotomies disappear or dis-
perse, so much so that "Adult" is ungendered and a war ship feminized: "Lullaby. / Adult and child / sink to their rest. / At sea the big ship sinks and dies, /
lead in its breast." We find ourselves in "Insomnia," another poem of A Cold
Spring, with an injunction to "Drop the silly, harmless toy, / pick up the
moon." The penultimate stanza of the song makes a plea for iconoclasm and
difference: "Lullaby. / If they should say / You have no sense, / don't you
mind them; it won't make / much difference."

Much difference is coveted. "Four Poems" disclose as they conceal the
problems and advantages of marginalization involved with a lesbian identity.
The futility of rationality and sense-making is a perception that intensifies
through the quartet as the poems grow more concrete and sensual. "Conversation," the first poem of the set, is unusually abstract for Bishop but has a
compellingly enigmatic texture as will "Varick Street" or "Faustina." The
opening stanza shows the dissociation and split of the body from the mind
and heart:

> The tumult in the heart
> keeps asking questions.
> And then it stops and undertakes to answer
> in the same tone of voice.
> No one could tell the difference.

The questions must be of love, considering the "tumult in the heart," and we
appear to have a Barthian lover, solitary, in dialogue with himself. Yet a
monologic binarism reveals its "uninnocence" and inexorably leads to a condition of engulfment, loss of borders. "Sense," in spite of the tone, dissipates
as it did in the lullaby, until meaning drains out of symbolic language and
"until a name / and all its connotations are the same." No subject, at least no
unified or identified one, appears in "Conversation."

In contrast to the stark unconversational abstraction of "Conversation,"
"Rain Towards Morning" engages us with an implied metaphor; a rainstorm
with its dramatic electrical explosions and the return of calm parallels a
building up and release of sexual tension. In fact, we come to the poem at

the moment of orgasmic pleasure: "The great light cage has broken up in the air, / freeing, I think, about a million birds." She indicates the beloved through indirection, not opposition; the lover and beloved merge into one "face":

> No cage, no frightening birds; the rain
> is brightening now. The face is pale
> that tried the puzzle of their prison
> and solved it with an unexpected kiss,
> whose freckled unsuspected hands alit.

Whose, indeed. We are given a puzzle, like the body, that cannot be solved by intellectual mastery. Goldensohn finely connects this poem in its imagery of cage, storm, and passion to the already mentioned unpublished piece, "It is marvellous to wake up together," to suggest that imprisonment as a continuing motif in Bishop underlines the kind of constriction a lesbian might feel in writing, in the 1940s and 1950s, about her sexuality. Yet in this poem, the possibility of breaking down unnameable barriers exists, and if only temporarily, prison becomes permeable.

"While Someone Telephones" adds a further element of constriction and distress to the sequence. She continues to elide the "I" (the previous poem only casually inserts, "I think," which rather than asserting a stable subjectivity makes it stand out as postulation). The title indicates a simultaneity of subjects without distinguishing them; the poem confounds these subjects throughout. As already mentioned, her scenario resonates with Barthian overtones, in her depiction of the lover(s) chained to the telephone, already going through the process of mourning. One, the one who waits, seems to anticipate a call, while the line is kept busy by some mysterious other: "Wasted, wasted minutes that couldn't be worse, / minutes of a barbaric condescension." Condescension implies a hierarchy or imbalance in feelings, or disparity: "the uncondescending stranger" is the hoped-for lover, "the heart's release." In its obfuscation and blurring of identities, the poem appears to describe, more than a vocal interaction, a physiological response. The feeling of abandonment conjured up, one could say, finds an objective correlative in the exterior landscape, but it is perceived not by any integrated identity as the poem breaks forth:

> —Stare out the bathroom window at the fir-trees,
> at their dark needles, accretions to no purpose

> woodenly crystallized, and where two fireflies
> are only lost.

This pair of fireflies (signals in the title poem, "A Cold Spring," of sexual energy and passion) turn into the "green gay eyes" of "these minutes' host," the one who enchains the other in waiting, the sacrificial lover. Bishop emphasizes the absence left by a loved one as a part of the lover's identity: "Hear nothing but a train that goes by, must go by, like tension; / *nothing*. And wait." Waiting becomes the tension that found release in "Rain." With the last three lines appearing with the word "and" to mimic the ending of "A Cold Spring," she reiterates the sense of simultaneous action indicated by the title: "And while the fireflies / are failing to illuminate these nightmare trees / might they not be his green gay eyes." We have entered a dangerous landscape with too many accretions, the green eyes indicating that these fireflies might well be the kind that devour one another. "Not to be devoured is the secret goal of a whole life," knows the smallest woman in the world, a figure from a story by Clarice Lispector, translated by Bishop (to be discussed at the close of this chapter). We seem in the throes of a relationship between a male and a female: fated to devour one another? While Bishop could be substituting a "he" for a "she," I think her male personas here (unlike those artist figures of *North & South*) are masks donned to mock heterosexual romance as well as to play with those power relations of dominance and submission, typically inscribed within male / female bonds, in homosexual contexts.

The last of the sequence, "O Breath," with its title and its first line's "celebrated breast," seems to reinscribe a traditional romantic paradigm, while it also invites us to laud female sexuality. The first poem of this sequence baffled with its heady abstraction, the second with its compacted conceit spiraling upon itself, and the third with its discovery of the phallacy in a predatory, enchaining love. By this fourth poem, she projects another version of love, one that could operate as "equivocal" exchange. The very form of her lines, broken and divided by spontaneous caesuras (in the manner of Rich's love poems in "Splittings" in *The Dream of a Common Language*, 1978), allows breath to circulate through the poem. She begins with the dilemma of the subject / object division—taking on a traditional male role of voyeur and overseer as she watches her lover sleep. Bishop risks objectifying the loved one whose sphinxlike body "blindly veined" "lives and lets / live" yet she admits to the loved one's impenetrability (what the Barthian lover cannot), saying "I cannot fathom   even a ripple." With the fragment, "why restrained," she works toward release. The close-up scrutiny of the lover's breast animated by breath reveals a bluntness not usually credited to Bishop: "(See the thin flying   of nine black hairs / four around one   five the other nipple, / flying almost intolerably   on your own breath.)" "Intolerably" might incline us to share Williamson's view that Bishop's love poems (though he does not discuss this one) refute the ultimate possibility of love and connection. But it is the desire to "bargain" and negotiate with another—rather than to master or penetrate the other—that allows her to acknowledge, even accept, the difficulties that inevitably come with cathexis. The lover does fear that she cannot be significantly present to the slumbering one, yet counting the hairs belies an exactitude, as it demonstrates an undisguised loving proximity, a reassessment of "flaw" (a key word from "A Cold Spring") and the signs of intrusive corporeality. Even if she gives up the dream of complete fusion, she recognizes an "equivocal" bonding that exists through the mingling of their breath, both inside and outside the breast:

> Equivocal, but what we have in common's   bound to be
>   there,
> whatever we must own   equivalents for,
> something that maybe I   could bargain with
> and make a separate peace   beneath
> within   if never with.

The language throughout this poem is typically Bishopian, and I would say, feminine in its anti-absolutist and vigorous indeterminacy ("something" and "maybe," for example, let the poem float around signification), in its *feeling around for* rather than in any linear or definitive assertion. Stubbornly vague, Bishop wants us to feel with her for the ineffable other. Aware of the problematics of making "a separate peace" that accommodates both self and other, the poem, nevertheless, affirms connecting. Language, her language, is spoken with the breath of the other, or could be an attempt to approximate its rhythm. There is hope of common "bounding," an escape from identity or sameness into an intimacy of equivalence bargained for through immersion (within) or subversion (beneath). These propositions allow us to read the love relationship in terms of nurturing, as the lover's posture approximates both the child "within" the mother's womb and "beneath" her breast. She can say "if never with"—asserting both possibility ("if") and impossibility ("never"), and though the poem ends on a potentially depressed note, "if never with" implies that a "without" exists, that the lover does not simply unite symbiotically with a projected beloved. Bishop insists that we waver in our interpretation: such oscillation in language is part of an imperative to disestablish rigid boundaries.

These four poems take up a love situation, and through the sequence, Bishop subverts her own archaic impulses. She often inserts herself into the male tradition, camouflaging her identity and exchanging hats, to show its limitations and liabilities for the woman practitioner; to reveal the loneliness and isolation involved in the choice of poetic undertaking, especially within a tradition that extols the powerful and controlling isolated ego. Margaret Homans in *Women Writers and Poetic Identity* discusses the impact of Romanticism upon women writers and suggests that the contribution of women Romantics was in their search (where it succeeded) for a transcendence recognizing collectivity rather than the essential egoism that governed male Romantics; the difficulty lies, according to Homans, in writing transcendence without reinscribing female as mother, as earth, as death, but instead as collective power and energy.[11] Bishop reveals the Romantic search for transcendence as egomaniacal and deluded, and she finds strength through her bonding with other women even as she shows the obstacles to such bonding. Needlessly self-denigrating, she writes, on a stay in Maryland, "I find I'm really a minor female Wordsworth."[12] Different from the male Wordsworth, but not minor. More like Dorothy Wordsworth, Emily Brontë, and Emily Dickinson (writers Homans examines), Bishop does not seek to find the imprint of her consciousness staring back at her, whole and legitimized from the landscape; instead she may see herself as interdependent with others and the natural world, not in the position to subdue them or it but ready to follow and trace the "conspiring root." Women turn to other women for survival and support in their marginalization.

The first and title poem of *A Cold Spring* is dedicated to Jane Dewey, a resident of Maryland, a locale Bishop often visited in her travels across the country. The title suggests a new phase in Bishop's career, an awakening, if tentative, to feeling. It is not only a decade that separates the composing of her two volumes: if *North & South* is a highly cerebral revision of past influences and traditions, her next volume consciously moves toward openness and emotion. Instead of being consumed by the threat of isolation, instead of feeling herself as a woman poet pitted against an unaccommodating tradition, she allows herself the freedom to comment upon the difficult aspects of that tradition that interfere with an exploration of her sexuality and her relationship with others.

Though "A Cold Spring" is dedicated to Jane Dewey and charts an awakening of passion and warmth, metaphoric of the change in phases in her poetic presentation, two male figures haunt the poem tellingly. One is John Dewey (Jane's father), the famous social psychologist and author, best known for *Human Nature and Conduct* (from which Bishop took notes), a valorization of reason and practical intelligence in ordering actions and morals.[13] He writes: "We can recognize that all conduct is interaction between elements of human nature and the environment, natural and social" (14). We must pay attention to the physical sciences if we are to understand how to negotiate with our realities. Morality does not spring from some innate good, or through the conditioning of the self through cultivation. The internal and external must interact; habits involve "cooperation of organism and environment" (16). Such a view "brings morals to earth, and if they aspire to heaven it is to the heavens of the earth, and not to another world. Honesty, chastity, . . . are not private possessions of a person. They are working adaptations of personal capacities with environing forces" (17). This conception of human behavior and the self as bound up with a sociality rather than an insulated spiritual essentialism is certainly comparable to Bishop's earth-centered reasonableness, her "miracle for breakfast," her sense of the necessary cooperation between human beings and the natural world. Yet sensibility and restraint in conduct are the very forces this poem works against.

Rich considers "A Cold Spring" to be "a recording of a slow, deliberate, erotic unfolding," though she does not pursue a detailed analysis of this unfolding. A cursory reading of the poem might indicate that Bishop has turned her descriptive powers decidedly outward, abandoning the surrealist partiality of *North & South*. But even if this piece is read as descriptive poem—indeed, especially if it is—a peculiar rendering of nature surfaces that celebrates connection, even as it is tenuous or flawed. Which leads to the other male within the poem: Gerard Manley Hopkins, one of Bishop's poetic heroes. It is Hopkins who provides the epigram for the poem: "Nothing is so beautiful as spring." Bishop admired Hopkins for the rapid transitions in the movement of his mind, portrayed so well in his poetry, and for his hearty spiritualism. Hopkins's poem of spring is tellingly different from Bishop's. Spring for Hopkins re-creates an unfallen Edenic moment: the locus of innocent procreation free from sin, boy and girl paired off, still fresh in their May-day. As much as Bishop venerates Hopkins, she cannot accept such a full-blown and unconditionally warm spring. Her spring is askew, and the relation between the sexes is not inflexibly defined as in Hopkins. Her spring emerges slowly, only gradually giving up its juice. The hesitancy and imperfection in her landscape reflect her own romantic uncertainties. And she seeks out a poetic diction more suited to a world out of touch with "[a] strain of the earth's sweet being in the beginning."

Ostriker reminds us of the "link between outcast words and outcast persons" (196). Since she must find another language to express her outsiderhood, Bishop's anti-Romantic description points up arbitrariness and fallenness with dust signaling the onset of spring:

> A cold spring:
> the violet was flawed on the lawn.
> For two weeks or more the trees hesitated;
> the little leaves waited,
> carefully indicating their characteristics.
> Finally a grave green dust
> settled over your big and aimless hills.
> One day, in a chill white blast of sunshine,
> on the side of one a calf was born.
> The mother stopped lowing
> and took a long time eating the after-birth,
> a wretched flag,
> but the calf got up promptly
> and seemed inclined to feel gay.

As Robert Pinsky has said, Bishop appears to have the gift of giving the illusion of simply representing reality, and Goldensohn even goes so far as to call her "the ultimate realist" (119). But hers is not an objective record even as her eye seems to note the exact moment of each shift in her environment. The continual mentioning of time markers throughout—"For two weeks or more," "Finally," "One day," "The next day," "Took a long time," "promptly"—only increases the viewer's uncertainty and produces the impressive sense of the incommensurable randomness of our markings or citings of time passing. Her alertness implies an anxiety, a waiting like that of the "little leaves," who are "carefully indicating their characteristics." The lover is the one who waits, according to Barthes. But her waiting involves her in a networked landscape embodying an emotional exchange.

Her "the violet was flawed on the lawn" suggests Bishop's own idiosyncrasy and mock self-deprecation. There is an enjoyment in the flaw (as there is in an uncle's "transvestite twist" in "Exchanging Hats"). She seems to be recalling or reusing details from a letter to Lowell, written at Cape Breton, where she describes a similar birthing, complete with vaudevillian surprise and pathos: "I was called out to see a calf being born in the pasture beside the house. In five minutes after several falls on its nose it was standing up shaking its head & tail & trying to nurse. They took it away from its mother almost immediately & carried it struggling in a wheelbarrow to the barn—we've just been watching it trying to lie down. Once up it didn't know how to get down again & finally fell in a heap. Now it seems to be trying *not* to sleep."[14] If nothing else, she draws upon the mother's separation from offspring for her poem, turning it into, perhaps the "long time" taken with the afterbirth, and the mournful "lowing"—as well as the almost perverse ways of this calf. In contrast, then, to Hopkins's spring, Bishop's revels, as does her letter, in eccentric naturalism. A calf born as if from a hill itself, "on the side of one," and the mother's lingering ingestion intensifies the sense of cyclical and contiguous, if partly absurd, relations within nature. There is a pleasure in the abject, if we want to use Kristeva's word for an apprehension of our corporeality, its incorporation and expulsion of matter; in this case, "the wretched flag" becomes the sign of waste in the generation of new life and the anguish of decathexis. The newborn, prompt and automatic, "seemed inclined to feel gay," suggesting sexual inclination just as the little leaves hesitating begin to "indicate" their inclination. All the signs of spring mirror the poet's own sense of otherness, of coming out or birthing emotional expression and desire.

Bishop moves away from Transcendentalism, which bestows upon the natural a hieroglyphic power to figure forth God, but instead of simply focusing upon the earth as drained of significance, she empowers the body, and her connection with the earth through the body. But she does so in a manner that avoids confirming the typical association with the transcendent eternal Mother—the womb and tomb of all—that Margaret Homans takes so much to task for its making woman into the silent other / object who, while outside man's complete control, is always subjected to his force, will, manipulation. A matter-of-fact tone ("The next day / was much warmer") serves as counterpoint for the sensuous language especially predominant in the second stanza where the body becomes linked to an eroticized landscape. The addressee is firmly synecdochic with it through "her big and aimless hills," though not metaphorical of it. A male sleeper most explicitly personifies nature, reversing our stereotypes of the earth as mother figure by resorting to Norse mythology instead of the traditional Greek, as "the sleeper awoke, / stretching miles of green limbs from the south. / In his cap the lilacs whitened, / then one day they fell like snow." We are not, by any means, in a "sober" environ, and all the liquid consonance of the second stanza prepares us for effusion and immersion. Bishop never loses sight that this location links her with Jane Dewey: "Four deer practised leaping over your fences." Second-person address makes the tone intimate and since she never uses the first-person, her own identity also seems in the process of disappearing or dissolving in the terrain.

We feel a tension build with the "[s]ong-sparrows were wound up" and with the whip of "the complementary cardinal" within a space now finely interwoven. She discovers an active blurring between elements rather than static shapes in isolation from each other, and in complementarity, cause to celebrate the corporeal:

> Greenish-white dogwood infiltrated the wood,
> each petal burned, apparently, by a cigarette-butt;
> and the blurred redbud stood
> beside it, motionless, but almost more
> like movement than any placeable color.

Colors meddle with one another. "Infiltration" suggests infusion, hinting maybe at the smokiness of the cigarettes outcast. "Apparently," a touchstone Bishop word, with the "butt" make the passage doublespeak of eternal appearance without definite substance or solidity.

The temporal shift to evening and "a new moon" softens and deepens a diffusion within the landscape. A druggedness overcomes the atmosphere, and we can see each cow-flop under the moon: we expect release with "The bull-frogs are sounding, / slack strings plucked by heavy thumbs." She closes in upon moths, opening as if in adoring prayer, "flattening" themselves as part of a surface interlayered and spreading:

> Beneath the light, against your white front door,
> the smallest moths, like Chinese fans,
> flatten themselves, silver and silver-gilt
> over pale yellow, orange, or gray.

Silver seems unnecessarily repeated. But the same emerges with a difference, "gilt." (Perhaps she puns upon "guilt," the guilt over writing that Cixous attributes to women, as they encode their forbidden bodies in secret.) The advent of spring sped up in one day and evening resolves itself in the steamy and close observance of fireflies engaged in a mating rite with a climactic "Now":

> Now, from the thick grass, the fireflies
> begin to rise:
> up, then down, then up again:
> lit on the ascending flight,
> drifting simultaneously to the same height,
> —exactly like the bubbles in champagne.
> —Later on they rise much higher.

The double colons prepare for a continuous or recurring climax—not closed (distinct from the economy of a "glorious phallic monosexuality," Cixous, 254). Guilt has been annulled. Champagne brought to the celebration. With the fireflies rising in wave-like patterns she offers a vision of effervescence almost limitless. Though these fireflies "drift," they have direction, coincidence, symmetry like the fanlike moths spread against the door. Her characteristic lines begun with dashes produce a sense of deferral, building up to the poem's moment of expansive, orgasmic "certitude," festive anticipation and fulfillment. The final three lines return to the body as landscape:

> And your shadowy pastures will be able to offer
> these particular glowing tributes
> every evening now throughout the summer.

An offering is being made—for whom and for what is kept unspecified. But as mating signals, these tributes are "particular." In "While Someone Telephones," fireflies reappear as a menacing "illumination" of nothing, of a lover's frustration: now they promise simultaneity, reciprocity and possible fulfillment.

Williams's evocation of the emergence of spring in *Spring and All* likewise rejects Romantic notions of nature and reverberates with Bishopic tentativeness.[15] "One by one objects are defined" he says, passing bush and plant in clear sharp outlines. But while he sees objects in apposition, he emphasizes their separation from each other. And like his Romantic predecessors, his focus is upon the power of the imagination antagonistically *apart* from the sensuous world, as seen, for instance, in his admiration of Juan Gris and his antirepresentationalism: "TO ESCAPE ILLUSION and stand between man and nature as saints once stood between man and the sky" (112). Bishop's poem, in contradistinction, redefines the parameters of the imagination, or in this case, of the limits of a love poem; it invokes a desire to infiltrate nature, a desire that does not objectify (because a subject is not asserted) but incorporates it in a subject's process of unfolding in relationship. By never resorting to first person, she expresses herself through the landscape and so avoids setting up a chimeric relationship that could make of the beloved a fixed object. Just as the cow eats the afterbirth, we are involved in a cycle of boundary erasure, not in a terrain that sets the artist in antagonism with the elements.

For Homans, the Romantic tradition prevents women from participating in a poetry that emphasizes the primacy of the self. Since the emergence of subjectivity rests upon constructing women as "other," the female is often associated with a powerful but objectified nature. For women writers, to embrace such a paradigm involves a denial not only of the feminine but of their very selfhood. To identify with nature and with the other, as demanded by high Romanticism, involves a destruction of the very subjectivity and selfhood seemingly necessary for poetic accomplishment. As Homans puts it: "To identify with the mother . . . would be to identify with nature, and to identify with nature would be to put an end to writing about nature." But such identification can signal a new economy if these terms do not remain trapped within the linguistic formulations of phallocentrism. To be "other" within the mainstream allows a woman the ability, as Homans recommends, to recognize the limitations of oppositional thinking, of custom and hierarchy. It also allows for a poetry not based on the self in opposition to nature or others, but on offering: the Cixousian gift that has no demand, which makes for amenable interchange. When Homans suggests that hierarchy in language might be undone "in other ways than by denying otherness" she opens the way for those like Bishop who forge new ground for a feminist imagination.

Jane Dewey does not get absorbed by nature; while she "possesses" the farm, she does so through dedication, metonymy, and contiguity. To identify with nature is not to embrace the inarticulate but to refuse to fix meaning in authorized ways. While such an identification may mean a refusal of the self that is pitted against nature, it does not demand an absolute disappearance of the self. Bishop does not achieve a facile harmony with nature nor does she try to close the gap between things and words, self and world.

Throughout, Bishop struggles with the difficulty of being lesbian in a dominantly heterosexual world and worries about how "otherness" affects relationships. Do they run the risk of miming the negative patterns of dominance and submission structuring heterosexuality? She parodies such patterns in at least the first three parts of "Four Poems." "A Cold Spring," however, proposes a nonhierarchical spontaneous relationship—"up, then

down, then up again" moving "to the same height." Yet Bishop's honesty in
dealing with relationships includes her recognition of the difficulties associated with having an "inverted" perspective. In "Insomnia," for instance, she
plays upon an archaic, but at the time, still-used word for lesbian, "invert,"
a term inherited from the sexologists Krafft-Ebing in nineteenth-century
Germany and Havelock Ellis in 1920s America to describe what was nar-
rowly and biologically considered "the man trapped in a woman's body" syn-
drome. But Bishop uses the term to invert it—to play with definitions, and
because it conjures up a spatial meaning—linking the term with vision itself.
Our erotics effect our sight.

Bishop's surrealist impulse still persists from *North & South* in poems such
as "Insomnia" in its suspension of logic, its transpositions and reversals.
Through the image of the well, she invokes Radclyffe Hall's famous lesbian
novel *The Well of Loneliness* (1928), which popularized Ellis's assessment of
sexual inversion. Gilbert and Gubar, aware of the revolutionary quality of
the book for its time, nevertheless regard Hall's work as still inscribing the
male assumption of defeat, desperation, and isolation for those in alternative, nonheterosexual relationships.[16] Bishop's well, however, is of loneliness
but it also becomes a resource, the transformative potentiality existing beneath and within the sorrowful and longing voice of the insomniac suffering
an unrequited love. That she can imagine an alternative world is her power
(as Cixous recommends through "Sorties," woman must take flight): the inverted world of sleep and dreams can make more sense to "a daytime sleeper"
than waking hours. The drop into the well becomes the imaginative space of
the looking-glass; she draws our attention to the way we read from left to
right; in a world inverted, ironically, language does not function or becomes
illegible and unnecessary. Dreams provide truth: "you love me" is a way of
saying "I love you," without saying it, to show the reversible and chiasmic
positions of "you" and "I." Here paradox survives without bafflement. And
here dialectical thinking loses its credit in the fluent exchange forwarded by
hypnotic anaphora:

> where left is always right,
> where the shadows are really the body,
> where we stay awake all night,
> where the heavens are shallow as the sea
> is now deep, and you love me.

The rhyme in the stanza enjambed to this one links "deserted" with "inverted"; it is as if, through the poem, the subject, identified only by the "other," the "you," escapes to a place of returning love.

The poem begins with the conventional love image of the moon, usually linked to the feminine; in this poem it is trapped "in the bureau mirror," and somewhat like the Gentleman divided by one, this speaker feels split. Another prisoner, she is unable to sleep and identifies with the moon who "never / never smiles" and who looks "far and away beyond sleep." A mirror pretends symmetry, depth, perfect reflexivity. But here both the moon and mirror distort. Think of the figure in "Man-Moth," described as "an inverted pin magnetized to the moon" who "always seats himself facing the wrong way," or of the figure(s) in "Love Lies Sleeping" (CP, 16):

> for always to one, or several morning comes,
> whose head has fallen over the edge of his bed,
>   whose face is turned
>   so that the image of
>
> the city grows down into his open eyes
> inverted and distorted. No. I mean
>   distorted and revealed,
>   if he sees it at all.

The threat of blindness persists. But if vision and revelation emerge, they do in this equation, from inversion, from seeing the world through peripheral glasses. Love does "lie" sleeping, but "Insomnia" wants to replace dormancy with the revelation of dream.

The final stanza of "Insomnia" (CP, 70) ends with the abrupt, almost incidental, "and you love me"—which makes this poem one of Bishop's most vulnerable; Moore has called it "a cheap love poem," probably because it is one of the rare moments Bishop's speaker openly requests love, even as she reticently admits her own. Before the last clauses, which depict an inverted world, she has already flown outside the universe and into another one (making of the first a linguistic myth of singularity and enclosure) that has a mirror and a body of water of its own (suggesting the infinite and eternal space Cixous allocates to woman's imaginary). Identifying with the moon, awake and cast into a well, abandoned by the sensible world, she wishes in the penultimate sentence to assume some of the moon's pride (or the deserting beloved) and its ability to relocate, defy the Universe and its conventional orbiting:

> By the Universe deserted,
> *she'd* tell it to go to hell,
> and she'd find a body of water,
> or a mirror, on which to dwell.

Such a notion leads her to tell herself in superstitious and ritual song (as she did to the child in one of the "Songs"): "So wrap up care in a cobweb / and drop it down the well / into that world inverted." The shadows that are really the body echo "the shadowy pastures" of "A Cold Spring" and bring us back to that enticingly blurred landscape. She deflects the possible Romantic sense of limitlessness invoked through the sea and heaven trading places, but substitutes the renewing yet limited figure of the well: feminized source of imaginative flight and, if nothing else, of the illusion of correspondences.

With "Faustina, or Rock Roses" (*CP*, 72), Bishop has broken the ice of solitary meditation and portrays another "inverted" relationship, this time a triangle. Black Faustina tending, a crazy white woman aging, a visitor closely seeing. The ambivalence about dependency between servant and mistress, as Goldensohn has so insightfully recommended, could also mirror Bishop's conflicted feelings about the binding of herself with her mother and with other women; this poem, perhaps, allows her the distance she needs to reckon with her difficulties of power and helplessness within love situations. The visitor (read as Bishop) "embarrassed / not by pain nor age / nor even nakedness, / though perhaps by its reverse" becomes part of the duo's interaction through her perception of the process of decay always going on seen almost at an atomic level, the poem stitching together transitional moments of relative perspectives and slants. She scrutinizes the metamorphoses at work not only between Faustina and her patient but in the setting itself, within even the wallpaper that haunts with its rose configuration, "betrayed" by an "eighty-watt bulb":

> violet-embossed, glistening
> with mica flakes.
>
> It exposes the fine white hair,
> the gown with the undershirt
> showing at the neck,

> the pallid palm-leaf fan
> she holds but cannot wield,
> her white disordered sheets
> like wilted roses.

The visitor feels her difference from her surroundings, but fears and understands identification. As all aspects of the setting reverberate in one another, complete distance is not possible.

> The visitor sits and watches
> the dew glint on the screen
> and in it two glow-worms
> burning a drowned green.

Are these glowworms reminiscent of the petals burned by unseen cigarettes? Are these worms not mating but just drowning, dying in each other? Nothing can be fully disentangled, purified, or made unambivalent; so the poem tells us. The patient's sheets recall the wallpaper "blooming above her head / into four vaguely roselike / flower-formations" and look forward to the "rust-perforated roses" the visitor "proffers" before she leaves.

Bishop's roses—and this poem—can be understood better by taking into account an unpublished poem called "Vague Poem (Vaguely Love Poem),"[17] written, it would appear, as part of the process of "Faustina," material seemingly repressed and incorporated within it. This makes "Faustina" an even vaguer love poem. Bishop plays upon our desire for permanence, and our desire to find it in symbols. She returns to the rose, an image inseparable from romance, and proffers it "rust-perforated." The second half of the published poem's title, "Rock Roses," never referred to explicitly within that poem—leads us to the roses that recur in "Vaguely Love Poem." A woman brings her home to see a rock-rose that fascinates her as it seems to harden to crystal, effortless and immediate, without intermediate stem or leaf. To see the process of the rock-rose blooming, apparently, requires hallucinatory ability. She seems to be waiting once more for some passion to emerge. The speaker has a near-vision, sensing something at work "inside": "I *almost* saw it—turning into a rose" she says and then wackily confesses to that "Crystalography and its laws" she had "once wanted badly to study," while in the margins she has written: "until I loved." It is as though love makes "laws" irrelevant or impossible. The final stanza provides her with a vision: the "she" of the draft converts to the more direct "you," and the nakedness missed in "Faustina" appears. She describes the woman's breasts as roses and then inscribes the whole body as sprouting roses. We are close to a polymorphous reading of the body with roses traversing the beloved:

> Just now, when I saw you naked again,
> I thought the same words: Rose-rock; rock-rose . . .
> Rose, trying, working, to show itself,
> forming, folding over,
> unimaginable connections, unseen, shining edges.
> Rose-rock, unformed, flesh beginning, crystal by crystal,
> clear pink breasts and darker, crystalline nipples,
> rose-rock, rose-quartz, roses, roses, roses,
> exacting roses from the body,
> and the even darker, accurate rose of sex—

We may feel with Irigaray that "[a] woman has sexual organs everywhere." She exults. Rainbow, rainbow, rainbow. Bishop figures the lover's body as having, as she imagined of the rock-rose, "unimaginable connections," hallucinated as "earth to rose and back again," a dream of recurrence not death.

Is it not strange then that rock-roses—which require so much to come into being—belong in the published poem's title with "Faustina"? Not when feelings are so mixed, so exacting. While Faustina lives by her role as caretaker, she also resents her position:

> complaining of, explaining,
> the terms of her employment.
> She bends above the other.
> Her sinister kind face
> presents a cruel black
> coincident conundrum.

Genuine care threatens to evaporate in the context of social inequality. Perhaps we should here think of Carol Gilligan's "ethic of care" attributed to female psychology; because of our roles as nurturers and caretakers, Gilligan contends, our morality is contextually and relationally based: we tend, in short, to base our ethics on the "other."[18] While Bishop's aesthetics does affirm this ethics, she also reveals the more sinister underpinnings of "care," especially in contexts of racial and social inequality. Faustina suffers from "the terms of her employment," a subservient position, and recalls an earlier poem, "Cootchie," which depicts another servant / mistress opposition: "Cootchie, Miss Lula's servant, lies in marl, / black into white she went" (*CP*, 46). Bishop exposes again in "Faustina" the danger of hegemony. Whiteness appears as if it might eliminate difference; the very weakness and powerlessness of the unnamed mistress "with her pallid palm-leaf fan" wilts and bleaches away into her sick room. The outsider or the marginalized figure, if we think of her in terms of Hegel's master / slave dialectic, gains a certain kind of power by being subordinated. But in Bishop's attempt to escape binarism, she reveals that "dialectic," understood only in terms of power, misses the nuances and "unimaginable connections" ("Vaguely Love Poem") that make all our impulses impure and ambivalent, multiple and "proliferative," like the roses of "Vaguely Love Poem." Faustina's death-wish for the woman she cares for shades into an "unimaginable nightmare," a dependency as dangerous for the ego as it was for the sisters in "The Baptism." Freedom from employment is both alluring and frightening. And the question of whether or not the death of her mistress will bring peace or more pain expands, almost as the rock-rose of the unpublished poem, growing outward, vulviform—with its "unseen, shining edges, / forming, folding over" ("Vaguely Love Poem").

> The acuteness of the question
> forks instantly and starts
> a snake-tongue flickering;
> blurs further, blunts, softens,
> separates, falls, our problems
> becoming helplessly
>   proliferative. ("Faustina")

Bishop's rose is exfoliating—both expansive and disintegrative, unlike H.D.'s, whose trademark sea-rose possesses the hardness and edginess of the rock-rose, yet stands alone, embattled. To become "helplessly proliferative," to "say only either," means to lose complete control over limitedness and finitude, to see oneself in a more generative scheme. The visitor's final offering of "rust-perforated roses," shot through with the holes made by time, are not the roses of conventional romance; they break down the association of femininity with softness and delicacy. One remembers the skin in "The Fish" compared to "ancient wallpaper" with "shapes like full-blown roses" about to flake off and blur, "stained and lost through age." One of Bishop's gifts is to see the "coincident conundrum," the not-to-be resolved but united doubleness. Pain and loss, love and possibility.

In spite of the dangers of connection, Bishop never forgets our interdependence, nor does she underplay connection between individuals and their environments. The predatory factories of "Varick Street" (*CP*, 75) intrude the industrial and commercial into a love situation, and possibly corrupt it. The italicized songlike refrain: "And I shall sell you sell you / sell you of course, my dear, and you'll sell me"—this is not Cixous's exchange but rather the violent prostitution and cupidity of love evoked in "Three Valentines," or in "Love Lies Sleeping," an anti-aubade with the lover waking isolated in a city to address the covert and destructive character of love: "queer cupids of all persons getting up, / whose evening meal they will prepare all day, / you will dine well / on his heart, on his, and his." "Varick Street" precedes a quartet of poems dealing more directly with the amatory voice; here the personal involvement of the speaker remains oblique. The first stanza depicts the factories with "elongated nostrils / haired with spikes" writhing and veined like a live beast suffocating, "trying to breathe" while it pollutes the air. A following stanza increases in surreality as does the sense of the speaker's possible love-sickness:

> On certain floors
> certain wonders.
> Pale dirty light,
> some captured iceberg
> being prevented from melting.
> See the mechanical moons,
> sick, being made
> to wax and wane
> at somebody's instigation.

To be "prevented from melting" is stagnation (as with her "Imaginary Iceberg"). Yet somewhere "On certain floors / certain wonders" are taking place without definite source, wonders that allow for the possibility of intimacy that emerges, however compromised, in the last stanza. Bishop's phrasing and syntax suggest emotion rather than sense: "Lights music of love / work on." The "music of love" keeps working, transfiguring the assemblage of factory lights, and she moves out of the room on Varick Street in imagining the pressing and printing of calendars, a "certain wonder"; the "mechanical moons" now "make medicine / or confectionary" (looking forward to "Sestina" where the moons change to tears and seeds). Do we see Donne's lovers, their compact world a microcosm for the universe so there is no need to go outside, all miniaturized in the Beloved:

> Our bed
> shrinks from the soot
> and hapless odors
> hold us close.

The bed both shrinks and withdraws from the world of soot and odors, and that world also draws them close. The site of intimacy and comfort is both bombarded by a hapless environ and made possible by it.

"The Shampoo," which closes *A Cold Spring,* is the most vivid example of Bishop's transformed love poem of desire and intimacy, written with Lota in mind near the beginning of her residence in Brazil; instead of the "I" and "you" of "Insomnia," the hectic subjects are now in the first-person plural, "our memories." In rough drafts the poem was called "Gray Hairs" (the change in title reflects a change in emphasis while still exploring the relation between time and love). Carpe diem demands the lover seize the day, insisting on the primacy of youth, denying the necessity of loss and age. This is a love poem written in a time of possible conflict ("shocks") to a "dear friend" who has been "precipitate and pragmatical," acting with characteristic Bishopian ambivalence. Like the poem to Marianne Moore, this is also an invitation to "Come flying." "The Shampoo" turns to everyday experience to find the art of love. Bishop feels the pressure of days and distance, but accepts and immerses herself in temporality and flux. Come, let's bring in May, proclaims Herrick. Here she sings, simply, come, let me wash your hair. Metaphysical conceit flattens. The moon, drawn into the tin basin as into a well, becomes domestic, "battered and shiny." Correspondence with any divine is snapped: more important are the correspondences within earthly, intimate—even flawed—relationships. With "the still explosions on the rocks," stillness and turbulence occupy the same image, and she continues this doubleness with the lichens (as with the sea-lice in "The Fish," which in Bishop's reclaiming, turn into beautiful, possibly sublime, embroidery), which "grow / by spreading, gray, concentric shocks." The comma between "spreading" and "gray" makes "spreading" both adjective and verb, description and action; spreading is always amenable.

In traditional love poetry, the grey hairs of the beloved get ignored, but here the loved one's hair becomes a flock of sheep, shooting stars that are seen in the process of concentricity and disintegration, opening into the world—not self-enclosing or withdrawing. That the circles made around rocks in the sea "have arranged to meet the rings around the moon" imply an apocalyptical and fantastical tryst and symmetry while "within our memories they have not changed" (the circles under the eyes, signs of time passing). The image of hair greying is celebrated, and the shampooing of it imitates another coming, the orgasmic moment of "A Cold Spring" when the fireflies begin to rise "exactly like the bubbles in champagne"; here "the shooting stars" are moving ungoverned, dispersing ever outward. Cixous's sense of woman's writing as a giving and an offering up annotate this poem well:

> She gives more, with no assurance that she'll get back even some un-expected profit from what she puts out. This is an "economy" that can no longer be put in economic terms. Wherever she loves, all the old concepts of management are left behind. At the end of a more or less conscious computation, she finds not her sum but her differ-ences. I am for you what you want me to be at the moment you look at me in a way you've never seen me before: at every instant. When I write, it's everything that we don't know we can be that is written out of me, without exclusions, without stipulation, and everything we will be calls us to the unflagging, intoxicating, unappeasable search for love. In one another we will never be lacking. ("Laugh," 259)

This is hardly the "selling" in "Varick Street" or the semicannibalism of "Love Lies Sleeping." The "search for love" involves us in an amenable un-conditional process, an act and art of fluid overlap between subject and object.

Without being at all definite about its subject or object, Bishop's very thin, short-lined "Sonnet" (CP, 192) provides the conventional form for a love poem only to undermine it—to allow for a kind of intoxicating release. While this valedictory poem is not, of course, directly associated with the pieces discussed from A Cold Spring, it does, nevertheless, represent a kind of fulfillment of impulses in "Insomnia" or "The Shampoo" as a self-portrait of unexplained passion, without any need for an "I":

> Caught—the bubble
> in the spirit-level,
> a creature divided;
> and the compass needle
> wobbling and wavering,
> undecided.
> Freed—the broken

> thermometer's mercury
> running away;
> and the rainbow-bird
> from the narrow bevel
> of the empty mirror,
> flying wherever
> it feels like, gay!

Measurement and compass "computation" are turned awry; there is no stiff-
ness here, no fear of mirror slippage, but an exuberant "running away." She
reverses the positions of octet and sestet, using form only to show it broken
and reformed. No longer have we a dividing or reflecting mirror, but an
empty one, a "virgin mirror" ("The Riverman," 105) so that identity becomes
untrammeled in flying and feeling, a "rainbow-bird" free from the "narrow
bevel." If the thermometer is the body in this nearly metaphysical conceit,
the trapped and divided creature within, the bubble at "spirit-level," the mercurial spirit, can be released only as the enclosing rod shatters. Hermes can
fly, steal back the essential multiplicity of language. The invert is now gay.

IV

Bishop concerned herself in North & South more with breaking down
boundaries for an interactive aesthetic experience ("The Monument," "The
Map," and "Large Bad Picture" are good examples); her inclusion or wel-
coming of the reader into the text remains. But by the time of A Cold Spring,
another poet emerges: Bishop as lover, more personal and vulnerable. She
asserts the "imperative of intimacy" even as she continues to illumine states
of uncertainty, striving, separation, and loss. Her emphasis is not, nevertheless, on separation but upon how we can pursue connection and bonding.
Several layers of this pursuit resonate in A Cold Spring: she is concerned
with the lover's desire for the other, not to subdue or dominate but to feel in
contiguous interchange with; in another way, she also shows the loss of a
Transcendentalist ethos with a remainder—the desire of the poet as lover to
merge, nevertheless, with the landscape, to find within it some spiritual immanence. These two figures—the lover and the mystic (Cixous's femininity,
recall, carries in it the "cosmic")—obviously cross paths; the desire for the
other is often the desire to feel an oceanic oneness with the world. In a re-

view of Emily Dickinson's letters to Dr. and Mrs. Josiah Gilbert Holland, she says of the poet: "To her, little besides love, human and divine, was worth writing about and often the two became fused."[19] The same impulse to fuse the two loves could be said of Bishop, with of course, different valences.

Language marks a separation of the self from the mother to a state of alienation and articulation, as Lacan has articulated. But as Nancy Chodorow discovers, the Freudian model we have inherited emphasizes this alienation and ignores the continuing and developing bonding between girl and mother that cuts through a sense of ultimate separation; thus Chodorow proposes fusion and permeability as a basis of female experience. If nature does not in itself possess the hieroglyphic sensibility Emerson thought it did, if it does not bear the "thumbprint of God" ("Over 2,000 Illustrations," *CP*, 57), Bishop still feels an indefinable and indeterminate sense of spirituality without being able to confirm or codify it, this "spirit-level"; she feels permeable with nature. Language becomes a way to explore our sense of connection, and to find from within our corporeality the ability to connect through and within language.

Four major poems—"Over 2,000 Illustrations and a Complete Concordance," "The Bight," "At the Fishhouses," and "Cape Breton"—revise transcendental thinking. Hariette Chessman's assessment of Gertrude Stein and Transcendentalism applies to Bishop; she says that the "concept of correspondences becomes irrelevant. [Stein] shifts the focus from the poet's relation to divine nature to the poet's relation to language itself in which a form of divinity resides, not wholly beyond words, but within them."[20] The act of writing in these poems becomes a way of absorption, incorporation, diffusion, weaving, even loving—an overtaking of boundaries or an enlarging of them that makes the necessity for a definable transcendent divinity less pressing. She turns away from metaphor and hierarchy toward metonymy, parataxis, anaphora. These poems, not evidently love poems, still speak a feminine aesthetics, or in Ostriker's terming, an erotics.

"Over 2,000 Illustrations" emerges from the intimate examination of a family Bible and—as many have pointed out—it mourns a lost or missing family security in the last seven lines:

> Why couldn't we have seen
> this old Nativity while we were at it?
> —the dark ajar, the rocks breaking with light,
> an undisturbed, unbreathing flame,
> colorless, sparkless, freely fed on straw,

and, lulled within, a family with pets,
—and looked and looked our infant sight away.

In a poem mended with "ands," this vision lulls us "within," back to an inti-
mation of an original state of coordination and intimate domesticity within
the liminal dark and unrent light. The poem provides a sequence of glances
within consecutive sentences, disparate in content. She laments the repetition of the conjunction "and" and its lack of signifying power, but then
proceeds to rejuvenate it. Fluctuating between "or" constructions, simple
untelling "to be" verbs, and transparent comparisons using "like"—all reveal
an inability to reach beyond words, as in these evocative lines:

> The cobbled courtyard, where the Well is dry,
> is like a diagram, the brickwork conduits
> are vast and obvious, the human figure
> far gone in history or theology,
> gone with its camel or its faithful horse.
> Always the silence, the gesture, the specks of birds
> suspended on invisible threads above the Site,
> or the smoke rising solemnly, pulled by threads.
> Granted a page alone or a page made up
> of several scenes arranged in cattycornered rectangles
> or circles set on stippled gray,
> granted a grim lunette,
> caught in the toils of an initial letter,
> when dwelt upon, they all resolve themselves.

Resolution is very much like dissolution, as Bishop takes us back through let-
tering, history, and theology to the yet-to-be envisioned world. But we have
"always the silence." She may imagine a centrifugal moment of first creation:

> The eye drops, weighted, through the lines
> the burin made, the lines that move apart
> like ripples above sand,
> dispersing storms, God's spreading fingerprint,
> and painfully, finally, that ignite
> in watery prismatic white-and-blue.

"Dispersing" is painful but seemingly imperative for the imagination, drop-

ping with the weight of history. Her next stanza begins: "Entering the Narrows at St. Johns / the touching bleat of goats reached to the ship." We have
been taken to a world of "touching"; she makes ambiguous who or what is
"entering" other than the sound, "the touching bleat of goats." Vision becomes tactile, a spreading beneath the fingerprint.

   In this second stanza of the poem, a "we" is introduced as an ungendered
pronoun of joining. Often she will do away with all pronouns, but here the
"we" allows for an intimacy between speaker and reader. She only introduces
"I" when she shows herself in opposition and fear of ego-dissolution: "It was
somewhere near there / I saw what frightened me most of all: / A holy grave."
"And" appears as fragile hinge between experiences, yet she claims for parataxis the nondominating, nonoverpowering virtue which hierarchical subor-
dinating language stifles. We must make do with our linking "ands." We may
want to find, she implies, ultimate concord, but nothing is ever complete or
tallied inalterably as the first half of her exuberant title ("Over 2,000 Illustrations") indicates. We cannot forget that all the seeing that takes place in the
poem is mediated by the book, which we are instructed to handle as well:

>   Everything only connected by "and" and "and."
>   Open the book. (The gilt rubs off the edges
>   of the pages and pollinates the fingertips.)
>   Open the heavy book. Why couldn't we have seen
>   this old Nativity while we were at it?

Only through cross-pollination of book and reader can we see the family and
its pets; representation connects even as it separates, "points to the Tomb, the
Pit, the Sepulcher."

   "The figure of osmosis is the emblem of female desire" (179), Ostriker
claims and within Bishop's poems "osmosis," liquefaction, pervades. Liquids
passing between membranes, apparently effortless absorption of ideas and
feelings, gilt spreading on the fingertips. Again, we should probably think of
Chodorow with her sense of feminine identity as having "permeable ego
boundaries." Such thinking potentially romanticizes loss of identity or death
but can signal potential communion with others. Bishop's pleasure in osmosis builds in the other three poems, which seek concordance through language, not beyond it.

   Although we are told in a parenthetical epigram that Bishop wrote "The
Bight" (CP, 60) on her birthday and therefore feel the poem resonant with
the personal, the perceiving "I" is strictly kept out of the poem; except for the

stilted use of "one," she banishes pronouns altogether. Absorbing the landscape, she is absorbed by it and, spongelike, needs not assert any false objectivity or distance maintained by a lordly "I." The bight refers to a space
between two headlands that makes for a receding bay, but we cannot not hear
the homonym "bite" within a poem brimming with orality—the dredge's
"dripping jawful of marl," "the blue-gray shark tails" being prepared for the
restaurant trade, the pelicans "like pickaxes / rarely coming up with anything." Wetness and dryness are shown as mysteriously apart—while also in
intimate collaboration. "Absorbing, rather than being absorbed, / the water
in the bight doesn't wet anything": the water exerts an active force (displacing
the association of a feminine energy with the passive), pulling everything
into its attractive kinesics.

The kinds of correspondences possible in Bishop's landscape are drained
of Symbolist conviction: she confesses outright her inability to reiterate
Baudelaire's vision of nature as a temple of symbols in conversation with
man. She turns the water to the "color of gas flame," and she manages, "One
can smell it turning to gas; if one were Baudelaire / one could probably hear
it turning to marimba music." She envies exotic synesthesia, but not too
much, at least not when it pretends to mirror some divine other, more coherent, world. At the bight, in view of the dredging, we are hardly in a sublime
setting—though it is "awful," it is also "cheerful," and its sheerness, its transparency, reveals more absorption than transcendence. The unromantic and
even repellent dredging she parallels to poetic thinking; she does not elevate
her own work as she seems to identify plurally with the pelicans and their
"humorous elbowings," with the "frowsy sponge boats" that "keep coming
in / with the obliging air of retrievers," with the "little ochre dredge" (recall
"the little rented boat" of "The Fish") that "plays the dry perfectly off-beat
claves." The archaic past-tense of cleave is "clave," and cleave means both to
cling to and to separate; her activity brings together and retrieves even as it
reveals discontinuities, brokenness, lack of correspondence. Her description
of the bight, which invokes Baudelaire as a letter she can no longer read,
could just as well be of a writer's desk (a landscape defamiliarized as it will be
in "12 O'Clock News, CP, 174):

> Some of the little white boats are still piled up
> against each other, or lie on their sides, stove in,
> and not yet salvaged, if they ever will be, from the last bad
>   storm,

like torn-open, unanswered letters.
The bight is littered with old correspondences.

The poet, on her birthday, could be aware of those letters she has not had a
chance to answer, aware that not responding to mail denies the power of language to connect. As Barthes's interpretation of the love letter insists, "Like
desire, the love letter waits for an answer; it implicitly enjoins the other to reply, for without a reply the other's image changes, becomes *other*" (158). A
Cold Spring can be read as a series of correspondences with significant
others. "Letter to N.Y." (*CP*, 80) is an explicit demand for continued and intimate correspondence: "In your next letter I wish you'd say / where you are
going and what you are doing." And her "Invitation to Miss Marianne
Moore" (*CP*, 82–83), buoyant and hearty in its request that her friend "please
come flying," is at once a recognition of Moore's "otherness"—her "soft un-
invented music," and an absorption of the other's style—the formality of address ("Miss"), the quirky stanzas replete with Moore-like images such as
"countless little pellucid jellies / in cut-glass epergnes dragging with silver
chains."

But here the beloved is the landscape itself, and she abandons the dream
of ultimate transcendence (this is an important step in seeing others in unfixed relationships as equal and not subordinate); instead she is caught up in
the process, never neat, of salvaging from among what remains, absorbing
the landscape in sensuous enjoyment.

If the elements in "The Bight" seem only connected through metonymic
absorption by the viewer, the landscape in "At the Fishhouses" (*CP*, 64–66)
shows itself in the process of osmosis, so much a signature of feminine identity. The landscape will not allow for a rigidly bounded or isolated ego. The
sea decorates and warps everything in the environment with its offerings,
making it into a kind of tapestry or quilt:

> All is silver: the heavy surface of the sea,
> swelling slowly as if considering spilling over,
> is opaque, but the silver of the benches,
> the lobster pots, and masts, scattered
> among the wild jagged rocks,
> is of an apparent translucence
> like the small old buildings with an emerald moss
> growing on their shoreward walls.

The big fish tubs are completely lined
with layers of beautiful herring scales
and the wheelbarrows are similarly plastered
with creamy iridescent coats of mail,
with small iridescent flies crawling on them.
Up on the little slope behind the houses,
set in the sparse bright sprinkle of grass,
is an ancient wooden capstan,
cracked, with two long bleached handles
and some melancholy stains, like dried blood,
where the ironwork has rusted.

"Lined," "plastered," "rusted"—all suggest incorporation and blurred boundaries. Even "iridescent coats of mail" blend with the "iridescent flies." We exist in terms of embroidery and interlayering. The fisherman becomes
inseparable from his environment: "There are sequins on his vest and on his
thumb." Just as "The Moose" will present us with the momentary intersection of natural and human, here Bishop communes with a seal, even as she
recognizes the gulf between them. She says of him that he is "like me a believer in total immersion," but immersion includes the seal's emergence out
of the water and into the human realm. Immersion is a baptism, but not an
orthodox one. She can only sing the Baptist hymn, "A Mighty Fortress Is
Our God," with humor. Metaphors of immolation only counteract her experience of immersion, and therefore also of temporality. She doubles metaphor back upon itself in the closing section:

It is like what we imagine knowledge to be:
dark, salt, clear, moving, utterly free,
drawn from the cold hard mouth
of the world, derived from the rocky breasts
forever, flowing and drawn, and since
our knowledge is historical, flowing, and flown.

In usurping and reversing the usual functions of tenor and vehicle, deliques-
cence becomes the central term and knowledge a way to convey *it*. Bishop's
epistemology makes knowledge "utterly free," makes it a diffuse and unlimited entity. The juxtaposition within the phrase "forever, flowing" heightens

our sense of endless solubility and flux. And what force is "drawing" the paradoxically "dark" and "clear" water of knowledge? The only *agent* in this
stanza is our imagination, which is deferred through the introductory "It is
what." We only have approximation *in time,* not possession or final certitude; all knowledge is "derived." If our experience links up somewhere, it is
with those "rocky breasts," the originary source of our knowledge, both feminized and resistant. The "cold, hard mouth" tells us nothing. Our language
and imaginative act shows us *own*ership only in fluidity: Bishop has us flowing and flown at once.

History and knowledge further conflate with the loss of a transcendent
spirituality apart from natural processes in "Cape Breton" (*CP,* 67–68) where
"rotting snow-ice sucked away / almost to spirit; the ghosts of glaciers drift /
among those folds and folds of fir." The way the landscape includes and incorporates everything in it is perhaps a synecdoche for the woman writer's
craft:

> The silken water is weaving and weaving,
> disappearing under the mist equally in all directions,
> lifted and penetrated now and then
> by one shag's dripping serpent-neck,
> and somewhere the mist incorporates the pulse,
> rapid but unurgent, of a motorboat.

We are no longer in a forest of symbols that we must penetrate, to find correspondences and meanings; we find ourselves folded and refolded in the vast,
always alterable, absorbing: "the mist, and meshing / in brown-wet, fine,
torn fish-nets." Even as the weaver is an old man in "At the Fishhouses" who
"sits netting, / his net, in the gloaming, almost invisible," the activity of netting suggests the more "female" activity of weaving, and since both represent
impulses to connectivity, Bishop works against the sense of an entrenched
gender identity. The old fisher himself looks as if he is about to dissolve "in
the gloaming," become "invisible," an image that links him with the "man
carrying a baby" in "Cape Breton," who gets off a bus and then cuts through
a meadow toward "his invisible house beside the water." That he holds a
baby suggests that this man is not like the hermit of "Chemin de Fer," for ex-

ample, with his unreachable retreat, but is instead a potential nurturer. "In-
visibility" implies a less ego-centered or appropriative household.

V

The surrealist and survivalist aspects of Bishop's work have long been overshadowed by an emphasis upon an assumption of her pellucid style. But at
every turn she teases us out of our sense-making petrifaction. Thus, her persistent piling up of alternatives, the "or" without the "either," her exponential
qualifications of but and but and but. "Lights music of love," ("Varick
Street") we cannot quite divine. She is not after an exactitude of finality, only
a precision of uncertainty and multiplication. She blurs and softens boundaries, showing their permeability. Enclosures are often invoked in order to
deny their viability. In "Twelfth Morning; or What You Will," translated
from Cabo Frio, are the lines: "Don't ask the big white horse, *Are you supposed / to be inside the fence or out?*" (*CP*, 110). Like this horse, Bishop "remains in doubt," with the cross-dressing of *Twelfth Night* implied by the
title. She says of a courtyard in "Paris, 7 A.M.," "It is like introspection / to
stare inside, or retrospection, / a star inside a rectangle, a recollection" (*CP*,
26–27). To look outside is to look inside, and to look within is to look backwards. It is no wonder that her vortical opacity comes to the forefront in matters of love; and it is not simply a modesty or reticence, but more a testimony
to her challenge of male-centered readings.

In its choice not to hierarchize or enclose or limit signification, the postmodern is assimilable to the feminist project. Julia Kristeva in *Tales of Love*
declares that "love" is the site where meaning is most troubled.[21] Because
"love" happens between two subjectivities, it is difficult to know if there is
any equivalence between the two, or if their discourse is only fictively complementary because so alien, as Barthes might argue. At the outset, Kristeva
says: "The ordeal of love puts the univocity of language and its referential and
communicative power to the test," and she implies that this test results from
the "abyss separating the sexes." (But Kristeva, in extolling a new kind of
antipatriarchal writing arising from the semiotic in *Desire in Language*, concentrates her praise upon such male writers as Joyce, Artaud, Mallarmé and
does not deal with love between women or expressed by them.) Yet in
Bishop's decision to surround us with a language of insistent repetition and
parataxis, phrases "spilling over" and incorporating with others, she meets

her landscapes as a lover. She strives for and generates, moreover, an intimacy between herself *as she describes* and us much in the way she muddles
the subject / object, lover / beloved splits in poems such as "A Cold Spring,"
"O Breath," or "The Shampoo."

French feminists, including Hélène Cixous and Luce Irigaray, more readily recognize patriarchy as a systematic repression and underrepresentation
of woman's sexuality and turn to the female body as a means of locating a
new writing not regulated by masculinist thinking. The rigorous linking of a
focus upon language and feminism makes these writers more assimilable to
the postmodern. By validating and expressing her bodily impulses, by coming into contact with her own body and other "sexts" (to use Cixous's word),
woman may liberate a voice silenced by the limits set by male tradition. In
spite of criticism, such as that raised by Anne Rosalind Jones and more recently, Rita Felski, that the French feminists do not take social issues into account, and sacrifice politics to the overflowing of their own libidinal energies
and flows, perhaps even reinscribing binary essentialist and biological notions that have historically confined women to the roles of gestation and nurturing, I think their recognition of the sexuality repressed in female writing
in the past and their encouragement to women to seek alternate modes of
writing (and of reading) itself becomes a potentially vitalizing political position.[22]

Cixous and Bishop intersect in subverting patriarchal binarism and in emphasizing a mode of loving that "unhoards." They also both celebrate—a fascinating coincidence—marginalized, Brazilian writers. Living in Brazil for
more than fourteen years confirmed Bishop as an expatriate and outsider.
Not only did she translate *The Diary of Helena Morley* and edit an anthology
of Brazilian poetry (some of which she translated), she also translated several
stories of Clarice Lispector. For the last decade, Cixous has had a literary
love affair with Lispector, translating her extensively. Of Cixous's translations, Jones admires the "peculiarly female attentiveness to objects, the ability to perceive and represent them in a nurturing rather than dominating
way."[23] This aptly describes Bishop's visual technique, which never tries to
ascertain, solidify, or pin down but allows the rock-roses to exfoliate, freeing
words from the enthrallment of an illusory stasis.

"The Smallest Woman in the World," the most significant of Lispector's
stories that Bishop translated, can be read as a parable of the dangers and fol-
lies in the masculinist attempt to reduce or constrict female sexuality and
subsume love in an economy of power and force.[24] Lispector's story tells of
Marcel Petre, "hunter and man of the world," who in quest of the smallest

woman in the world discovers what he believes to be "the smallest of the smallest pygmies in the world." The ironic perception of phallocentrism surfaces here in splendid clarity:

> Probably only because he was not insane, his soul neither wavered nor broke its bounds. Feeling an immediate necessity for order and for giving names to what exists, he called her Little Flower. And in order to be able to classify her among the recognizable realities, he immediately began to collect facts about her. (501)

Not only does he find out that "her race will soon be exterminated," but that her tiny race is "retreating, always retreating" (a phrase Bishop will use in her poem "Brazil, January 1, 1502" to describe the terrorized Indian women) into "the heart of Africa."

The explorer publishes his findings and we are given glimpses of various readers of the paper who want to possess this smallest of African women. One lady reflects, thinking of her "perverse tenderness," her desire to tend the anomaly: "Who knows to what murkiness of love or tenderness can lead?" (502). (Think, perhaps, of Faustina.) We are then told of "a clever little boy" with "a clever idea" who wants to make the smallest woman into the family's toy. The child's mother wonders about this "cruel necessity of loving," to what extent we will go to possess and infantilize another. In yet another household, there grows "the desire to have that tiny and indomitable thing for itself. . . . To tell the truth, who hasn't wanted to own a human being just for himself?" (504).

But what Lispector's story reveals is that no human can truly possess or own another. The smallest woman in the world, pregnant, defeats the explorer by her indomitable nature: he has simply to see her for one moment out of the context of his scientific inspection and "instead of curiosity, or exaltation, or victory," he feels sick. With "the secret of her own secret" within her, in her delight with living itself, the smallest woman in the world laughs warmly, with the laugh of another kind of Medusa, while Petre, "adjusting his symbolic helmet" attempts to regain self-control through prolific note-taking. Through the parable we can understand Bishop's resistance to patriarchy and the conquest of marginalized others, themes further pursued in *Questions of Travel.*

The title of "Argument" (*CP*, 81), creates the expectation that it will present a logical statement in traditional terms; instead, it is a poem that wants to suspend spatial and temporal categories, the opposition of "never" and "forever," and "argues" for a writing that is a weaving and loving, rather than a dominating and subduing. The characters of the "argument" are "days" and "distance"—both threatening to keep lovers separate just as commercialism and industrialism try in "Varick Street.": "argue argue argue with me / endlessly / neither proving you less wanted nor less dear." Time and space markers disrupt emotional currents, and the repetition in an unseparated stream of "argue" seems to interfere with the "imperative of intimacy," yet the coastline observed from a plane as "stretching indistinguishably / all the way, / all the way" does not reflect any essential separations or demarcations. As "Days" speaks, Bishop's resistance to phallocentric systems of ordering surface along with her call for another kind of love poetry, one of affirmation instead of annulment:

> And think
> of all those cluttered
> instruments,
> one to a fact,
> canceling each other's experience

She recommends the primacy of feeling and the sharing of separate experience. The poem resonates finally, with a Cixous-like utopianism, as if she were about to glimpse the end of the "false theater of phallocentric representationalism" (Cixous, 254):

> The intimidating sound
> of these voices
> we must separately find
> can and shall be vanquished:
> Days and Distance disarrayed again
> and gone
> both for good and from the gentle battleground.

4

Imagined Places and the Questions of History

Not a form so grotesque, so savage, nor so beautiful but is an
expression of some property inherent in man the observer—
an occult relation between the very scorpions and man. I feel
the centipede in me—cayman, carp, eagle, & fox. I am
moved by strange sympathies, I say continually "I will be a
naturalist."
—Emerson, *Journal*, 13 July 1833

It was the furthest point of my experience. It seemed
somehow to throw a kind of light on everything about me—
and into my thoughts. It was sombre enough, too—and
pitiful—not extraordinary in any way—not very clear either.
No, not very clear. And yet it seemed to throw a kind of light.
—Joseph Conrad, *Heart of Darkness.*

I

Marlow's spatial journey in *Heart of Darkness* cannot be separated from his
retelling of its psychological impact; he returns home with a knowledge that
both enlightens and obscures. Joseph Conrad here writes with the approxi-
mating and tentative language of Bishop. As traveler, her experience becomes irreconcilably clear and unclear, unspeakable and endlessly iterable.
Not only a record of personal travel and history, *Questions of Travel* addresses
the difficulty involved in the process of conveying otherness, the "furthest

point" away from the self. She considers how we might appreciate another culture and its history without projecting our own image on to it, and in the process, reveals that our language always prevents complete comprehension, that we must rearrange experience to give it sense and coherence. At the same time, she demands an escape from narcissism, from the "love" of these explorers like Petre, from even the "naturalism" of an Emerson—who, enchanted by the "hummingbirds little & gay," stuffed to offer the ornithological sublime, strolls through the Cabinet of Natural History taking down observations.[1] Bishop knows the temptation to be "determined to rush to see the sun the other way around" and "the tiniest green hummingbird in the world" ("Questions of Travel," CP, 93–94). And she recognizes that it is only in the *trying* that we gain any light upon otherhood—thus the act of the traveling mind she requires.

The volume known as A *Cold Spring* in *The Collected Poems* never appeared on its own but in conjunction with *North & South* under the serviceable title, *Poems*, in 1955. Within the section of A *Cold Spring*, Bishop included "Arrival at Santos," later to be the opening piece in *Questions of Travel* (1965). Presentation for print allows for an imposition of order that denies or hides "original" chronology. Because of the time lapsed after the publication of *Poems*, questions of travel inevitably become also questions of time as well as place. The volume, however, generates a definite impression of "composition," intentional calm and collectedness: she divides the book in two sections, "Brazil" and "Elsewhere," with the story "In the Village" acting as telling partition. The grouping of her poems is aesthetically logical: the poems in "Brazil" all deal with her physical presence in the country, those in "Elsewhere" take up places of her New England past; because the poems in the latter section are more obviously personal and take an inward turn, the autobiographical story between the volumes allows us to adjust to the shift. Yet many of the poems in *Questions of Travel* were written in the years 1956–57 (spurred on by Lowell's *Life Studies* in 1956) with a few composed in the early 1960s. "Arrival in Santos" (1952) coincides oddly enough with her arrival in Brazil, but as signaled by the last line of that poem, "we are driving to the interior," she becomes preoccupied with prose autobiography between 1953 and 1956, writing both "Gwendolyn" and "In the Village" in 1953, working on a larger, never-to-be finished piece drafted as "Homesickness" (later to fuse with "Memories of Uncle Neddy," 1977), and translating *The Diary of Helena Morley*.

The movement from outward to inward is not so continuous and smooth as the volume might like us to think. While I agree with David Kalstone that

Bishop's "deepening assimilation to Brazil not only recalled her Nova Scotia childhood but helped her to recapitulate and reclaim it," reclaiming is not the result of the necessary "repression" (one of the "twin reflexes" Kalstone attributes to *Questions*) of the private that "Brazil" appears to be. Rather, Bishop's attention to location and "impression" (the other reflex) oscillates with inner exploration, so that outward and inward become always questionable categories.[2] Attention to the self becomes attention to the Other, the "not me" of different landscape and culture, and the two appear inextricable. Even attention to the autobiographical in "Elsewhere" looks to a more mythic past—as in its first three key poems "Manners," "Sestina," and "First Death in Nova Scotia," possessing the logic of fairy tale and fantasy more than simply confessional reportage.

No matter how much the introspective and autobiographical aspects of *Life Studies* influenced Bishop, Kalstone emphasizes that her work offsets the indulgence and lack of perspective occasionally present in Lowell. But it is not merely confession that bothers Bishop; it is Sexton's "egocentrism," Eliot's "resignation" (which she warns Lowell against) and Lowell's "morbidity." She rejects, ultimately, the cramped space of the solitary mind dwelling upon itself, and continues to challenge the Romantic model of the isolated poet. Lowell's "The Scream," a poetic adaptation of "In the Village," is for Kalstone testimony to the essential "differences in self-presentation" (200) of Bishop and Lowell; his poem waxes "melodramatic" and awful, undiluted by the delight in impression, the cheerful.

What Bishop finds "superb" in *Life Studies*, however, is a kind of willing cheerfulness, the ability to attain through art at least a temporary and tentative sense of well-being. She writes to him in 1957:

> They all have that same feeling, as if you've been in a stretch (I've felt that way for very short stretches once in a long while) when everything and anything suddenly seemed material for poetry, seemed to *be* poetry, and all the poems are illuminated in long shafts here and there, like a long-waited for sunrise. . . . It seems to me it's the whole purpose of art, to the artist (not to the audience)—that same feeling of control, illumination—*it is all right, for the time being.*[3]

Bishop's residence in Brazil offers such a sunrise for her, or more of one than she seems to have ever thought possible, and makes her autobiographical investigations and personal struggle deeply tempered by good humor. For the time being. She can advise Lowell in 1957: "Sobriety & gaiety & toughness will do the trick, or so I hope for myself and hope & pray for you too."[4] Yet *Questions* marks a shift in her emotional status, one she always understands as precarious and tentative. Before her letters to Lowell from Brazil, she complains frequently of loneliness and depression. In one letter of 1948 while hospitalized for her asthma, she is reading Proust's letters (the parts about his asthma really "get to her") and offers from them two quotes she really likes: "Les gens les plus gentils ont quelquefois des périodes odieuses," and "Mais l'art est un perpetual sacrifice du sentiment a la vérité."[5] Self-pity and valorization of the sacrificial artist seem more in character with the later Lowell. While staying in Maine (Bishop is beginning "Homesickness" at this point), she repeats to Lowell what a hairdresser tells her upon learning she is an "orphan": "kind of awful, ain't it, ploughing through life alone—feels like ploughing up and down stairs," and then later that year bemoans "solitude and ennui—the kind of suffering I'm most at home with and helpless about"; she confesses in December, "my loneliness comes in attacks—rather brief— sometimes two or three a day, and then I don't have any for a week."[6] She is not without health problems and depression in Brazil, but the relocation provides her a stability and sense of home she had never before experienced. Even the cortisone prescribed for her asthma allows her to see the world re- filtered, so much so that "the mountains look exactly as if floating in vin rosé, with a white kind of milk below us."[7] It would be fair to say that a sense of home fortifies her so that she may travel to imagined places.

Movement and unsettlement characterize the period before her trip to South America: Key West and then Yaddo in 1947, Maine in 1948, a post at the Library of Congress in 1949–50, with visits to Maryland and Nova Sco- tia. In 1951, she begins her travels in South America. On 26 November 1951, she writes to Lowell: "Somewhere off the coast of Brazil . . . at present we're approaching Santos."[8] She did not intend to "arrive." But an accident (the quirkiness of which resounds with surrealistic appropriateness) inter- venes and alters her plans to travel to the Straits of Magellan. Eating a cash- ew fruit produces in her an allergic reaction so she stays in Brazil to recover. By 1952, she is living with Lota de Macedo Soares, whom she had met ear- lier in New York, and to whom she dedicates this volume. In 1953, she writes to Lowell that she is "happy, for the first time in [her] life," and that "here I've been able to stop drinking about entirely."[9] While *Questions of Travel* is appropriate as title for the volume, her questions occur as she at- tempts to stop traveling, to settle down, and to partake of a provisional sense of belonging and home. Yet she continues to be aware that "standing still" or being "stationary" can only be illusions: arriving and departing moment to moment. Her Brazilian period is one of self-expatriation and an exploration of otherness. The pieces of "Brazil" appear, at first, to be topographical poems such as "Florida" or "Cape Breton," but as in those poems, place recedes to give in to questions of epistemology and language: What is it to know another culture, and can one? Can we escape imagining or making the "other" up as we record our observations? What is the self in relation to a place? How is our sense of time and history affected by "travel"?

II

There is an imperative, moving in dual directions, suggested by Bishop's antichronological rearrangement of her poems; an imperative to look to the outside, to find oneself in the other, and at the same time, a realization that looking out always leads to looking in. The dangers of solipsism contemplated throughout *North & South* recur, but with a difference: a belief that we can, if only partially, overcome narcissism. Thus she orders her volume with a desire to foreground attention to the outside, to the other. She opens outward (even as she acknowledges that such a movement also requires "interior" exploration) in "Brazil," then with her stories (she had thought about including "Gwendolyn" in *Questions*), and finally "Elsewhere" turns the mirror around.

Because so concerned with otherness (and not just her own), *Questions* is perhaps her most political work; in it surfaces again and again an attempt to give voice to the Brazilian culture she appropriately feels outside of. While many of the poems "feel" calm, they unsettle us with open questions—a tension emerges in her voice, a struggle with a historical guilt for oppression, social inequality, poverty. She never forgets her potential for being a "tourist" and the dangers involved in such a position.

Kalstone remarks how differently Bishop relates to the past than does Lowell. Of him, he sees "the present cripplingly shadowed by the burden of the past" (213); of Bishop's *Questions*, he declares: "The poems record an awakening to a world almost as if Bishop had no previous history: they are 'life studies' in a new transparent key, the bright C major of discovery in the present tense" (214). But even as it is true that the first three poems are "shucking off habitual notions of culture and history," and that they are probably, as he puts it, "poems of method," they are so with an eye for acknowledging stories of pasts other than the personal. If Lowell is weighted by the "burden of the past," Bishop's historicity allows her to carry the past into the present and still keep moving: she is not crippled by remembrance. The personal unconscious so significant to an interpretation of many of her poems gives way to the collective: we must here step away from Freud to Lévi-Strauss.

But first back to Emerson, whom Bishop read much of in Brazil. In "Circles," history is a series of ever-widening circles where "around every circle another can be drawn."[10] Instead of a linear progression, "there is no outside, no inclosing wall, no circumference to us" (405). Emerson forsakes fixation upon the past and focuses on the continuously disclosing and volatile present:

> In nature every moment is new; the past is always swallowed and forgotten; the coming only is sacred. Nothing is secure but life, transition, the energizing spirit. No love can be bound by oath or covenant to secure it against a higher love. No truth so sublime but it may be trivial to-morrow in the light of new thoughts. People wish to be settled; only as far as they are unsettled is there any hope for them. (413)

This grand essay closes with the dictum: "The one thing we seek with insatiable desire is to forget ourselves, to be surprised out of our propriety, to lose our sempiternal memory, and to do something without knowing how or why; in short, to draw a new circle." His is not a simple erasure or denial of the past but a commitment to change and movement. Every new sphere in our serialized history derives from and even coexists with previous ones.

Bishop's arrival in Brazil draws a new circle, and even as she throws off part of her own history, she redresses it as she looks to the history of another culture. Her epigraph prefacing the volume is from the sonnets of Camões, which obligate the individual to give of herself as much as she can—somehow that is how much she owes: "O dar-vos quanto tenho e quanto posso, / Que quanto mais vos pago, mais vos devo." (Give how much you have and how much you can, / That's how much you pay, how much you owe.) Her poems pay the debt of an observer. Taking on the guise of explorer, placing herself in an alien environment, she embraces unsettlement.

Claude Lévi-Strauss uses a similar figure to Emerson's concentric circles to describe the collective memory of humanity. Because every present moment becomes the expanding ridge of countless other moments, we live as if only in the present, unable to comprehend our connection with more distant times:

As he moves forward within his environment, Man takes with him all the positions that he has occupied in the past, and all those that he will occupy in the future. He is everywhere at the same time, a crown which, in the act of moving forward, yet recapitulates at every instant every step that it has ever taken in the past. For we live in several worlds, each more true than the one within it, and each false in relation to that within which it is itself enveloped . . . but the apparent contradictoriness of their co-existence is resolved by the fact that we are constrained to accord meaning to those worlds which are nearer to us, and to refuse it to those more distant.[11]

Time becomes spatial for Lévi-Strauss with the present, past, and future in coexistence; "contradictoriness" emerges with our clashing temporal worlds and cultures, those we cannot fold within our nearest circle.

An impersonal history allows Bishop access to personal history, without sacrificing the one for the other. In "From Trollope's Journal, " dated "Winter 1861," Bishop re-creates a dramatic monologue (similar to those in *Life Studies* of Ford Madox Ford, George Santayana, and Hart Crane) to give voice to Civil War experience. Trollope mirrors Bishop's position, in his transcontinental crossing and position as outsider. He can't see much difference in the American statuary: "As far as statues go, so far there's not / much choice: they're either Washingtons / or Indians, a whitewashed, stubby lot." Artifice converts difference into the same, this is Trollope's sentiment, and war makes everyone—the president, doctor, cattle, foreign tourists alike— ill. To cut out this passage from this English writer's journal is paradigmatic of Bishop's collage impulse, and her desire to show the past as present. She discovers her own traveler's journal in "Questions of Travel"; in discovering otherness outside herself she discovers it within, and by making the past present, shows their collaboration in our continual modification of history.

With the insistent use of "here" in the opening of "Arrival at Santos" (*CP*, 89–90), the effort at immediacy and orientation is evident—our introduction or departure into the poem, primed by a deadpan pointer, strips topography of the romance of travel and arrival:

> Here is a coast; here is a harbor;
> here, after a meager diet of horizon, is some scenery:
> impractically shaped and—who knows?—self-pitying
>   mountains,
> sad and harsh beneath their frivolous greenery,

with a little church on top of one. And warehouses,
some of them painted a feeble pink, or blue,
and some tall, uncertain palms.

"Meager," "impractically," "self-pitying," "sad," "harsh," "frivolous," "feeble," "uncertain": such adjectival language seems uncharacteristic of Bishop in both its judgmental tone and excessiveness. The descriptions in "The Map," for instance, caress the object and permit contact ("We can stroke these lovely bays"); an encounter in "reality," it would seem, has less substance, or offers less excitement. "Arrival" becomes disappointing deferral. "Uncertain" usually has unmitigated positive value in Bishop (the map's shadows and indeterminacy contribute to its glamour), but among the other less favoring words, it contributes to an almost scornful valence. Almost immediately, however, she turns this voice into self-criticism of "immodest demands," a motive running a course throughout *Questions*:

> Oh, tourist,
> is this how this country is going to answer you
>
> and your immodest demands for a different world,
> and a better life, and complete comprehension
> of both at last, and immediately,
> after eighteen days of suspension?
>
> Finish your breakfast. The tender is coming,
> a strange and ancient craft, flying a strange and brilliant
>   rag.
> So that's the flag. I never saw it before.
> I somehow never thought of there *being* a flag,
>
> but of course there was, all along.

The enjambed question contains a self-reprimand of naive expectations that an "arrival" will signal some kind of final destination. "Arrival," in Bishopic terms, must be taken with irony, and as the passage from Emerson's "Circles" suggests, "complete comprehension" is neither desirable nor possible. There will be no relief from "suspension." In the curt admonition to "[f]inish your breakfast. The tender is coming," "tender" is, of course, an auxiliary boat come to take the passengers ashore (yet another arrival), but it also denotes the sympathy required of the tourist and even the payment of an obligation (this accords with the Camões quote). The flag startles the narrator into a realization of otherness. She describes the tender as "strange" as well as the "flag," emphasizing her surprised acknowledgment of another continent's "being."

Though this poem originally was published with *A Cold Spring*, it conforms to the other pieces in "Brazil" in its turn back to rhyme and toward a more narrative mode. The stanzas are never end-stopped, a maneuver that works against her regular rhyming and the arrangement of the poem into near quatrains. She wants her poetics to approximate the immediate process of experience, in the way of Kalstone's "present tense," as she introduces dramatic narrative into the piece:

> And gingerly now we climb down the ladder backward,
> myself and a fellow passenger named Miss Breen,
>
> descending into the midst of twenty-six freighters
> waiting to be loaded with green coffee beans.
> Please, boy, do be more careful with that boat hook!
> Watch out! Oh! It has caught Miss Breen's
>
> skirt! There! Miss Breen is about seventy,
> a retired police lieutenant, six feet tall,
> with beautiful bright blue eyes and a kind expression.
> Her home, when she is at home, is in Glens Fall
>
> s, New York. There. We are settled.

We are only "settled" provisionally, on the first line of another stanza. "Gingerly," Bishop allows each stanza to slip into the next, allowing for the "catching" of Miss Breen's skirt and unhooking it with a satisfying "There!" only to find this character's home to be insolidly falling into the next quatrain. The depiction of Miss Breen's idiosyncrasies highlights our usual blindness to apparently "familiar" strangeness, (and as Millier uncovers through letters, represents for Bishop "a vision of an accomplished successful lesbian life" (238–39), though this aspect of Breen is fairly well hidden in the poem). Breen is another version of herself as outsider. Revealing the desire for the habitual, regular and customary, she enjoins: "The customs officials will speak English, we hope, / and leave us our bourbon and cigarettes."

Santos, however, becomes an emblem of temporariness and passage, rather than static arrival:

Ports are necessities, like postage stamps, or soap,

but they seldom seem to care what impression they make,
or, like this, only attempt, since it does not matter,
the unassertive colors of soap, or postage stamps—
wasting away like the former, slipping the way the latter

do when we mail the letters we wrote on the boat,
either because the glue here is very inferior
or because of the heat. We leave Santos at once:
we are driving to the interior.

Will the letters we write on the boat arrive at their destination? Will we,
"driving to" rather than "into"? These are questions that inform Derrida's
The Post Card—a metaphor for the nonarrival of meaning and the link between identity and arrival: "arriver," he reminds, means to happen, to suc-
ceed—to reach a culminating point where meaning and destiny are insured,
and therefore suspicious and untenable.[12] Such is the deconstructive doubt
Bishop also passes to us. Freud's model of "fort-da" (an important concept
for Derrida as he proposes that his "discovery" models Freud's own relationship to psychoanalysis: a process of departure and return, a compulsion to repeat his own autobiography through his theory) resurfaces in the context of
Bishop's travel as a larger metaphor for the enactment of personal loss and
chance discussed in Chapter 1. Our letters slip the way our stamps do.
She generalizes with "ports" (which resemble "posts," the anterior guards between different locales): they introduce territories, but also function as after-
thoughts or torn open letters, the stamp upon the delivery of a new land,
postdated by the time of our arrival, our reading.

The climate of Santos itself seems unfavorable for permanence. Bishop offers us her customary "or" clauses (she tends to string along "or" phrases without any limiting "either" in sight), but without her usual open-endedness; she
now puts herself in the position of a traveler who desires an assertion of a
"different world." Yet when she decides in the final uncharacteristic "either /
or" clause that the stamps on our letters slip "either because the glue here is
very inferior / or because of the heat," we cannot be sure that it is for either
reason. Knowledge and "comprehension" do not go far in this port, and
Bishop, taking on all the ethnocentric tics of superior feeling and peevish dissatisfaction with the lack of postcard "impression," recognizes the limitations
in the tourist's apprehension of a place. The landscape extends a "meager
diet" (the "twenty-six freighters / waiting to be loaded with green coffee

beans" suggests something more abundantly exportive), but the narrator inti-
mates that the tourist receives what she puts forth. (Bishop recommends to
Lowell E. H. Gombrich's *Art and Illusion*, a work that postulates that our
expectations and our previous experience determine and predicate our vision.)[13] In writing a letter to the country, the tourist cannot read the reply.
We are left with "who knows?" in our sighting the horizon, a horizon that recedes evermore as if in one of her uncle's paintings.

If the voice in "Arrival in Santos" is a calculated analysis of the tourist
mentality and its flaws, other poems in the volume become even more definitely critical of the Eurocentric mind. Eight Januaries after she dates "Arrival," she writes the exquisite "Brazil, January 1, 1502" (*CP*, 91–92;
apparently written New Year's day 1959), telling Lowell that she "finally had
to do something with the cliché about the landscape looking like a tapestry."[14] In his conservative yet enlightening *Landscape into Art*, Sir Kenneth
Clark traces the history and evolution of landscape painting.[15] From this
work, Bishop takes as epigraph to her poem the phrases: "embroidered nature . . . tapestried landscape." That she does not even retrieve a whole sentence from her source again indicates a vision of poetry as collage, bringing
together (or taking apart) different pieces of material. Bishop wants us to see
the poem as fabrication. Perhaps this is what Kalstone means when he calls
the poem one of "method"; it is self-reflexive: writing as tapestry.

Sir Kenneth Clark contends that to see the landscape as tapestry is a particularly medieval construction of nature. As he tells us: "Parallel with [their]
mistrust of nature was the symbolising faculty of the medieval mind. We
who are heirs to three centuries of science can hardly realize a state of mind
in which all material objects were thought of as symbols of spiritual truths or
episodes in sacred history" (5). To regard nature as symbol undervalues representationalism: "The less an artifact interests our eye as imitation, the
more it must delight our eye as pattern, and an art of symbols always involves
a language of decoration" (6). Early medieval art disregards nature as either
irrelevant or shuns it as either irreverent or terrifying; it is only the domestication of nature into garden that allows landscape to emerge:

> Natural objects, then, were first perceived individually, as pleasing in
> themselves and symbolical of divine qualities. The next step towards
> landscape painting was to see them as forming some whole which
> would be within the compass of the imagination and itself a symbol
> of perfection. This was achieved by the discovery of the garden—be
> it Eden, or the Hesperides, or Tir-nan-Og—it is one of humanity's

most constant, widespread and consoling myths; and its reappearance
in the twelfth century is only a part of the general reawakening of the
imaginative faculty. The very multiplicity of sensations which St.
Anselm had believed to be so dangerous now became accepted by the
Church as a foretaste of paradise. (6)

While Clark provides the historical basis for landscape as paradise, he does
not (as it is not in the scope of his investigations) look to the political ramifi-
cations of such a reconstruction. I quote him at length because it is this very
myth or "cliché" of paradise, the hope of a "different world" that informs the
conquest of Brazil, at least in Bishop's rendering of it.

The conquistadors cannot "see" the landscape: it appears before them as a
tapestry, and Bishop implicates herself along with the present-day colonizers,
as caught up in the same composition of the landscape as paradise. Landscape presents itself, or rather, *absents* itself as artifact, already written over
and posted: immediacy being impossible. Bishop begins with the "event" of
conquest, which mirrors on the psychological level the moment of rupture
from a presymbolic state when we enter language, and as she collapses "us"
with "them," she positions us always at that moment of a postsemiotic "greet-
ing." History, as re-created, is inseparable from fiction and myth. As decorative painting, as tapestry, Bishop's first stanza puts history in the narrative
present:

> Januaries, Nature greets our eyes
> exactly as she must have greeted theirs:
> every square inch filling in with foliage—
> big leaves, little leaves, and giant leaves,
> blue, blue-green, and olive,
> with occasional lighter veins and edges,
> or a satin underleaf turned over;
> monster ferns
> in silver-gray relief,
> and flowers, too, like giant water lilies
> up in the air—up, rather, in the leaves—
> purple, yellow, two yellows, pink,
> rust red and greenish white;
> solid but airy; fresh as if just finished
> and taken off the frame.

Even as she collapses 1960 into 1502 (as if the whole enterprise of conquest could be reduced to the single day of an arrival, or as if the deferral of arrival has been going on for more than four centuries), Bishop shows newness and freshness as a thing "worked" up, with plenitude a myth continually refurnished, "every square inch filling in with foliage." She claims for the two Januaries the same "Nature" "exactly," but her descriptions, always as if in the process of present modification ("blue, blue-green," "yellow, two yellows," "solid but airy"), call exactitude into question; what she reveals is the mind constructing and decorating the landscape and history, a process that has no originary or "real" model to measure itself against.

Yet the tapestry, here, is not, even as the first stanza might suggest, of an idyllic garden, though symbol and allegory make of the hellish wilderness a tantalizing challenge to the conqueror to make it habitable and tame under Christian banners:

> Still in the foreground there is Sin:
> five sooty dragons near some massy rocks.
> The rocks are worked with lichens, gray moonbursts
> splattered and overlapping,
> threatened from underneath by moss
> in lovely hell-green flames,
> attacked above
> by scaling-ladder vines, oblique and neat,
> "one leaf yes and one leaf no" (in Portuguese).

Bishop invokes an eternal moment as "the big symbolic birds keep quiet, / each showing only half his puffed and padded, / pure-colored or spotted breast." Pure or spotted, the conquistador's mission is inscribed as indeterminate, his presence in this New World questionable even by the leaves that neither bless nor curse, but do affirm and deny, "'one leaf yes and one leaf no' (in Portuguese)." Is half enough? But the language is of the conqueror, not the conquered, and it is these unnamed others and their suffering we must finally acknowledge. The "symbolic birds" here recall the "fine black birds / hanging in n's in banks" of the early "Large Bad Picture." The impulse to animate, to reveal the inextricable intertwining of language with our perception of artifacts recurs in this poem as politicized and historicized.

Even as the first stanza of the poem *places* us in a "present," with the first two lines, we cannot separate "us" and "them": "Januaries, Nature greets our eyes / exactly as she must have greeted theirs." By the third stanza, analogy joins us and Bishop with the arriving Portuguese:

> Just so the Christians, hard as nails,
> tiny as nails, and glinting,
> in creaking armor, came and found it all,
> not unfamiliar:
> no lovers' walks, no bowers,
> no cherries to be picked, no lute music,
> but corresponding, nevertheless,
> to an old dream of wealth and luxury
> already out of style when they left home—
> wealth, plus a brand-new pleasure.

Temporal movement becomes more convoluted with her reinforced paralleling of current and past attitudes toward the landscape. The transition between thoughts slips uncertainly as previous to this portion of the poem, she supplies a haunting image:

> The lizards scarcely breathe; all eyes
> are on the smaller, female one, back-to,
> her wicked tail straight up and over,
> red as a red-hot wire.

Are we meant to think of the Christians as these lizards cornering, ready to pounce on "the smaller, female one," who, in fact, does not appear defenseless—with her "wicked tail," she taunts the breathless males. Her presence somehow deflates the impulse to conquer and possess, reveals it as ridiculous, fantastical even. Bishop's characteristic word repetition ("red as a red-hot wire") within the same morpheme forces us in our reading to circle back and postpone arrival. The Christians appear on the scene and face the "not unfamiliar." Through a double negative, Bishop alerts us to the absence of the myth of paradise: it is this absence that is "not unfamiliar." Instead, what they discover is another dream "already out of style." *The Great Gatsby* reiterates this temporal, almost archetypal, predicament, its last line foreseeing, not arrival, but continual retrogression, "So we beat on, boats against the current, borne back ceaselessly into the past."

American literature seems compelled to reproduce the moment of originary discovery, fascinating to us because our history is con-founded on it.

We romanticize the conquest of the land by not seeing those who occupied it before us as subjects; such is Nick's blind spot in his elegy for the "green breast" of the New World in the final movement of Fitzgerald's novel mourning the dream for regeneration:

> And as the moon rose higher the inessential houses began to melt away until gradually I became aware of the old island here that flowered once for Dutch sailors' eyes—a fresh, green breast of the new world. Its vanished trees, the trees that had made way for Gatsby's house, had once pandered in whispers to the last and greatest of all human dreams; for a transitory enchanted moment man must have held his breath in the presence of this continent, compelled into an aesthetic contemplation he neither understood, nor desired, face to face for the last time in history with something commensurate to his capacity for wonder.

Bishop turns us, one could say, back to one such "transitory enchanted moment" and reveals the darker side of discovery, the lust for a "brand-new pleasure," the conquest, enslavement, mastery ("each out to catch an Indian for himself"), which has little to do with contemplation, much more to do with imposition and force. Present strivings to "arrive" or attain fulfillment always take us back to our old expectations, our ever-receding or retreating ideals. Rape of the land is connected with sexual exploitation of women: the two imply blindness to the Other; the conquerors doom themselves, living out their delusions, cutting away at the very barrier they themselves persistently erect. With insight, Robert Dale Parker, in discussing the connections between Lispector's story and this poem, asserts that "the use of gender to intensify colonial trespass suggests not that gender conflict is secondary, but rather that, as a discord of both Old World and New, the conflict between genders is even more constant than the conflict between explorers and explored."[16] Gender domination, indeed, emerges as the gradually revealed crux of the poem. The pivotal moment shuts the armed men out from the collusive women:

> Directly after Mass, humming perhaps
> L'Homme armé or some such tune,
> they ripped away into the hanging fabric,
> each out to catch an Indian for himself—
> those maddening little women who kept calling,

> calling to each other (or had the birds waked up?)
> and retreating, always retreating, behind it.

This moment of confrontation that takes place "[d]irectly after Mass" unravels into an endless future, always anterior. An earlier poem, "Cape Breton," offers us similar post-colonial knowledge about a landscape marked by conquest, which withholds its secret: "Whatever the landscape had of meaning appears to have been abandoned, / unless the road is holding it back, in the interior, / where we cannot see"; but Bishop's revelation is also about a kind of rhetorical return of respect to the earlier meanings, eroded and erased by conquerors and Christians. As Jane Shore has explained, Bishop's metaphors can be revolutionary in their ability to propose simultaneous images; in "Cape Breton," when Bishop writes "The little white churches have been dropped into the matted hills / like lost quartz arrowheads," Shore alerts us that "[b]y changing churches into arrowheads, Bishop is inverting the historical order of things—she's giving the land back to the Indians."[17] This, I think, is the kind of giving back that occurs in the final stanza of "Brazil, January 1, 1502," and it is a returning that promises us otherness, and a questioning of conquest.

In his brilliant re-history *The Conquest of America*, tellingly subtitled *The Question of the Other*, Tzvetan Todorov traces the establishment of "our present identity" in the modern era to the conquest of America because it was then that "men discovered the totality of which they are a part, whereas hitherto they formed a part without a whole."[18] Todorov chooses the narrative of the confrontation between the Spaniards and the Indians in America, realizing that this choice is one among many, in order to respond to the question: "How to deal with the other?" (4–5). By the end of his chapter on Columbus, Todorov asserts: "The entire history of the discovery of America, the first episode of the conquest, is marked by this ambiguity: human alterity is at once revealed and rejected" (49–50). Todorov suggests that Columbus's journals postulate discovery as an "intransitive action," the desire to come upon an earthly paradise, not simply as a means to fulfill the ends of greed or conversion; and this desire "to discover" finds its basis in literature rather than in an immediate reality. Todorov asks, "but is not a travel narrative itself the point of departure, and not only the point of arrival, of a new voyage? Did not Columbus himself set sail because he had read Marco Polo's narrative?" (13). (Bishop's own travels are based on literature she read as a child, and the myths handed down of her uncles who went off to sea, and of her maternal great-grandfather whose ship foundered in a storm off Sable Island, a place

Bishop visited just before setting out for Brazil.) The conquest of America is paradigmatic, for Bishop, of the conquest of South America.

The problem Columbus has in relation to the Other sets up the predicament Bishop herself faces, or recognizes as threatening our encounters with alterity. Todorov summarizes the double attitude Columbus has in regard to the Indians:

> Either he conceives the Indians (though without using these words) as human beings altogether, having the same rights as himself; but then he sees them not only as equals but also as identical, and this behavior leads to assimilationism, the projection of his own values on the others. Or else he starts from the difference, but the latter is immediately translated into terms of superiority and inferiority (in his case, obviously, it is the Indians who are inferior). What is denied is the existence of a human substance truly other, something capable of being not merely an imperfect state of oneself.(42)

Later Todorov will say the same of both Cortés and the missionary historian Las Casas: "difference is corrupted into inequality, equality into identity. These are the two great figures of the relation to the other that delimit the other's inevitable space" (146). Even when a man comes with "love," "good intentions," and "sympathy," problems arise if perception operates on the basis of these two figures. Of Cortés, he marvels that destructiveness displaces conservation and wonder so entirely:

> There is a dreadful concatenation here, whereby grasping leads to taking and taking to destruction, a concatenation whose unavoidable character we want to question. Should not understanding go hand in hand with sympathy? And should not the desire to take, to profit at another's expense, imply a desire to preserve that other as a potential source of wealth and profit? (127)

Todorov uncovers "the paradox of the understanding-that-kills" (127): even as Cortés praises the Indians for their workmanship and artistry, he fails to regard the Indian as subject. He says of Cortés's "admiring observations":

> They all concern *objects*, the architecture of houses, merchandise, fabrics, jewelry. Like today's tourist who admires the quality of Asian or African craftsmanship though he is untouched by the notion of

sharing the life of the craftsmen who produce such objects, Cortés goes into ecstasies about the Aztec productions but does not acknowledge their makers as human individualities to be set on the same level as himself.(129)

Of Las Casas's supposed Christian "love" for the Indians, Todorov exacts these commanding questions:

> Can we really love someone if we know little or nothing of his identity; if we see, in place of that identity, a projection of ourselves or of our ideals? We know that such a thing is quite possible, even frequent, in personal relations; but what happens in cultural confrontations? Doesn't one culture risk trying to transform the other in its own name, and therefore risk subjugating it as well? How much is such love worth? (168)

Such questions seem to underpin Bishop's own of travel; her poems alert us to the fine and difficult line between desire for unity and the danger of making difference into identity: she has had the opportunity to confront such a dilemma in her questions of "personal relations" previously. Motifs of domination and dependency must have surfaced in her relationship with Lota, and appear as a submerged reflection of her questions of cultural relations, as Goldensohn incisively suggests in her discussion of the Brazil poems. Bishop prefers that boundaries between self and other dissolve to erase the painful imposition of hierarchy, as she does in "Song for the Rainy Season," when she bemoans, "(O difference that kills, / or intimidates, much / of all our small shadowy / life!)" As an exile in Brazil, she realizes the fragility of her position there; yet all "homes" take on an artificial character because of her painful awareness of the ever-surrounding otherness and "not-me" of the world. While she constantly writes herself in environments as outsider, she wants to avoid being the kind of outsider or tourist who stays safely on the periphery, appropriating the objects of another culture without discerning their unique connections to their makers. In "Questions of Travel," she opens her situation up to ethical consideration: "Is it right to be watching strangers in a play / in this strangest of theatres?" Is it possible to come upon the Other without projection? At the very least, Bishop reveals the act and process of projection (as she does in constructing "Brazil" as tapestry), and shows how our perception configures and shapes what we discern. In this way, she heightens our sense of otherness.

The virtual impossibility of comprehending the outsider's position is expressed vividly through another travel narrative—Lévi-Strauss's *Tristes Tropiques*, a work recommended as further reading of geography in the bibliography of the Time-Life *Brazil* Bishop wrote. Lévi-Strauss subjects his own motives and profession to interrogation, in much the same spirit as Bishop does in terms of her poetic craft. The first chapter of his book, "Departure," opens with the paradoxical confession: "Travel and travellers are two things I loathe—and yet here I am, all set to tell the story of my expeditions. . . . [f]ifteen years have passed since I left Brazil for the last time and often, during those years, I've planned to write this book, but I've always been held back by a sort of shame and disgust" (17).

Lévi-Strauss's jaded tone is partly postwar cynicism: traveling had become a personal necessity to avoid persecution. Military preparation and occupation underlined a larger sickness in civilization, what for him appeared as the movement toward "monoculture," the homogenization of all cultural difference, a world gone flat, to use the language of "Visits to St. Elizabeths." He writes of a "familiar shipboard scene" of "a military mission on its way to Paraguay": "Officers and wives alike seemed to mistake the transatlantic voyage for a colonial expedition; and although they were to act as instructors to what was, after all, an army of no great pretensions, they behaved as if they were about to occupy a conquered country" (38). This experience indicates to him just "how thoroughly the notion of travel has become corrupted by the notion of power." Travel becomes an opportunity to assert force. In traveling as in conquest, we tend to step between ourselves and our vision of another's culture. Again and again, he informs his readers that he cannot present the "real" Brazil, but only a version of one.

"Arrival at Santos" reverberates with like sentiments to Lévi-Strauss's recollection of his departure, in its disappointment and ambivalence toward travel; he says, "I understand how it is that people delight in travel-books and ask only to be misled by them. Such books preserve the illusion of something that no longer exists" (39). Yet all we have in our modern age, it would seem, are these falsifying books, "album[s] in 'full colour'": "now that the Indians' masks have been destroyed, these albums have taken their place" (43). He states, in Bishopic modulation, "I should have liked to live in the age of *real* travel," knowing that such an age exists only as illusion. Bishop's own disenchantment hinges upon her fascination with gilt volumes of strange and distant lands, as the first lines of "Over 2,000 Illustrations and a Complete Concordance" testify: "Thus should have been our travels: / serious, engravable." She begins with the knowledge that our travels, as they are, do not come up to snuff, and full-color representations are always, from a certain perspective, lies. Lévi-Strauss despairs that no culture remains intact and authentic so he must regard himself as "archaeologist of space, trying in vain to repiece together the idea of the exotic with the help of a particle here and a fragment of debris there" (44). In advance of Todorov, he points to the paradox: while a culture is alive and vital, we cannot see it for itself without ruining it with our own values: "the less one culture communicates with another, the less likely they are to be corrupted, one by the other; but, on the other hand, the less likely it is, in such conditions, that the respective emissaries of these cultures will be able to seize the richness and significance of their diversity"; either we are faced with what we cannot comprehend, or we are "hastening in search of a vanished reality" (45).

Like Todorov, Lévi-Strauss demonstrates that we cannot understand a culture without changing it, adjusting it to fit our own image. In his quest of the tropics, he confesses that even as he tried to catch the "primitive," it always escaped him: the "savage" is either domesticated or is "too strange," "too savage" (326–27). Lévi-Strauss's rhetoric unwittingly resounds with the ethnocentrism Bishop assigns to the Christians depicted in "Brazil" "ripping away at the fabric"; turning away from individuals with their foreign tongue, he turns to the earth's speech: "What lay behind those confused appearances which are everything and nothing at one and the same time? If I take any particular scene and try to isolate it, that tree, that flower, could be any other tree, any other flower. Could that also be a lie, that whole which gave me such delight, that whole whose parts vanished as soon as I tried to examine them individually? If I had to admit that it was real, I wanted at last to master it, all of it, down to its smallest detail" (327). As anthropologist, he cannot refrain from the desire and duty of mastery, just like Lispector's Petre in his quest to "understand" the smallest woman in the world. But in his conclusion to *Tristes Tropiques*, Lévi-Strauss again acknowledges the essential impossibility of "comprehension," in his restatement of a Buddhist injunction: "When we make an effort to understand, we destroy the object of our attachment, substituting another whose nature is quite different" (394), similar to Todorov's "understanding-that-kills." Yet "substitution" eventually, from this Eastern point of view, becomes "Presence": "The other object requires of us another effort, which in its turn destroys the second object and substitutes a third—and so on until we reach the only enduring Presence, which is that in which all distinction between meaning and the absence of meaning disappears: and it is from that Presence that we started in the first place"(394). We come full circle, face to face with the incomprehensible Other.

What makes *Tristes Tropiques* so significant in connection with Bishop is not only its rendition of experiences in the tropics but also its realization that "truth" and "presence" are elusive; Lévi-Strauss works, riveted to the intractable and contradictory understanding of his profession, swiveling upon the two figures Todorov warns of—equality as assimilationism or difference as superiority: he cannot be a distant outsider, without becoming too much of the condescending tourist, and he cannot be too much of an insider, adopting the customs of the culture he studies, for fear of losing all objectivity (382). Because Lévi-Strauss knows he cannot truly penetrate to the authentic, he at one point exclaims of his interaction with some natives (in the mode of "Questions of Travel" when Bishop asks, "Should we have stayed at home and thought of here?"): "No sooner are such people known or guessed at, than their strangeness drops away, and one might as well have stayed in one's own village" (326–27). But the strangeness, of course, reappears, making it even more plausible that to stay in one's own village would amount to the same imagining of the Other.

The first stanza of "Questions of Travel" (*CP*, 93–94) reiterates the impatience of "Arrival at Santos." The narrator has "arrived" at an unsettling and volatile setting requiring superlatives.

> There are too many waterfalls here; the crowded streams
> hurry too rapidly down to the sea,
> and the pressure of so many clouds on the mountaintops
> makes them spill over the sides in soft slow-motion,
> turning to waterfalls under our very eyes.

By the end of this sentence, clouds becoming waterfalls invite our awe. She employs the adverb "here," meaningful and functional really only in the moment of utterance. Instead of being placed, we are disoriented, which involves a distortion of our sense of time. Temporality is different "here," but how seems uncertain: "—For if those streaks, those mile-long, shiny, tear-stains, / aren't waterfalls yet, / in a quick age or so, as ages go here, / they probably will be." Ages, apparently, move swifter "here." The "streaks" can figure as "tear-stains" or waterfalls or as they quicken, "the mountains look like the hulls of capsized ships, / slime-hung and barnacled." Her tears and the overturned ships reflect, as will "Sestina," personal sorrows and anxieties about loss. Determining what is in a landscape, distinguishing it from how we construct it, she seems to insist, is the difficult thing. All is variable and unpredictable, especially for the traveler, and Bishop's characteristic indecisiveness and agility in qualifying any assertion best express this discovery.

The questions of the second stanza rebuke the traveler who needlessly ventures away from home, lusting to possess the exotic:

> What childishness is it that while there's a breath of life
> in our bodies, we are determined to rush
> to see the sun the other way around?
> The tiniest green hummingbird in the world?
> To stare at some inexplicable old stonework,
> inexplicable and impenetrable,
> at any view,
> instantly seen and always, always delightful?

Her questions are no longer recriminating; they become a longing, open-ended invocation that acknowledges the compulsion we have to project our fantasies onto the world, trying to possess it. She celebrates the multiplicity and mystery of nature, as does Emerson. But her hummingbird is vital and alive, and she recognizes that the "inexplicable," retreating tapestry is "always, always delightful":

> Oh, must we dream our dreams
> and have them, too?
> And have we room
> for one more folded sunset, still quite warm?

She converts a commonplace such as "we want to have our cake and eat it too" into a profoundly resonant question of our desire to have and ingest and yet still to have and possess. The final portion of the poem responds with Prufrockian ("would it have been worth it, after all?") languor and meditation:

> But surely it would have been a pity
> not to have seen the trees along this road,
> really exaggerated in their beauty,
> not to have seen them gesturing
> like noble pantomimists, robed in pink.

This apprehension of beauty elevates the traveler, and somehow brings her in closer connection with the landscape. What follows are fragments introduced by dashes—as if we are watching Bishop's thought processes—of all the traveler would have missed, as she looks to uncover the history behind the visible, rather than simply taking in its sensory splendor. First, she thinks:

> —Not to have had to stop for gas and heard
> the sad, two-noted, wooden tune
> of disparate wooden clogs
> carelessly clacking over
> a grease-stained filling-station floor.

This "grease-stained filling-station" and all its homemade elements re-emerge in "Filling Station," written a year earlier, probably about a New England setting, and included in "Elsewhere." These "disparate wooden clogs" appeal for their particularity and uniqueness; they are "inexplicable and impenetrable," but the traveler who listens is able to catch something of the "two-noted, wooden tune." In parentheses, she warns of the assimilationist trend elsewhere to eliminate the "disparate": "(In another country the clogs would all be tested. / Each pair there would have identical pitch.)" Of his own method of creation, Robert Pinsky has commented that it is impossible for him to look at an object purely from an aesthetic standpoint and not try to trace its history and origin, to appreciate the labor and suffering that have contributed to its existence.[19] Pinsky, it would seem, would have the same curiosity about the factory where the clogs are tested and the origin of the more "disparate" music.

Bishop does not address persons in her survey in this poem of valuable memory, and instead of examining some monumental work of art, she turns away from the stereotypical sites of touristic "beauty" to the homeliest of environments and with Pinsky, concerns herself with an object's history; she discovers the earmarks of an inscrutable (though it does throw a kind of light) presence. She looks past and through the incalculable landscape. The clogs make their "wooden tune," but there is also "the other, less primitive music of the fat brown bird / who sings above the broken gasoline pump." We have come upon a makeshift shrine, "a bamboo church of Jesuit baroque: / three towers, five silver crosses." With numerical and architectural accuracy, she discerns the diverse and unique; transcending its material in the hands of others, woodwork becomes an emblem of struggle and care:

> —Yes, a pity not to have pondered,
> blurr'dly and inconclusively,

on what connection can exist for centuries
between the crudest wooden footwear
and, careful and finicky,
the whittled fantasies of wooden cages.
—Never to have studied history in
the weak calligraphy of songbirds' cages.

Just as "[s]omebody embroidered the doily," a doily seemingly excessive and improbable, in "Filling Station," somebody "whittled" the cage above the broken pump, unusable but enduring somehow. The study of such history and art is bound to be inconclusive, but the faded signature upon the songbird's cage gives proof of an empowered voice singing through time and colonization.

At this point in the poem, we have drifted far from "the hulls of capsized ships," the peril and uselessness of travel. Or have we? The value of traveling has not yet been confirmed, even with her blurred reconstruction of a fragmented culture. It is, after all, to the traveler and his notebook that we return in "a sudden golden silence," an opportunity she would have missed had she not traveled. Bishop is careful not to insert herself, but instead an anonymous thinker, whose fragmentary writing has been lifted from an erased context, as those words of Sir Kenneth Clark. Language cannot be told apart from the tapestry of the nature it describes. We have circled back to the questions earlier in the poem, only now they are italicized: we seem doomed or freed (depending on perspective) to our inconclusive inquiries. With its questions foreclosing any possible immediacy in experience, the notebook entry outlasts any "folded sunset." These questions are like a series of Chinese boxes, one within the other, except that the enclosures keep moving outward, discovering limitation as well as new potential for expansion:

"Is it lack of imagination that makes us come
to imagined places, not just stay at home?
Or could Pascal have been not entirely right
about just sitting quietly in one's room?

Continent, city, country, society:
the choice is never wide and never free.
And here, or there . . . No. Should we have stayed at
   home,
wherever that may be?"

Ultimately, travel becomes not a choice between movement and stasis, imagination and direct experience: "home" is an artificial construction, "sitting quietly in one's room" does not end the activity of the mind; and in moving city to city, one never ends up face to face with the Other, always either culturally constructed or personally imagined.

III

A significant aspect of the drift in Bishop's orientation away from the personal or even philosophical to the political and historical reveals itself in her preference for narrative over lyrical in this volume. The narrative technique appears everywhere but most predominantly and fully in the three poems "Manuelzinho" (CP, 96–99), "The Riverman" (CP, 105–9), and "The Burglar of Babylon" (CP, 112–18). As a narrator, she becomes a self-acknowledged outsider of events, a position permitting greater recognition of otherness. Integral to these poems written narratively is her desire to portray difference with sympathy: the difficulty of this should be now clear from Todorov and Lévi-Strauss. Also essential to these narratives is their impulse to incorporate folk tradition, invoking an oral culture that passes down a generational lore through experience. In attempting to move into an "interior" of another culture, she always bears the knowledge that she cannot fully penetrate it; thus, her narratives respect and evoke the sense of a system of respected yet unelaborated mystical beliefs.

If Bishop in her previous poems aimed at simple and clean language, she drives this tendency to a further limit here, using the most homey, unpretentious, and seemingly transparent diction possible. Most often she is monosyllabic; no complicated syntax demands the reader strain after abstruse meaning. Through this method she enhances the effect of folk telling; and she refuses to call attention to her own subjectivity (as if that were not a way of highlighting it). As in translating Helena Morley's diary, she wants to raise the voices of others—even as those others ultimately may reflect her own concerns.

In order to position herself beyond the relationship of colonizer / colonized or spectator (tourist) / spectacle (tour), and the opposition inside / outside or center / periphery, she utilizes another narrator with the epigraph in "Manuelzinho,": "(Brazil. A friend of the writer is speaking)." By having a full tenant render the character portrait of Manuelzinho, a "[h]alf squatter,

half tenant," she highlights the differences between them and in this way reveals that perhaps another way exists of apprehending the liminal or half, a
way that escapes the befuddled narrator missing Manuelzinho: his identity
slips from her bluff categorization. The poem ends with Bishop's friend
questioning and doubting herself, realizing her deficiencies in knowing the
Other:

> You helpless, foolish man,
> I love you all I can,
> I think. Or do I?
> I take off my hat, unpainted
> and figurative, to you.
> Again I promise to try.

And for Bishop, it must be all in the trying, as we have only the figurative. In
revealing the distortions involved in dialogue, Todorov dismisses it entirely at
one point, and suggests that otherness might best be apprehended through a
triangle: "The touchstone of alterity is not the present and immediate second
person singular but the absent or third person singular" (157). As she removes
the possibility for immediacy or comprehension from the friend, she provides Manuelzinho as an absence, a third person introduced by a conflicted
understanding. Speculation is inconclusive, but the conjectures that surround Manuelzinho proffer him an irreducible uniqueness. The follow-up
to "I think" is "Or do I?": this is not an expression of epistemological certainty.

Exasperated, the narrator wants to understand Manuelzinho. Even as she
finds his ways "foolish," she admires an aspect of them that could only be
called spiritual or mystical. She stands at the threshold of a universe operat-
ing with alternate values; his family emerge in a kind of vision "twined in
wisps of fog" near the end of the poem:

> —All just standing, staring
> off into fog and space.
> Or coming down at night,
> in silence, except for hoofs,
> in dim moonlight, the horse
> or Formoso stumbling after.
> Between us float a few
> big, soft, pale-blue,

> sluggish fireflies,
> the jellyfish of the air . . .

This is an arena without ordinary boundaries, a moment shaped by filmy silence and moonlight, something like the moment when the bus confronts the moose in her poem of that title in *Geography III*—a moment "between us" made somehow sacred because it partakes of at least two worlds.

Drawing lines and making boundaries amount to property, up for question in this volume. The narrator's genealogical guilt (as well as her unconsciousness about her own displacement) for Manuelzinho's disinheritance surfaces in her illogical assertion of ownership and avoidance of facing another's subjectivity:

> I watch you through the rain,
> trotting, light, on bare feet,
> up the steep paths you have made—
> or your father and grandfather made—
> all over my property,
> with your head and back inside
> a sodden burlap bag,
> and feel I can't endure it
> another minute; then,
> indoors, beside the stove,
> keep on reading a book.

Indoors and outdoors, inside and outside: such distinctions only perpetuate comfort and safety at the expense of perceiving border states. One of Manuelzinho's idiosyncrasies is to blear these distinctions—to be inside a bag and outside in the rain, for instance. Later, after going over Manuelzinho's "Dream Books," the narrator will identify with his disinheritance but still reasserts her ownership: "In the kitchen we dream together / how the meek shall inherit the earth— / or several acres of mine."

Bishop reinscribes the motif of the earthly paradise with Manuelzinho as "the world's worst gardener since Cain." As disenfranchised dweller, he takes on the role of Cain, rebel to an order that excludes and marginalizes him. Instead of conforming to his role as vegetable supplier, he acts as more of an artist, or like a bricoleur free of scientific method, improvising with his environment; the practical or durable does not concern him in his adjustable relationship to the earth. Manuelzinho even dresses improvisationally, with

the help of his seamstress-wife, renewing and covering him through what is
at hand, by the homemade:

> Patch upon patch upon patch,
> your wife keeps all of you covered.
> She has gone over and over
> (forearmed is forewarned)
> your pair of bright-blue pants
> with white thread, and these days
> your limbs are draped in blueprints.

This is the architectonics of Jerónimo, whose house is put together by whatever materials become available, paradigmatic of a patchwork kind of writing, as collage or tapestry, decorative not denotative.

As if upside-down, the tenant regards Manuelzinho's landscaping with
awe and perplexity:

> Tilted above me, your gardens
> ravish my eyes. You edge
> the beds of silver cabbages
> with red carnations, and lettuces
> mix with alyssum. And then
> umbrella ants arrive,
> or it rains for a solid week
> and the whole thing's ruined again
> and I buy you more pounds of seeds,
> imported, guaranteed,
> and eventually you bring me
> a mystic three-legged carrot,
> or a pumpkin "bigger than the baby."

Vegetable and flower mingle shamelessly in Manuelzinho's garden, and his
relationship with the earth cannot be predetermined—cause does not trace
to "guaranteed" effect; it is as if a secret communication within his environment went on, the "umbrella ants" somehow prepared for rains. The "mystic
three-legged carrot" remains among other signs that indicate a disposition toward the world distinct from the landowner's and therefore unreadable to
her. Manuelzinho has another language she has no entry to, or at least,
Bishop lets the narrator imagine a language of immediacy and possibly tran-

scendent meaning: Manuelzinho's account books are dream books, "one with flowers on the cover, / the other with a camel," and are "honeycombed with zeros," accounts beyond the grasp of the overseer and that cannot be settled. As an entity beyond her categorizations, Manuelzinho's signs are productive and iterable without being comprehensible, as in this remembered "interaction":

> And once I yelled at you
> so loud to hurry up
> and fetch me those potatoes
> your holey hat flew off,
> you jumped out of your clogs,
> leaving three objects arranged
> in a triangle at my feet

We readers are introduced to play in the triangle of poet / friend / subject and take the friend's "unkindly" appellation of Manuelzinho as "Klorophyll Kid" as apt and kindly; he becomes a figure for metamorphosis and creative substitution. His "holeyness" will not allow him to see his father as dead or limited by his mortality; the shocked narrator, however, reads this as a sign of foolishness: "The family gathers, but you, / no, you 'don't think he's dead! / I look at him. He's cold. / They're burying him today. / But you know, I don't think he's *dead.*'" In spite of herself, the narrator must call Manuelzinho's father "superior," and describe his moustache in the posture of flight, "like a white spread-eagled gull."

The narrative technique of "Manuelzinho" forces us to realize our implication in storytelling; we recognize our limits and a language that always excludes a point of view. "The Riverman" presents an even more decisive representation of Brazil and spiritualism, but by using first-person confession, Bishop deliberately nears herself to otherness. (According to Millier, Lota "hated it" because it was written without firsthand experience of the Amazon (304), which from my point of view, underlines Bishop's very effort in writing it—to demonstrate imaginative construction.) Prefaced with an acknowledgment of Charles Wagley's *Amazon Town* as source for "factual" details, the poem continues to show, however, that information is "relayed" and mediated, escaping absolute comprehension.[20] Although Wagley as an anthropologist and social scientist discusses the transition within the Amazon from supernatural belief to naturalistic explanation as a matter of course, he writes with a sympathetic regard for the magical practices and folk beliefs of

Brazilian culture, and distinguishes between novice and experienced sha-
mans in terms of their mystical powers. The *sacacas*, as they are called, of his
study were known for their association with water spirits and their ability to
travel enormous distances under water. He tells of a young *pagé* (another
name for the *sacaca*), apparently the inspiration for Bishop's character, who
aspires to be as powerful as the legendary Joaquim Sacaca. Bishop removes
some details for her portrait almost straight and unchanged from this text:

> Satiro is still learning his profession. Though he wanted a rattle
> very badly, he told us that first he must have the power to travel
> under water. In the depths he expects to receive his *maraca* (rattle)
> from the very mouth of a giant water snake. A more powerful pagé
> told Satiro that he also needs a "virgin mirror"—one into which no
> one has ever looked—so that he could see his spirit companions
> without danger to himself while traveling under water. He has tried
> successfully several times to buy such a mirror, but someone always
> looks over his shoulder as the box containing them is opened in the
> store.

This is just the kind of homey anecdote that appeals to Bishop. She makes
much of the mirror, which would seem to represent undiluted self-presence,
without a troubling split engendered by language. The riverman declares:

> I need a virgin mirror
> no one's ever looked at,
> that's never looked back at anyone,
> to flash up the spirits' eyes
> and help me recognize them.

But all the multiple mirrors the riverman buys become spoiled by human
glances that insert distance between reflected and reflection.
   Other details that contribute to Bishop's portrait of a shaman, taken from
Wagley, are the importance of smoke from painted cigars and alcohol, both
necessary in provoking trance. Bishop's riverman naively recounts:

> They gave me a shell of *cachaça*
> and decorated cigars.
> The smoke rose like mist
> through the water, and our breaths

didn't make any bubbles.
We drank *cachaça* and smoked
the green cheroots. The room
filled with gray-green smoke
and my head couldn't have been dizzier.

Such is the setting for the initiation by Luandinha, "a female spirit said to have been a large water snake" (Wagley), "a river spirit associated with the moon" (Bishop in her epigraph). The riverman's initial encounter with this spirit approximates a return to the womb and to an impossible language of direct understanding:

She complimented me
in a language I didn't know;
but when she blew cigar smoke
into my ears and nostrils
I understood, like a dog,
although I can't speak it yet.

While the Dolphin plays the central role in the first movement of the poem, all Bishop says of him in the epigraph is that he "is believed to have supernatural powers," and she includes neither the danger and malevolence often connected with the "boto," as the dolphin is called, nor its strong sexual associations (Wagley, 238–39). Bishop illustrates, instead, pure belief—a state of mind set apart from colonization and the implantation of scientific explanation. By adopting the voice of the riverman, Bishop speaks for a past generation—or one in the midst of transition (as she does when rescuing the pre-industrial moment of Helena Morley's diary for us to see); the use of first person lends the poem an immediacy and presence it might not otherwise have, and in its anaphoric use of "I" in simple declarative sentences, reminds one of the narrative "The Fish," another poem about the encounter between two worlds and the impulse toward empathy and revelation rather than isolation and cynicism.

I got up in the night
for the Dolphin spoke to me.
He grunted beneath my window,
hid by the river mist,
but I glimpsed him—a man like myself.

I threw off my blanket, sweating;
I even tore off my shirt.
I got out of my hammock
and went through the window naked.

The dolphin "grunted" just as her fish does when taken from the water. Intermediate positions and entities attract Bishop: the dolphin is like a man but is not one; the riverman passes from home "through the window naked." Leaving his home above water he finds another below, drawn by the correspondence between a "burning bright" moon and a "gasoline-lamp mantle / with the flame turned up too high, / just before it begins to scorch," counterpointing the other extreme, "the gas flame turned down as low as possible" in "The Bight": here correspondence tries to be much more sure. The imagination represents itself as possible belief.

I heard the Dolphin sigh
as he slid into the water.
I stood there listening
till he called from far outstream.
I waded into the river
and suddenly a door
in the water opened inward,
groaning a little, with water
bulging above the lintel.
I looked back at my house,
white as a piece of washing
forgotten on the bank,
and I thought once of my wife,
but I knew what I was doing.

Being able to give up one place for another, to stand within a threshold, is part of Bishop's strength; her riverman shares this ability to inhabit imagined places, places of otherness. Below is a world of playfulness and imagination, movement and displacement:

When the moon shines on the river,
oh, faster than you can think it
we travel upstream and downstream,
we journey from here to there,

> under the floating canoes,
> right through the wicker traps,
> when the moon shines on the river
> and Luandinha gives a party.

Luandinha's quarters become "like at the cinema," with the powerful moonlight. The landscape neither "here" nor "there" becomes a site of transformation. Living between two worlds, the *sacaca's* life above water shows signs of his alternate one below:

> I don't eat fish any more.
> There is fine mud on my scalp
> and I know from smelling my comb
> that the river smells in my hair.
> My hands and feet are cold.
> I look yellow, my wife says,
> and she brews me stinking teas
> I throw out, behind her back.

An essential aspect of the riverman's spirituality is his relationship to nature. Bishop's poem is as much about respect for the environment and ecological balance as it is about otherness; many of the spirits in Brazilian folklore and superstition guard against exploitation of nature, protecting it from hunters and fishermen who kill too much, as we learn from Wagley (234–35). The riverman's "study" is of the rhythms of nature ("The river breathes in salt / and breathes it out again") and his coming to intimate terms with "the deep, enchanted silt." Commonsensical, this initiate mystic tells us:

> Look, it stands to reason
> that everything we need
> can be obtained from the river.
> It drains the jungles; it draws
> from trees and plants and rocks
> from half around the world,
> it draws from the very heart
> of the earth the remedy
> for each of the diseases—
> one just has to know how to find it.

"One just has to know how to find it" is a bricoleur sentiment; being a witch-doctor requires imagination and improvisation as sympathy with the environment; such a spiritualism demands feeling for otherness. Most of the poem (after his introduction to Luandinha, a female presence—for Bishop, an unusual place to locate obvious power) is told in present tense, blurring the mythical component of the text. By the poem's close, the riverman has become as one with the river, surpassed his landed relatives, though still linked to them as medicine man; he is powerful and elusive, not commensurate with the physical:

> I'll be there below,
> as the turtle rattle hisses
> and the coral gives the sign,
> travelling fast as a wish,
> with my magic cloak of fish
> swerving as I swerve,
> following the veins,
> the river's long, long veins,
> to find the pure elixirs.
> Godfathers and cousins,
> your canoes are over my head;
> I hear your voices talking.
> You can peer down and down
> or dredge the river bottom
> but never, never catch me.

What evades capture is, in part, the magical "other," understood better in transit and immersion than in fixed place; these sorcerous words could also be Manuelzinho's, as a motto of inscrutability, opacity, lubricity.

IV

"The Riverman" is a political poem that argues like "Manuelzinho" for the place of the marginal, peripheral figure, and also for respect for the natural as powerful Other; these poems do not want, necessarily, to make margin center, for it is their outsiderhood and liminality that gives these two characters their spiritual power. The turn to narrative and the insistence upon a simple and conversational diction ground this volume, which, fitting for Bishop's social and political gestures, is never dogmatic or didactic. Nevertheless, Bishop is interested in the political. Bishop complains, for instance, that the Time-Life *Brazil* did not turn out the way she had wanted it to because of the interference of the editors who, for instance, changed all her chapter headings and did not allow her to use as many or the kind of pictures she had hoped to.[21] Though she never specifies the direction she wanted to take with the edition, it seems likely that the published one was more of a "tourist's" version of Brazil that could not address in detail the difficult issues of slavery, colonization, and poverty, so inherent to the history of the culture. Yet George Starbuck tells Bishop in his interview with her that even a task like the Time-Life book she made "wholly [her] own"—her choice of what to include is distinctive—for example, her printing the suicide note of the dictator Vargas or a photograph of Dom Pedro at Niagara Falls (132). *Brazil* informs us in journalistic style but with a Bishopian selectivity of an essential doubleness in the Brazilians:

> Exploding birth rate and high infant mortality rate, great wealth and degrading poverty—these are the two big paradoxes. But along with them come many smaller ones repeating the pattern, overlapping and interacting; passionate patriotism combined with constant self-criticism and denigration; luxury and idleness (or admiration of them) combined with bursts of energy; extravagance and pride, with sobriety and humility. The same contrasts even appear in Brazilian history, periods of waste and corruption alternating with periods of reform and housecleaning.[22]

Though her desire to write a geography and history of Brazil indicates an interest in diachronic rendering, Bishop presents the country as living synchronically:

> Men from two, three or more eras of European history live simultaneously in Brazil today. The coastal cities, from Belem at the mouth of the Amazon River to Porto Alegre in the south, are filled with 20th Century men with 20th Century problems on their minds: getting on in the world and rising in it socially; how to pay for schools and doctors and clothes. Then in the surrounding countryside is a rural or semirural population who lead lives at least half a century behind the times, old-fashioned both agriculturally and socially. And for the

people of the fishing villages, for those living on the banks of the great
rivers, for cowboys and miners—all the backlands people—time
seems to have stopped in the 17th Century. Then, if one ventures
even a little farther on, one enters the really timeless, prehistoric
world of the Indians.

Is this simply a poetic understanding of history? It is as if the present were layered with tapestry hangings, and if ripped away at, would reveal those "mad-
dening" Indian women. The quote explains her interest in figures such as
Manuelzinho and the riverman, those living in "out-moded" fashions. Time
becomes place; the one defines the other, in her rendering of Brazil. She re-
covers a cultural past, makes it present, knowing that every revealing is also
a new concealing. Just so with personal history, as poems such as "Manners"
and "Sestina" will demonstrate; not on a quest to preserve or glorify the past,
she establishes its ongoing and *changing* presence.

   In resorting to the ballad (from Latin, *ballare*, "to dance") in "Burglar of
Babylon," Bishop returns to an oral, folk technique of passing stories down
(or around). The author of a ballad is traditionally anonymous, and different
versions of the story told are presumed to exist. Babylon as a site for events in
this "dance," from this perspective, becomes telling: the poem can be read,
on one level, as paradigmatic of the corruption of the word—with language
comes the multiple. By the end of the poem, after the "criminal" Micuçú is
buried, "They're after another two." The fall away from an Edenic oneness
leads to poverty and exposes the ongoing necessity of its retelling. The envoy
repeats the first and fifth stanza:

> On the fair green hills of Rio
>   There grows a fearful stain:
> The poor who come to Rio
>   And can't go home again.
>
> There's the hill of Kerosene,
>   And the hill of the Skeleton,
> The hill of Astonishment,
>   And the hill of Babylon.

The multiple hills show the unfair stain of poverty and death with allegorical
trenchancy. "The poor who come to Rio" seem trapped within the circle of
their historical and topographical presence.

If Bishop is anyone other than the anonymous speaker, she must identify with those watching the scene of action from binoculars:

> Rich people in apartments
> Watched through binoculars
> As long as the daylight lasted.
> And all night, under the stars,

And later:

> The rich with their binoculars
> Were back again, and many
> Were standing on the rooftops,
> Among TV antennae.

While she did not see Micuçú himself, she admits in her forward to its publication in 1968: "The story of Micuçú is true. It happened in Rio de Janeiro a few years ago. . . . I was one of those who watched the pursuit of Micuçú through binoculars. . . . The rest of the story is taken, often word for word, from the daily papers, filled out by what I know of the place and the people."[23] While Bishop is not among the rich of Rio, she certainly regards herself as privileged, cannot but see herself in the position of those protected from the poverty of those on the hill of Babylon. Rio lures Brazilians away from their homes in the countryside with the promise of wealth; in the process, they lose their "home," become eternally displaced: with this Bishop also must identify.

In "Pink Dog" (CP, 190–91), begun near the end of her residence in Brazil, all displaced persons become figured in the hairless, naked dog; the poem becomes one of Bishop's most politically aggressive and satiric as she addresses society's treatment of the outcast poor, the burglar from Babylon included:

> Didn't you know? It's been in all the papers,
> to solve this problem, how they deal with beggars?
> They take and throw them in the tidal rivers.
>
> Yes, idiots, paralytics, parasites
> go bobbing in the ebbing sewage, nights
> out in the suburbs, where there are no lights.

> If they do this to anyone who begs,
> drugged, drunk, or sober, with or without legs,
> what would they do to sick, four-legged dogs?

The only solution, the poem satirizes, is to dress in carnival costume, disguise the bare state of things.

The theme of helpless homelessness woven so thoroughly into the fabric of *Questions of Travel* surfaces in even a minor poem of the volume, "Twelfth Morning; or What You Will" (*CP*, 110–11), taken from Cabo Frio, which discerns in an uncertain scene of "thin gray mist" these essential characters: "the black boy Balthazar, a fence, a horse, / a foundered house." To mark off boundaries again is the essential ill; here the fence shows itself ineffective:

> The fence, three-strand, barbed-wire, all pure rust,
> three dotted lines, comes forward hopefully
> across the lots; thinks better of it; turns
>   a sort of corner . . .
>
> Don't ask the big white horse, *Are you supposed*
> *to be inside the fence or out?* He's still
> asleep. Even awake, he probably
>   remains in doubt.

In *Brazil*, she emphasizes the country's doubleness, the wide chasm kept between rich and poor—with no substantial middle class—and provides a problematic picture of the slums of such a "hill of Babylon" with the caption: "the *favelas* of Rio are home to a quarter of its people, who live without running water or sewers literally a stone's throw from luxury apartment houses. Flimsy shanties built of odd scraps, they are inhabited mainly by rural people who come to Rio to find work. Although the *favelas* are no worse than many other city slums, they are more conspicuous—inescapable reminders of the rural squalor behind Brazil's industrial progress" (138). Homes are fragile on the hill of Babylon, about to topple down:

> On the hills a million people,
>   A million sparrows, nest,
> Like a confused migration
>   That's had to light and rest,

> Building its nest, or houses,
>   Out of nothing at all, or air.
> You'd think a breath would end them,
>   They perch so lightly there.
>   ("Burglar of Babylon")

In revealing the proximity and synchronous existence of the rich and poor, Bishop makes us aware of the lie that progress can represent. Micuçú (the name means "deadly snake," and as we learn from Wagley, supernatural powers are often attributed to snakes, who often have their vengeance upon those who exploit the natural world) is made into the anti-hero, the victim of a society that takes so little care of its poor. It is clear from the poem the answer to the aunt's question, "'Why did he have to rob?'" We are meant to blame unjust social conditions.

Though the story is taken from a newspaper, Bishop shows us how we are always in the process of mythologizing, distorting the Other. The ballad, typically overstated for effect, presents Micuçú as "An enemy of society. / He had escaped three times / From the worst penitentiary"; at the same time, Bishop includes in the ballad an internal criticism of such narrow mythologizing, which makes Micuçú either evil or good, without shading, either ingrate criminal or orphaned victim who dies with "two contos" in his pocket. She presents both possibilities, but no one knows the actual details of the boy's life or crime. While the poem centers upon the pursuit of Micuçú, it shuffles through a variety of perspectives: that of the touristic rich people, the aunt, the customers in the aunt's drink shop, the soldiers, Micuçú himself, and one of us. A customer leaving Micuçú's aunt offers, only after he has been killed, "'He wasn't much of a burglar, / He got caught six times—or more.'"

The soldiers themselves are subject to irony. Predatory, they far outnumber the solitary Micuçú, yet the poem reduces them, deflates their importance. They look ridiculous, vaudevillian:

> The soldiers were all over,
>   On all sides of the hill,
> And right against the skyline
>   A row of them, small and still.
>
> . . . .
>
> But the soldiers were nervous, even
>   With tommy guns in hand,

> And one of them, in a panic,
>   Shot the officer in command.

And then Micuçú's perspective minimalizes those lounging tourists:

> Far, far below, the people
>   Were little colored spots,
> And the heads of those in swimming
>   Were floating coconuts.

The pursuit of Micuçú on the hill of Babylon becomes an allegory for the state oppression of the poor, and ridding the state of one such as him will not abolish other outlaws in the impoverished economy—and the myths will go on, this time telling us that the new criminals are less feared:

> Micuçú is buried already.
>   They're after another two,
> But they say they aren't as dangerous
>   As the poor Micuçú.

The homelessness of the poor in Rio is a pronounced concern of Bishop's. Yet she often presents difficult issues in this volume in fairy-tale-like forms (such as "Visits to St. Elizabeths," its metrics modeled on a nursery rhyme), not so much to cloak painfulness as to provide a language both sparing and mythical; her childlike tone re-creates a sense of wonder, essential to an approach toward the Other. *Brazil* opens with a story of a child kidnapped by a woman who lost her own to miscarriage, illustrating the love for children so integral to Brazilian culture, and on the next page emends: "But there is more to it than that. The story immediately brings to mind one of Brazil's worst, and certainly most shocking, problems: that of infant mortality" (10). The fate of children in poverty-stricken families—or those disenfranchised of their homes—obviously compels a writer like Bishop, who underwent dramatic displacements. The question at the close of "Questions of Travel" is, therefore, poignantly personal, yet political: "Should we have stayed at home, / wherever that may be?" That this subject of child mortality possessed her interest can be seen in the elements—among them a doll, a pacifier, and a baby's sandal found on the beach—of her "Cornell" box, created while she lived in Brazil.[24]

These central narratives, "Manuelzinho," "The Riverman," and "The

Burglar of Babylon" attempt to venture into the interior, without claiming ownership, to extend beyond the tourist's arrival and hesitation on the borders, to seek some kind of "membership" ("Song for the Rainy Season," *CP*, 101). The interior is, of course, always on the move, partly an imagined place, contiguous with the interior of the observer's consciousness. The political and historical issues raised in this volume are not reduced because of this recognition, but are, in fact, heightened because of their connection to the genuine and personal, so relevant in Bishop's writing. Her excursion into dramatic monologue and narrative alleviates the personal without diminishing it, giving greater scope to her loss of home, connecting this loss with historical displacement.

V

The poem that follows "Questions of Travel," "Squatter's Children" (*CP*, 95), directly treats the issue of childhood displacement. The children playing appear in diminutive perspective, "a specklike girl and boy, / alone, but near a specklike house." Instead of making the house larger—to give scale to the children—her poem asks to be read as pictoral representation, such as the tapestry model in "Brazil, January 1, 1502." What is larger than the children in the picture is the movement of nature: "Clouds are piling up; / a storm piles up behind the house." Bishop wants to assert the primacy of nature over law, the kind of law that enforces ownership and possession. We are told "The children play at digging holes," to distinguish their activity from that of their father's work, signs of which indicate poverty and disuse: "they try to use / one of their father's tools, / a mattock with a broken haft." They make a home of their own in the natural world:

> But to their little, soluble,
> unwarrantable ark,
> apparently the rain's reply
> consists of echolalia

Solubility and unwarrantableness are for Bishop, we know by now, mostly positive terms. To be unwarrantable means to be unlawful, but the poem reverses this definition, as "Manuelzinho" did in its questioning of tenant-squatter rights. The closing prophetic stanza submits the children to a higher law of natural privilege:

> Children, the threshold of the storm
> has slid beneath your muddy shoes;
> wet and beguiled, you stand among
> the mansions you may choose
> out of a bigger house than yours,
> whose lawfulness endures.
> Its soggy documents retain
> your rights in rooms of falling rain.

The poem could well be called "Squatter's Rights," for she extends the figure of the house to the world, where each individual has a place; the poem seems to be a more serious commendation of "the meek shall inherit the earth" motif raised in "Manuelzinho."

Bishop's poetics affirms difference in order to diminish narcissism, but difference is also feared as the basis of segregation and oppression. To take down barriers, to reveal the room outside the walls, to expose an enfeebled fence motivates her blurring the boundary between the natural and the civilized. Such uncertainty of boundaries seems attractive in her poems of the Brazilian landscape. The house she shares with Lota in Petropolis, written about in "Song for the Rainy Season," partakes of the natural world, shows its indebtedness to it, and therefore, can never pretend to the security and solidity that are lies to our mortality. "Song" is an invocation that could possibly be spoken by someone like her riverman: her house possesses mystical properties in its intimacy with water and the rainy season, the source of life, mesmerizing the imaginative faculties:

> Hidden, oh hidden
> in the high fog
> the house we live in,
> beneath the magnetic rock,
> rain-, rainbow-ridden,
> where blood-black
> bromelias, lichens,
> owls, and the lint
> of the waterfalls cling,
> familiar, unbidden.

The abode described in this poem can be understood in Gaston Bachelard's terming of the "felicitous space"[25] in his examination of the house image, "a veritable principle of psychological integration"; using C. G. Jung's interpretation of the psyche as a structure of multiple temporal layers, he brings together the valuation of spaces with memory: "Not only our memories, but the things we have forgotten are 'housed.' Our soul is an abode. And by remembering 'houses' and 'rooms,' we learn to abide within ourselves . . . [houses] are as much in us as we are in them" (xxxiii).

The image of the house, for Bachelard, however, carries with it the value of being "the non-I which protects the I"; the places we inhabit and create in our dreams, he suggests, always possess this dynamic of the hope for preservation and shelter. Even the humble hut constitutes itself in our imagination as facing off the world:

> The hermit's hut is an engraving that would suffer from any exaggeration of picturesqueness. Its truth must derive from the intensity of its essence, which is the essence of the verb "to inhabit." The hut immediately becomes centralized solitude, for in the land of legend, there exists no adjoining hut. The image leads us on towards extreme solitude. The hermit is *alone* before God. His hut, therefore, is just the opposite of the monastery. And there radiates about this centralized solitude a universe of meditation and prayer, a universe outside the universe. The hut can receive none of the riches "of this world." It possesses the felicity of intense poverty; indeed, it is one of the glories of poverty; as destitution increases it gives us access to absolute refuge. (32)

Bishop's image of the house, in opposition to Bachelard's, which seems to participate in the enforcement of stricter ego boundaries, partakes of the non-I, questions the dialectic that separates place from surrounding. Her "hut-dwellers" in "Squatter's Children" are more at home in the outside; or at least, they regard their homes as risky. Her poetics counteract "centralized solitude" and her houses refuse to belong to such an image repertoire.

The poet's representation of the house in "Song for the Rainy Season" valorizes interpenetration of outside and inside, and the closeness establishing itself between the "I" and the "not-I," the human and the natural:

> House, open house
> to the white dew

and the milk-white sunrise
kind to the eyes,
to membership
of silver fish, mouse,
bookworms,
big moths; with a wall
for the mildew's
ignorant map;

darkened and tarnished
by the warm touch
of the warm breath,
maculate, cherished,
rejoice!

Certainly, "the warm touch" and "the warm breath" indicate that "Song for the Rainy Season" is also a love song, yet her representation of home does not denote security or complacent abiding. Her story, "Memories of Uncle Neddy," worked on throughout and after her residence in Brazil, epitomizes her attraction to the "tarnished" and "maculate." She opens the memoir with her experience of a period of continuous rain in Rio to confess her love of mildews, for the in-between state of life and death—"that gray-green bloom, or that shadow of fine soot," "a hint of morbidity, attractive morbidity" (228). Consciousness of mortality makes her aware of the essential doubleness in existence, and the overlapping of one thing with another. This translates into an experience of otherness that does not subject the "not me" to ostracism nor to elevated incomprehension. To see the self in the Other is not a narcissist incorporation of the Other into oneself nor a projection of one's desires on to the Other. Self and Other exist in cooperation and interaction.

Liquid is Bishop's preference, reflected in her poetics, as discussed in terms of love poetry in the last chapter. Rain and wetness appear throughout this volume as witness to the permeability of worlds, the warping and altering of boundaries, the questioning of the place of the self and the Other. "Song for the Rainy Season" is an exclamatory kind of prayer to dew and moisture, as in "The Riverman," for the ecological balance and the imaginative fluidity they mirror:

life!) Without water

the great rock will stare

> unmagnetized, bare,
> no longer wearing
> rainbows or rain,
> the forgiving air
> and the high fog gone;
> the owls will move on
> and the several
> waterfalls shrivel
> in the steady sun.

These could be the same waterfalls that were initially "too many" in "Questions of Travel," now discovered as necessary for imaginative survival. "Song for the Rainy Season" writes with a nostalgia for "membership," as if "the dim age" of shadows and mildew has already vanished or is on the point of disappearing (somewhat in the elegiac voice of Helena Morley). She sings to "rejoice" in the present "For a later / era will differ." The singer foresees a period of division (whether it be on a personal or political level is necessarily unclear):

> (O difference that kills,
> or intimidates, much
> of all our small shadowy
> life!) Without water

We depend upon water to blur difference, reflect unity, supply shadows. Exploitation of the forest, the division of lands, will drive the presiding and magical owls away.

Bishop writes "The Armadillo" (CP, 103–4) for Robert Lowell, who responds with his "Skunk Hour," dedicated to Bishop. The poem's occasion is a holy day celebrated with fire balloons for the "saint / still honored in these parts," and Bishop continues to show a nostalgia for disappearing traditions. Yet the poem establishes a relationship between the human and natural where again the owls are being driven from their home by the celebratory fire, as invasive as a conqueror or explorer figure unthinkingly disturbing the "membership" within the nest's shadowy life. For both Lowell and Bishop, the animals, armadillo and skunk, are made to appear "illegal," on the fringe of the natural and human world, and very much like artists, who, in spite of being endangered and threatened outsiders, discover a means of survival. Bishop identifies with her armadillo, who camouflaged, can leave "the scene" with the shamed posture of "head down, tail down," and in doing so, places her craft and position as artist alongside those displaced "others"— Manuelzinho, the Riverman, Micuçú—she has taken such pains to acknowledge. Without once exploiting the first-person singular, as Lowell does, this poem succeeds in being at once personal and ecological. The owls that preside over the house in Petropolis are driven away, their "ancient" home destroyed by the attack of a fire balloon:

> Last night another big one fell.
> It splattered like an egg of fire
> against the cliff behind the house.
> The flame ran down. We saw the pair
>
> of owls who nest there flying up
> and up, their whirling black-and-white
> stained bright pink underneath, until
> they shrieked up out of sight.
>
> The ancient owls' nest must have burned.

"My mind's not right," writes Lowell in "Skunk Hour," just before the last powerful movement of his poem when he identifies an emotional equivalent in his vision of skunks:

> I myself am hell;
> nobody's here—
>
> only skunks, that search
> in the moonlight for a bite to eat.
> They march on their soles up Main Street:
> white stripes, moonstruck eyes' red fire
> under the chalk-dry and spar spire
> of the Trinitarian Church.

The last stanza of the poem shifts from a view of the skunks as possessed, stalking and desperate to an image of a mother skunk as provider, a sign of the life force in defiance of the decay around her:

> a mother skunk with her column of kittens swills the
>   garbage pail.

She jabs her wedge-head in a cup
of sour cream, drops her ostrich tail,
and will not scare.

Kalstone compares the two poems to show Lowell's and Bishop's distinction from each other, and decides, even considering Lowell's indebtedness to
Bishop's style, that Lowell has written "a much more *historical* poem":

> Bishop's armadillo is viewed from a greater distance, is more crea-
> turely, a part of the whole natural scene rather than the human and
> historical one. She documents a prior creation, in contrast to Low-
> ell's stubborn and impressive refusal to believe in a world prior to his
> own. In 'Skunk Hour' the physical world is drawn into a historical
> drama of Lowell's re-enacted helplessness. In 'The Armadillo', the
> panorama is one of great attraction to and compassion for the physi-
> cal world of which the spectator-poet is only a small part. [26]

If a refusal to believe in a world prior to one's own is *historical*, I would like
to posit also that it is such a belief and respect, characteristic of Bishop, that
constitutes historical perspective. "Armadillo" begins by invoking the tradition of a culture she wants to understand; it is St. John's Day, a specific
occasion:

This is the time of year
when almost every night
the frail, illegal fire balloons appear.

Lowell's poem, on the other hand, suspends us in an uncertain temporality,
or one of the decayed past still striving to occupy the present; he begins with a
woman, an outmoded Victorian, stuck in the nineteenth century: "Nautilus
Island's hermit / heiress still lives through winter in her Spartan cottage; / her
sheep still graze above the sea."

The natural world, as Kalstone points out, is larger than the human one,
for Bishop, and as with Lowell, many past traditions are looked upon as de-
funct, misguided, or no longer promising security, permanence, or transcendence. Yet her identification with the armadillo does not only indicate
"attraction and compassion" for the natural world. The fire-balloons in this
human celebration, which represent the persistent yearning for transcen-

dence, "rising toward a saint / still honored in these parts," may resemble stars, "the tinted ones," but they simply fail, "receding, dwindling, solemnly / and steadily forsaking us," or, as she turns the poem, they are "suddenly turning dangerous." The balloons are dangerous; they interfere with the natural order of things. Though the poem begs allegory, it is not enough to say simply that men and their intrusive traditions run counter to the primal forces surrounding us. The armadillo is also made to seem "dangerous"; it appears guilty, conspiratorial with the fire balloons mimicking the stars and planets. Survival of one creature seems impossible without the expense of others.

Bishop's armadillo skirts the destruction of "the ancient owls' nest," a suggestion not of a history but of survival (one can't forget the burned "baby rabbit") over and through time:

> The ancient owls' nest must have burned.
> Hastily, all alone,
> a glistening armadillo left the scene,
> rose-flecked, head down, tail down,
>
> and then a baby rabbit jumped out,
> *short*-eared, to our surprise.
> So soft!—a handful of intangible ash
> with fixed, ignited eyes.

What makes "The Armadillo" such an intensely dynamic poem is its multiple positions, all taken up or identified with by the poet, whose craft, is in itself, an act of mimicry, exposed and mocked in the final stanza.

> *Too pretty, dreamlike mimicry!*
> *O falling fire and piercing cry*
> *and panic, and a weak mailed fist*
> *clenched ignorant against the sky!*

Mimicry works many directions. What is being apostrophized here? The fire balloons are, of course, the logical referent. But the armadillo, too, has camouflaged itself, and so, armored, can emerge unharmed. The "panic" belongs to the owls and the saved rabbit, and in defiance of their destruction, the armadillo becomes "a weak mailed fist / clenched ignorant against the sky!" But because the fist is "weak" and "mailed," we think of the human world, and also of Bishop's earlier poem, "Brazil, January 1, 1502," with the Christians in their "creaking armour" ripping into the tapestried landscape, their imagined place. The use or threat of power, as between nations, dwindles with this image of the armadillo. The artist or poet-spectator is implicated, as well, and Bishop enacts the similar gesture of self-criticism exercised throughout the volume, a reaction against un-self-conscious egoistic projection upon the "not-I." Disguise helps us to survive, and she hints that this is the strategy of the Indian women in endless retreat into the landscape in "Brazil"; it is also her own means of placing herself in the other's position, as she does for example, in "The Riverman."

All of Bishop's "Brazil" poems posit the limitations in our ability to know and understand otherhood. This position, I think, is a political one that demands that we review and question our methods of travel, that we realize that we occupy, for the most part, imagined places. Bishop may refute linear history and progress (as she does chronological storytelling), but she insists upon the present of the past, and its contribution to our misreadings and delusions of the Other. The mapmakers' colors are given to the historian, who must reflect upon boundaries and relationships. The period of *Questions of Travel* spans more than a decade of her exploration of another landscape and of her interior scape. The simultaneity of these processes surely caused great stress, as she writes to Lowell in 1962: "all this nostalgia and homesickness and burrowing into the past running alongside trying to write articles about the Brazilian political life—I can't—translating some Portuguese poems, etc.—are other writers as confused & contradictory? Or do they stick to one thing at a time?"[27] Bishop's "contradictory" impulses contribute to one another, and writing the poems of "Brazil" (which she herself does not term political) allows her to develop her methods for understanding her own "nostalgia and homesickness." Just as history shows itself in circular repetition through poems like "Arrival at Santos" (where there is no arrival) and "Brazil, January 1, 1502"—the recurrent quest, for example, of the earthly paradise—so does autobiography, the subject of Chapter 5. In tracking her personal history, Bishop actively imagines and constructs the self from memory. She also continues to insist upon repetition as a poetic and psychological necessity. We cope with the past by returning to it, over and again, in the present.

5

Remembering the Homemade

I could inform the dullest author how he might write an
interesting book. Let him relate the events of his own life
with honesty, not disguising the feelings that accompanied
them.
  —Letter from Coleridge to Thomas Poole, February 1797

    Omissions are not accidents.
    —Marianne Moore

Bishop would appear to agree with Coleridge's injunction to turn to autobiography for the most interesting of stories. As early as 1948, she was trying
to write about her childhood in Nova Scotia through visits and numerous
drafts of a piece called "Homesickness," which she was never able to finish.
Throughout her residence in Brazil, she wrote autobiographic pieces, constructed genealogies, attempted to piece together a past that had exiled her.
And throughout her career she was reading and later teaching, with almost
more interest than anything else, the letters and autobiographies of others:
Coleridge, Yeats, Dickinson, Juan Gris, Freud, Plath, to name a few. Even
as she interests herself in the domestic and private struggles of writers and artists, her range extends to lives as apparently obscure as that of Helena Morley, or as political as Rémy's *Memoirs of a Secret Agent of Free France*, which
she recommends to Lowell as the "most exciting book in years."[1]

 Although Bishop's period of exploration of otherness was most pronounced while she resided in South America, she also began to think more
about her own past and personal resources, about the meaning of origins and
home. Yet Coleridge's excerpted recommendation, oddly enough for him,
neglects to account for the necessary fiction that accompanies the "honest"
relation of autobiography, those distortions imposed by time and memory.

One of Bishop's last completed poems (1978), "Santarém" (*CP*, 185–87) begins midstream, offhand, with an admission that what follows must be questionable: "Of course I may be remembering it all wrong / after, after—how
many years?" An earlier draft (she had begun the poem on a river trip in
1960) had started less uncertainly, "I may remember it all wrong, / after two
years"; in the final draft, she doubles "after" and turns "two years" into an in-
distinct period and question; Bishop offers her own "I" and sense of temporal
perception (the two "so compressed, / they've turned into each other,"
"Poem") up for inquiry, an inquiry that irradiates her later work. Omissions,
what is not said, those unaccidental absences (she writes to Lowell, only part
jokingly, "I've always felt that I've written poetry more by *not* writing it than
writing it"), along with her highly conscious excavation of the twin processes
of excision and revision, propel Bishop's explorations of loss and the self.

When Edwin Boomer in "The Sea & Its Shore" discovers on his beach a
scrap of paper referring to "Averrhoe's catalogue of ANTI-MNEMONICS, or
weakeners of the memory" (*CPr*, 176), Bishop—as I have elsewhere pointed
out—is commenting on the necessity for the artist to forget, at least partially,
her tradition and to subvert it, burn up historical models in order to retextu-
alize and write from the experiencing self. Cultural forgetfulness, with its
stray, intentional lapses into memory, can be another way of remembering.
The need to cast off and turn to the interior, results, in part, from her is-
landed position as lesbian writer with minimal confirmed or canonized literary heritage. Along with others, Alice Walker has stressed woman's need to
seek out models; Walker discovers the most potent source of inspiration from
her mother, or from those individuals who become symbolic nurturers and
creators within oppressive or deficient environments through their strength,
patience, endurance. Such a model comes close to what I have called a poetics of the homemade, a returning to the self and all its "island industries."
But because a poet like Bishop is so aware of displacement on both a personal
and social level, her sense of the homemade requires the continual re-
making of "home" ("wherever that may be"); what comes nearest to the idea
of home is the almost always elegiac space created by a questionable and
imagining memory.

We remember not in terms of "duration" but through meditations of
place, proposes Gaston Bachelard; memory shapes our potent images of the
home, places of "protected intimacy," precisely because it functions as space:

> Memory—what a strange thing it is!—does not record concrete dura-
> tion, in the Bergsonian sense of the word. We are unable to relive

duration that has been destroyed. We can only think of it, in the line of an abstract time that is deprived of all thickness. The finest specimens of fossilized duration concretized as a result of long sojourn, are to be found in and through space. The unconscious abides. Memories are motionless, and the more securely they are fixed in space, the sounder they are. To localize a memory in time is merely a matter for the biographer and only corresponds to a sort of external history, for external use, to be communicated to others. But hermeneutics, which is more profound than biography, must determine the centers of fate by ridding history of its conjunctive temporal tissue, which has no action on our fates. For a knowledge of intimacy, localization in the spaces of our intimacy is more urgent than the determination of dates. [2]

While Bishop in her attraction to the idea of home, a space of heightened intimacy, would probably agree that we cannot "relive duration," her poetics protests, I think, against any such nostalgic belief that memories can be still or "motionless," or that the house as an image "appeals to our consciousness of centrality" (17). Bishop rejects the house as a symbol of permanence and wholeness, of the integrated self: we must keep inscribing homes, the intimacy and loss they imply, while the memory of them changes over time. She abandons, as well, firm "determination of dates," as her conscious and artful imprecisions of Santarém attest.

A literary tradition is not enough, and in Bishop's last works, she returns to the self and its primary resources, not to be clearly circumscribed. Richard Poirier in A World Elsewhere suggests that American writers seek within the self the vast spaces they discover in their environments. Distinguished from the English, the American temperament is "visionary":

One of the first English novels comparable to the American fiction of civilization and the frontier is Robinson Crusoe, but it is indicative of the American emphases of Cooper, of Mark Twain, of Thoreau, though Thoreau gives a whole chapter of Walden to bourgeois considerations of economy, that Defoe's novel is a sort of idyllic parable of man's gaining merely economic control over an environment out of which he could try to make anything he chose. A true born Englishman, he has no interest whatever in the merely visionary possession of the landscape. [3]

Of course Bishop's rewriting ("Crusoe in England," *CP*, 162–66) of Defoe's story reflects multiple concerns that exceed the issue of economic control, and her Crusoe does become a kind of visionary, instead of the colonizing figure from the novel.[4] She places her figure in England reviewing his past; her Crusoe feels, paradoxically, more of an exile at home than in the one he had to create from imagination, a familiar predicament from *Questions of Travel*. As castaway, Crusoe's survival demands ingenuity, but the utilitarian considerations of Defoe's character are not in Bishop's: survival, for her character, is a matter of the imagination. Bishop envisions the return of Crusoe to England as a loss of poetic power and her character mourns losing the immaterial "home," her Crusoe undergoing a kind of crucifixion:

> I'm old.
>
> I'm bored, too, drinking my real tea,
> surrounded by uninteresting lumber.
> The knife there on the shelf—
> it reeked of meaning, like a crucifix.
> It lived. How many years did I
> beg it, implore it, not to break?
> I knew each nick and scratch by heart,
> the bluish blade, the broken tip,
> the lines of wood-grain on the handle . . .
> Now it won't look at me at all.
> The living soul has dribbled away.

Defoe would never describe a knife with such intimate lovingness, but Bishop's poetics require that "the living soul," or the memory of one, make objects lively and interactive. Even as Crusoe's is an art similar to the Riverman's (who rejects the "stinking teas" of land) this poem must be about losing art, returning to "real tea."

Crusoe's survival here becomes also, of course, an emotional kind. As elegy, the poem is told in a kind of double recollection: at first the retrospective seems to account for everything, but the impetus behind memory—both permitting and blocking it—hinges upon the arrival of Friday, an event given seemingly only the perfunctory attention of a single, rather short stanza. In a quite compelling article on augury and autobiography in the poem, Renée R. Curry provides explicit and convincing correlatives between the poet's life and "Crusoe in England."[5] She decodes the narrative's subtext as "the muted story tells a tale of Lota de Macedo Soares and Elizabeth Bishop's lesbian relationship, de Macedo Soares's suicide, and Bishop's emotional life after the death" (74) and helpfully reminds us, "The 'now' of the Defoe Crusoe tale, presumably happens back in England after the twenty-eight years spent on the island. The 'now' of Bishop's life occurs in the mid 1970s, not yet a decade after de Macedo Soares's suicide" (88). Such a timeline should show how strenuous "now" can be, and show how imperative it is to read this poem as one of mourning, a mourning that sees no definite end (Bishop, Millier records [538], was working on an elegy for Lota in the last few years of her life); the details of overcoming the environment in a parable of economic victory are not so important for Bishop as the incoming of grief, the processes of a memory in recuperation.

Bishop nevertheless uses "Crusoe" to explore her relationship to tradition, as well as her experience of personal loss and exile, which in effect becomes the discovery of the absence of a fully usable literary past. But after all, which is which? to take a question from "Poem." Bishop's muted connection to tradition mirrors her silenced lesbian relationships, along with their eventual loss. The poem has its quiet debts, of course: aside from Defoe and the Wordsworth to be discussed later, Darwin and Jonathan Swift also figure significantly. Goldensohn reminds us that Darwin's "notes on the Galápagos, backed up by [Bishop's] own visit to the premises" (54) informs much of Bishop's description. And certainly *Gulliver's Travels* has parallels to Bishop's poem: both narrators' island displacements and the playing with misproportions in the landscapes. These debts notwithstanding, the poem recommends the "home-made," the reliance upon personal resource and experimental readiness. Her character revels with his "home-brew," a concoction derived through experience and not acquired by tested or recorded knowledge:

> There was one kind of berry, a dark red.
> I tried it, one by one, and hours apart.
> Sub-acid, and not bad, no ill effects;
> and so I made home-brew. I'd drink
> the awful, fizzy, stinging stuff
> that went straight to my head
> and play my home-made flute
> (I think it had the weirdest scale on earth)
> and, dizzy, whoop and dance among the goats.
> Home-made, home-made! But aren't we all?

Defoe models the self-made man, the new Adam, with no need of fore-fathers. What Bishop's Crusoe likewise prides himself on is the way the is-land has become his own project, especially now that he must remember it. From the very opening, with its "new volcano" reported in the paper, and the hearsay of an island's birth, the poem mocks the Adamic role of phallocen-tric naming:

> A new volcano has erupted,
> the papers say, and last week I was reading
> where some ship saw an island being born:
> at first a breath of steam, ten miles away;
> and then a black fleck—basalt, probably—
> rose in the mate's binoculars
> and caught on the horizon like a fly.
> They named it.

That naming follows such an uncertain gestation; does the island, after all, just exist in "the mate's binoculars"? Or is it a flyspeck just looking like a vol-cano? Naming never occurs as an original, inimitable event, but in a past act of personal possession, viable only as elegiac material; Bishop's Crusoe must confess:

> But my poor old island's still
> un-rediscovered, un-renameable.
> None of the books has ever got it right.

As Bishop even revokes Defoe's power to "get it right," she suggests the end-lessness of taxonomy since there is always "one kind of everything." The reg-istrar may never exhaust the possibilities of discovery: records erode, not the recording process or impulse to memorialize. When Crusoe describes his naming strategy for a volcano—"I'd christened [it] *Mont d'Espoir* or *Mount Despair* / (I'd time enough to play with names)"—Bishop refers to her own wordplay, her geography of erasure and reinscription, and to the doubleness of her own voice, woman impersonating a male narrator.

In spite of Crusoe's gender—indeed, because of it—the poem comments upon the position of the lesbian writer, castaway from the mainstream tradi-tion, thrown upon her own resources. By revealing lesbians as silenced and made unnameable by tradition, Bishop refutes the new Adam and inscribes the absence that books have not gotten right. (Later, of Friday's coming, she will reiterate, parenthetically, that "[a]ccounts of that have everything all wrong.") And it is the absences in her Crusoe's own accounting that direct us to a muted past, tragic because recorded in uneasy tranquillity. Crusoe explains that he cannot produce the monumental because of cultural deprivation or amnesia:

> Because I didn't know enough.
> Why didn't I know enough of something?
> Greek drama or astronomy? The books
> I'd read were full of blanks;
> the poems—well, I tried
> reciting to my iris-beds,
> "They flash upon that inward eye,
> which is the bliss . . ." The bliss of what?
> One of the first things that I did
> when I got back was look it up.

Such forgetting is, however, a way of remembering the homemade. Crusoe's looking up the blank leads us to do the same. Not only do we face "solitude"—the very state that made the line invisible and erased—but also what the poem at this moment confesses lies beneath blanks.

Bishop's choice of the recalled fragment is deliberate: the lines not only concern the consolatory aspect of memory, which makes absent objects present; they also appear in Wordsworth's "I Wandered Lonely as a Cloud," as an acknowledged appropriation of his wife's words, which William defended as the poem's "best lines."[6] A finely textured palimpsest appears: Mary Wordsworth speaks through William in a poem respoken by a Defoe character whose words Bishop dictates. Only in the arena of Wordsworth's poem can Mary find her outlet. Repossessed by Bishop, she finally speaks through the absences in Crusoe's literary memory, a kind of hidden mother's garden. Within these spaces resides the repressed feminine, homemade lyric—and Mary's solitude and mutation within the male community. Though Mary is not, assuredly, a prototypical lesbian, she alerts the attuned, remembering reader of literary suppression. Inasmuch as Bishop dismisses Defoe as unreliable and conveniently omits Crusoe's first name, the "I" of the poem is not Robin-son but can be interpreted as feminine maker of the self and world as home. Creativity, this poem confirms, does not emerge from comfortable acknowledgment of past traditions but from an exile's imaginings and re-creations.

What is absent or omitted—or rather embedded—deserves as much notice as what flashes on surfaces. "Solitude" is the missing word, and becomes, in opposition to our initial expectations, perhaps, not the state idealized by the poem: Crusoe functions creatively while alone, but suggests that Friday's appearance as other "saves" him, permits him to remember at all. Instead of the slave Defoe makes of him, Bishop makes him desired other, and subversively refers to homosexual passion by Crusoe's hoping Friday were a woman. The loss of the island, or the loss of "living soul," ultimately, does not devolve upon their rescue from this landscape. Friday's significance cannot be too much overplayed as Bishop always discards authority and tradition in favor of human relationship. The first introductory dashes regarding Friday forewarn his importance: "—Pretty to watch; he had a pretty body. / And then one day they came and took us off." How long Crusoe has been in England is not here indicated (so careful as her Crusoe is about most numberings), but he measures his time, his life, as the last jolting two lines indicate, by his loss of Friday: "—And Friday, my dear Friday, died of measles / seventeen years ago come March." We depend upon irretrievable others, upon absences, as they motivate us to reconstruct our pasts, even as memory cannot bear it.

As I have demonstrated, Bishop criticizes, through irony and polyphony, a silencing tradition. In the process, she discovers a dependency upon the personal forces in her own history only increasing over time, yet her poems postulate more and more a disunified ego, an acknowledgment, finally, of the power of the unconscious to disrupt surface cohesiveness. Her homemade, then, represents the remakings of a shipwrecked self. Because we do not have complete control over our identities or over the contents of our knowledge, we suffer slips and draw blanks, remembering this and forgetting that. We become like Bishop's Crusoe, in his self-questioning and partial amnesia; at one point, he recalls his self-pity with a confusion over the extent of his free-will:

> "Do I deserve this? I suppose I must.
> I wouldn't be here otherwise. Was there
> a moment when I actually chose this?
> I don't remember, but there could have been."
> What's wrong about self-pity, anyway?
> With my legs dangling down familiarly
> over a crater's edge, I told myself

> "Pity should begin at home." So the more
> pity I felt, the more I felt at home.

In misquoting a cliché, he makes himself more "at home," and at the same time, he recognizes the limitations upon his self-knowledge in lines resonant of these in "Questions of Travel": "*Continent, city, country, society: / the choice is never wide and never free.*" What constrains and liberates us in any place, whether traveling or at home, is those things we can tell or omit to tell ourselves, the homemade we construct from what we dimly misremember.

The processes of unknowing, then, become as important as those of knowing, since it is absences our consciousness slips upon and holds itself up against. Julia Kristeva's distinction between the semiotic as "a psychosomatic modality of the signifying process," a "rhythmic space, which has no thesis and position" (more noticeable and marked in poetic language), and the symbolic, the realm of law, of theses and positions, seems useful here.[7] Texts operate with a "genotext" that includes the semiotic and "can be detected in phonematic devices (such as the accumulation and repetition of phonemes or rhyme) and melodic devices (such as intonation and rhythm)," and a "phenotext," aligned to the symbolic:

> The phenotext is a structure (which can be generated, in generative grammar's sense); it obeys rules of communication and presupposes a subject of enunciation and an addressee. The genotext, on the other hand, is a process; it moves through zones that have relative and transitory borders and constitutes a path that is not restricted to the two poles of univocal information between two fully fledged subjects. If these two terms—genotext and phenotext—could be translated into a metalanguage that would convey the difference between them, one might say that the genotext is a matter of topology, whereas the phenotext is one of algebra. ("Revolution and Poetic Language," 120–21)

One could postulate this dual structuring in any signifying system—in any poem, in any sign, but it has more relevant application in appreciating the processes within texts committed to undermining thetic and symbolic knowledge or propositioning. While Bishop does not utilize "genotext" in ostentatious rebellion against "phenotext," she foregrounds "topology," the play within "relative and transitory borders," the only kind of home she can envision, and continues to posit the self as ephemeral and riveted by unconscious dislocatory processes, as when her Crusoe dreams of "things / like slitting a baby's throat, mistaking it / for a baby goat." Such mistakes appear to characterize Crusoe's waking life as well: "The goats were white, so were the gulls, / and both too tame, or else they thought / I was a goat, too, or a gull." "*Baa, baa, baa* and *shriek, shriek, shriek, / baa . . . shriek . . . baa . . .* I still can't shake / them from my ears." With the island's transitory borders of phonemic reiteration and even primal rhythms, of the "questioning shrieks, the equivocal replies," self remains in the process of remembering.

The dilemma of identity is linked in this poem with a painful solitude, interrupted by the arrival of a proto-lover. Apparently Friday cannot solve Crusoe's desire to reproduce: "I wanted to propagate my kind, / and so did he, I think, poor boy." Bishop shows her character caught in a paradox of kin. To achieve difference, one propagates: but the fallacy of this, she points out, is its result in "kind." The poem works through an anxiety over reproduction: first, by dyeing a baby goat "bright red" so "his mother wouldn't recognize him," and then, through a nightmare of murdering a child, mistaking it for a goat. Because of the singleness and uniqueness of everything on this island—"one kind of everything," and the limitless expanse of isolated islands—Crusoe craves the difference, the self, that emerges through relationship. But since connection can only be remembered by Crusoe's mourning, selfhood is shown as re-created, moment by moment, through memorial sacrifice.

Almost fanatically, Bishop highlights epistemological maneuvers—those fraught with unsettling self-questioning and uncertainty. "Poem," for instance, which contemplates the power of memory in the constitution of self and family, begins with characteristic noncommitment and approximation:

> About the size of an old-style dollar bill,
> American or Canadian,
> mostly the same whites, gray greens, and steel grays
> —this little painting (a sketch for a larger one?)
> has never earned any money in its life.

As the poet examines the painting—the details of the poem offered and then retrieved in part—precision becomes a gesture in the service of refutation, as when she cannot decide whether she sees bird or fly: "A specklike bird is flying to the left. / Or is it a flyspeck looking like a bird?" This indeterminacy, ultimately, reflects Bishop's mistakes of the self. Kristeva's semiotic is "inseparable from a theory of the subject that takes into account the Freudian

positing of the unconscious" ("Revolution and Poetic Language," 98);
Bishop's self, more the idea of a self, exposes the unconscious processes of
poetic activity. Her insistent return to early childhood (scenarios enacted primarily through repetition and metonymy) as a source for poetry becomes a
method, finally, for transgressing symbolic signification through the signifiers of loss and homing desire. But while her earlier investigations of the personal demand repetition in the experience of loss, her poems in *Geography
III* question the ability to remember, and become commentaries upon the
interpretive processes of memory, and the attempts to construct a self.

II

One's "home" is often not the home of one's birth, but as we have learned
from Bishop's "Crusoe" and her own restless navigations, a place created in
exile. Bishop's return to questions of her childhood, after her emigration
from Brazil, reflects a looping or circular movement: no place—England or
another island, Brazil or Nova Scotia—possesses the resilience or permanence of originary or final home. (Bishop's sense of home, as by now must
be evident, is early on a problematic one; when describing her childhood to
Elizabeth Spires she talks about her frequent displacement among family
members, saying movingly that she "was always sort of a guest, and I think
I've always felt like that.")[8] Yet Bishop's stay in Brazil gives her the perspective
of an unrescued Crusoe—not a house guest—trying to remember a lost self
and home. Even if, like her narrator in the early "The Prodigal," "it took
him a long time / finally to make his mind up to go home" (*CP*, 71), she must
attempt it, those "shuddering insights, beyond his control, / touching him."
The poems of *Elsewhere*, for the most part, are about prodigal, homecoming, insights—those inevitable, volcanic returns of the repressed.

Like the story, "In the Village," which precedes it in *Questions of Travel*,
"Manners," a retrospective poem that looks forward to the memory poems to
come in *Geography III*, is elegiac. And like *The Diary of Helena Morley*, it is
nostalgic for a pre-industrial historical period when decorum governed interaction with "[m]an or beast." Her grandfather's injunction, "'Be sure to remember to always / speak to everyone you meet,'" belongs, by the dating of
the poem addressed to a child of 1918, to the past; and "manners," in a period of anonymity and automobiles, is like the displaced wagon on its last leg:

> When automobiles went by,
> the dust hid the people's faces,
> but we shouted "Good day! Good day!
> Fine day!" at the top of our voices.

Longing for such an earlier period appears also in "Memories of Uncle Neddy" where she records the alteration in Neddy's tinsmith business: "Meanwhile, the shop was changing. First, there were many more things for sale and less and less work seemed to be done at the old black-and-silver glinting workbench. There were many household effects that came ready-made: can openers, meat grinders, mixing spoons, gray-mottled enamel 'sets' of saucepans" (*CPr*, 247–48). As the homemade diminishes, so does a connection with personal history; objects crafted by individuals, no matter how slipshod or homely, provoke an intimate connection between viewer and thing, and we make ourselves through our imaginative relationship with these objects.

"Manners" (*CP*, 121–22), as the first poem in "Elsewhere," escorts us delicately into the more painful memory poems and personal histories, in particular "Sestina" and "First Death in Nova Scotia," both written earlier than most of the Brazil poems. The poems of "Elsewhere," while perhaps less cohesive than those of the first section, "Brazil," are precursory to the theme of loss as memory in *Geography III*. As the title "Elsewhere" suggests, the poems revolve around the continual displacement Bishop experiences as memory crosses into our understanding of places, becoming much more imagined places. Fairy-tale diction and childlike simplicity characterize these poems and delude the reader into the illusion of "pure" confession; encoded, however, in them are the strategies always already remaking memory. An unnamed pain, more present and real because of its absence, moves through these ultimately self-reflexive poems. History becomes glaringly lightweight, floating above us like those dangerous fire balloons in "The Armadillo."

Written originally in 1951 for Ezra Pound after her 1949–50 post with the Library of Congress, "Visits to St. Elizabeths" (*CP*, 133–35) combines many Bishopian devices—anaphora, repetition with transformation through metonymy, the hypnosis of simple monosyllabic diction—to touch indirectly upon early experience, what is shudderingly, closest to home. Modeled on the nursery rhyme, the poem has the compulsive form of "This was the House that Jack Built." The algebra of each stanza—all beginning with "This"—adds one line with a different word ending; they gather force, alter yet retain previous morphemes, without the sense that we will come to any sheltering end in this expanding topography. More reasonably, stanzas present different perspectives, as if we were watching a turning prism; Pound is "tragic," "talkative," "honored," "old, brave," "cranky," "cruel," "busy," "tedious," "the poet, the man," "wretched," depending upon the position of the describer; other words change in the poem, but the stanzas pivot upon these labile epithets.

Embedded in the visits to St. Elizabeths is also Bishop's own history. Her name significantly inscribed in the title compels identification, and the poem and the visits necessitate a connection between her own relationship with her mother's institutionalization, and the absence and possible guilt that it represents (Bishop never visited her mother before her dying). All of the twelve stanzas become like positions on an unreadable clock, and time, skewed and arbitrary, is central to this piece, from the first four stanzas:

> This is the house of Bedlam.
>
> This is the man
> that lies in the house of Bedlam.
>
> This is the time
> of the tragic man
> that lies in the house of Bedlam.
>
> This is the wristwatch
> telling the time
> of the talkative man
> that lies in the house of Bedlam.

This wristwatch falls through the poem, like her mother's watch in "One Art," summoning us into a present that contains a tortured history, as if we are meant to stop, not time, but *before* it, face to face with the suffering of this man in *this* particular moment. Bishop modifies the tense of the nursery rhyme from "This was" to "This is," increasing the immediacy of her visits. She wants also to produce the sense of synchrony within chaos—this *is* Bedlam; yet even as we are in the present, we participate in the flux of a psyche trying to come to grips with itself. Even as Bishop must see herself in the story of "Visits," she also writes this poem with some distance from Pound and the tradition of high modernism he so emphatically represents. In endorsing the personal so fervently, her antimonumental humble poetics is provocatively not of the "Pound era."

"Brazil" marks a reexploration of form as A *Cold Spring* had marked a hiatus in form and exploration of a freer verse. In "Elsewhere," Bishop discovers how form can reinforce psychological impulses, even act them out, not transparently record them; as a kind of Kristevan genotext, her formal tactics point to the "relative and transitory borders" they cannot finally contain. The forms of particular interest to her are the sestina and the villanelle—at least, these become the most vivid enactments of her poetic measures; and the nursery-rhyme structure has vestigial resemblance to these other forms in its corresponding reliance on ritual repetition. She likes to discover what she can manage within limitation, and because these poems are usually so metrically regular, they alert us to the "timing" and topographical placement of each word. "Visits," based on accretion and substitution, experiments with process and flux as integral to formal constraints. Because we find ourselves in an unpredictable world, we cherish regularity, may even fetishize it. But as the unknown is as compelling as the known, she invites it more vigorously into view as contrasting undertow to compulsive iteration of the key word "house," a figure so resonant for Bishop. The eighth through tenth stanzas of "Visits," which illustrates her methodical *and* explosive operations, incant:

> This is a Jew in a newspaper hat
> that dances weeping down the ward
> over the creaking sea of board
> beyond the sailor
> winding his watch
> that tells the time
> of the cruel man
> that lies in the house of Bedlam.
>
> This is a world of books gone flat.
> This is a Jew in a newspaper hat
> that dances weeping down the ward
> over the creaking sea of board
> of the batty sailor
> that winds his watch
> that tells the time
> of the busy man
> that lies in the house of Bedlam.
>
> This is a boy that pats the floor
> to see if the world is there, is flat,

for the widowed Jew in the newspaper hat
that dances weeping down the ward
waltzing the length of a weaving board
by the silent sailor
that hears his watch
that ticks the time
of the tedious man
that lies in the house of Bedlam.

The stanzas interlock, the "weaving board" she must walk and balance within, while a potent uneasiness keeps resurfacing.

This is Bishop's postwar poem, without the absolute hopelessness and despair of other such poems. She wants "to tell the time" of this outsider. The first line of the last stanza indicates as much: "This is the soldier home from the war." Not eulogy, the poem appreciates mental struggle and an inevitable fragmentation of identity. Earlier, the ninth stanza began: "This is a world of books gone flat." The flatness of anomie has taken over the imagination. We find ourselves in an age of ontological uncertainty; the boy, anticipating the child Bishop of "In the Waiting Room," tests the environment trying to find solidity: "These are the years and the walls and the door / that shut on a boy that pats the floor / to see if the world is there and flat." Finally, the boy "pats the floor / to see if the world is round or flat." We have Bishop's characteristic splintering of choice. Discovery is exploration and choice of perspective. We come back to Columbus's moment rejoined upon a Crusoe.

To "tell the time" of St. Elizabeths is to tell the passing time of Pound and modernity; moreover, it is to tell her own time of historical investigation, her own attempt to employ personal memory. History, for Bishop, becomes the reliving and inevitable refiguring of experience possible in art. Both "Sestina" and "First Death in Nova Scotia" present in poems what Bishop had been struggling with in her prose, an examination of early pain and loss; these poems, in their return to childhood as the source of current experience, presage *Geography III*; and while these two pieces are less concerned with the memory's imaginative *reshaping* of experience than is her later work, they establish the process of *recovering* (both looking at anew and covering over) the past with Bishop's characteristic childlike tone and acute perceptivity.

The title shift of "Sestina," originally "Early Sorrow," highlights her turn to form not only as an aesthetic device but as a method of reliving and covering over painful experiences (a motivating impulse, as shown in Chapter 1,

of the villanelle "One Art"). The sestina allows for ritual repetition, a going
back over, to recuperate and modify, to cast out and bring back. By making
the present past, in one way, Bishop abolishes the past, and in another, perhaps more important, she makes the past so inextricably a part of the present
that she reveals the falseness of separating tenses: the past haunts the present,
and if we make the past the present we can potentially live within it.

A nursery rhyme is a game, playing with substitution to hypnotize the lis-
tener; just as in a fairy tale, the grim or sinister cloaks itself in the homely and
innocuous; such a rhyme pretends naiveté. As with Freud's "fort-da," Bishop
knows that games are seriously therapeutic; anecdotally but significantly, she
writes Lowell of a story she likes of a child in third grade, faced with a first
death, who says: "I told my little brother that when you die you cannot
breathe and he did not say a word. He just kept on playing."[9] (Especially considering Bishop's lifelong struggle with asthma, such a story seems quite self-
reflexive.) Playing, in such circumstances, must be a dramatic response, not
simply unfeeling avoidance. "Visits" denies uncomfortable painfulness even
as it reveals, and revels, in it. "Sestina" (*CP*, 123–24) functions similarly, ad-
dressing a more particularly personal history. Bishop generates a state of
wonder and play. In her world, objects possess life, and the boundaries between ourselves and the things around us diminish and blur: "The iron kettle
sings on the stove," just as "The grandmother sings to the marvellous stove"
in the final three-line stanza. The almanac is "clever": it "hovers half open
above the child," and even the phrase "the house / feels chilly" marks
Bishop's world as full of feeling. A sorrow *is* being hidden and repressed, but
informs every aspect of the child's environment. We do not need to know the
specific "early sorrow" that lies within this poem, but we can assume from
the grandmother's sadness that Bishop's poem returns to the early events of
loss, of the separation enforced by her mother's insanity and subsequent removal to an institution.

> September rain falls on the house.
> In the failing light, the old grandmother
> sits in the kitchen with the child
> beside the Little Marvel Stove,
> reading the jokes from the almanac,
> laughing and talking to hide her tears.

Paul Fussell, in his handbook on poetic form, says that the sestina has "dubious expressiveness in English," and that "regardless of the way it is tailored,

[it] would seem to be [a form] that gives more structural pleasure to the con-
triver than to the apprehender." But Bishop endows the form with high
expressivity: its ritualism includes the reader in a process of compulsive
ongoing sense-making of personal history, the necessity to "write it!" at all
costs.[10] Time, as in "Visits," is central to the poem; we begin in the fall, in
September rain, and with the almanac's insistence, end with the prospect of
spring. The almanac commands, *"Time to plant tears."* We are in the time
of mourning that must occur belatedly, as it does for Bishop in her writing of
the poem. The sestina form then becomes subject of the poem, a formula for
writing and revising the self and its losses through repetition.

The child has a "magical" understanding of the world which tries to make
sense of sorrow and separation:

> She thinks that her equinoctial tears
> and the rain that beats on the roof of the house
> were both foretold by the almanac,
> but only known to a grandmother.

This accords with the imaginative belief of a supernatural conception of the
world, such as that of Manuelzinho or the riverman of her Brazil poems. An
immanence resides within each aspect of the environment, and a communication hangs between them; the present foretells the past. The grandmother,
bearer of knowledge, in an effort to provide a place of protection from loss,
attempts to bring the child into the "now," but the child's acuity reads, inscribed in her surroundings, her mother's madness.

> The iron kettle sings on the stove.
> She cuts some bread and says to the child,
>
> *It's time for tea now;* but the child
> is watching the teakettle's small hard tears
> dance like mad on the hot black stove,
> the way the rain must dance on the house.

But the child does not just react to the world: she helps create it. Apprehending the fatalism of the stove and the almanac, she also reconstitutes her
loss through making a home, complete with absent father:

> *It was to be,* says the Marvel Stove.
> *I know what I know,* says the almanac.

> With crayons the child draws a rigid house
> and a winding pathway. Then the child
> puts in a man with buttons like tears
> and shows it proudly to the grandmother.

The "rigid house" resembles the poem's proud form, yet testifies to the flexibility and adaptability of the imagination that can create new possibilities with limited materials.

In a poem so rigorously indebted to detailing familiar household items such as stove, kettle, bread, while at the same time, pointing to the fearful and unfamiliar through the undercurrent of hidden emotion, Bishop satisfies Freud's requirements for his definition of the uncanny, a term quite useful in describing her ventures with the homemade.[11] As Freud explains it, the uncanny "is that class of the terrifying which leads back to something long known to us, once very familiar" (124), a conclusion substantiated by etymology: "heimlich," defined as familiar, intimate, belonging to the house, homely, also contains within it the opposite, "unheimlich," through its secondary meaning of "concealed, kept from sight, so that others do not get to know about it" (128). He sums it up: "Thus *heimlich* is a word the meaning of which develops towards an ambivalence, until it finally coincides with its opposite" (131). Helen Vendler, with such terms in mind, argues that the familiar becomes strange for Bishop since home, in her economy, must always engender something of the uncanny, as an intimately loved object that repeatedly seems to recede from her.[12] Those who are "oriented in [their] environment" are less apt, in Freud's assessment, to feel the uncanny (124): and as we have seen, Bishop often courts disorientation as poetic method. Vendler has succinctly put it, "As in the midst of life we are in death, so, in Bishop's poetry, in the midst of the familiar, and most especially there, we feel the familiar as the unknowable."

Through the interaction in "Sestina" of stove, almanac, and drawing—all homey objects—the child "secretly" mourns, following the "careful" and rigid requirements of a superstitious relationship with the world:

> But secretly, while the grandmother
> busies herself about the stove,
> the little moons fall down like tears
> from between the pages of the almanac
> into the flower bed the child
> has carefully placed in the front of the house.

Time to plant tears, says the almanac.
The grandmother sings to the marvellous stove
and the child draws another inscrutable house.

The envoi does not really conclude the poem. It manages to include all the key line ending words, all simple, strictly denotative (as far as this is possible) words, for tremendous effect as the form and the subject of the poem rest only upon the prospects of metamorphosis. Through the previous fluid stanzas, rain turns tears turns tea turns buttons turns moons turns seeds and then again turns tears. Within limitation and facing the apparent finality of loss, the imagination empowers us with the potential for remaking. Tears of mourning irrigate a creative impulse—the child's recasting of a house—that tentatively helps shelter sorrow and painful memory. The poem does not resolve itself or find closure; in a continuing process of coming to terms with our history, "the child draws another inscrutable house." Bishop does not want to drain the mystery of human existence out of creative activity, so it makes sense that she utilizes forms or formulas such as the sestina or a nursery rhyme, which do not rest upon ultimately predictable effects. Like the "inscrutable houses" the child draws, they comfort the mourner / writer / reader because she can predict what comes next linguistically, but the evocation remains like a charm or spell; the stanzas may be rooms, but not closed or sealed ones, as they guard, dimly, a familiar secret of loss.

The title "First Death in Nova Scotia" (*CP*, 125–26) suggests that she will retell the "first death" ever of that province and so looks forward to the naive narrator of "Sestina." With five ten-line mostly unrhymed stanzas laced with repetition, the poem holds us and "something" back. The pre-positioning admission of the first stanza, so straightforward and prosaic, appears only to numbly record setting:

> In the cold, cold parlor
> my mother laid out Arthur
> beneath the chromographs:
> Edward, Prince of Wales,
> with Princess Alexandra,
> and King George with Queen Mary.
> Below them on the table
> stood a stuffed loon
> shot and stuffed by Uncle
> Arthur, Arthur's father.

Not much later (1962), Bishop would begin her story "Uncle Artie," worked up into "Memories of Uncle Neddy" in 1977. This poem, focusing upon the death of her cousin Arthur, allows her to treat a subject of charged significance in the child's life since her father had already died and her mother was suffering breakdowns.

Bishop's aesthetic often destroys the stasis of pictorial representation, as Chapter 2 demonstrated. The chromographs allow Bishop to imagine the dead Arthur entering a landscape of luxury and wealth with the loon, as well, becoming a central object, animated like the almanac and stove in "Sestina"; dead and "stuffed," this loon, with its slang connection with the mad, exerts a lively impression upon the child. But unlike the almanac and stove, it won't speak:

> He kept his own counsel
> on his white, frozen lake,
> the marble-topped table.
> His breast was deep and white,
> cold and caressable;
> his eyes were red glass,
> much to be desired.

The loon oddly turns into desirable artifact, an uncanny image of life-in-death, mute and "caressable." This sense of indeterminate borders and images predominates in a story Bishop wrote earlier, "Gwendolyn" (1953, discussed briefly in Chapter 1) which also deals with her confrontation of death. Gwendolyn, a childhood friend who dies, is described through the course of the story as a doll, staring and mute, whose attractiveness makes her seem edible: "solid candy if you bit her, and her pure-tinted complexion would taste exactly like the icing-sugar Easter eggs or birthday-candle holders, held to be inedible" (CPr, 216). The inedible is edible, the strange the familiar: isn't that partly what Bishop convertibly proposes? In "First Death," she writes:

> Arthur's coffin was
> a little frosted cake,
> and the red-eyed loon eyed it
> from his white, frozen lake.

Arthur is made into an artifact, just as the loon has been, and Gwendolyn prematurely: "Arthur was very small. / He was all white, like a doll / that

hadn't been painted yet." She leaves him between states of nature and artifice, before he has been "stuffed"; to forever suspend her cousin between the
animate and the inanimate is the only way she can visualize his death, or be
true to its strange, unfamiliar appearance.

Similarly in "Gwendolyn," Bishop cannot face the reality of her friend's
death:

> The two men in black appeared again, carrying Gwendolyn's
> small white coffin between them. Then—this was the impossibil-
> ity—they put it down just outside the church door, one end on the
> grass and the other lifted up a little, to lean at a slight angle against
> the wall. Then they disappeared inside again. For a minute, I stared
> straight through my lace curtain at Gwendolyn's coffin, with Gwen-
> dolyn shut invisibly inside it forever, there, completely alone on the
> grass by the church door.
>
> Then I ran howling to the back door, out among the startled white
> hens, with my grandmother, still weeping, after me. (224)

The compression of the child's existence into a small coffin makes death un-
bearable. But at the end of the story, taking her aunt's doll "well wrapped in
soft pink tissue paper," she repeats a funeral ceremony with the doll newly
christened Gwendolyn. She and another friend undress the doll and make a
wreath for her and then "laid her out in the garden path and outlined her
body with Johnny-jump-ups and babies'-breath and put a pink cosmos in one
limp hand" (226). Such a ceremony breaks down distinctions between life
and death, and makes the fact of dying more tolerable. Yet even as she places
a lily of the valley in Arthur's hand, she is not sure even her imagination can
revitalize him or send him away, even as Arthurial legend makes the child a
good subject for court:

> The gracious royal couples
> were warm in red and ermine;
> their feet were well wrapped up
> in the ladies' ermine trains.
> They invited Arthur to be
> the smallest page at court.
> But how could Arthur go,
> clutching his tiny lily,

> with his eyes shut up so tight
> and the roads deep in snow?

As the child narrator gives life to the chromographs—animates them, places temporality into their spatial fixedness, she realizes the limitations of the mannerly fairy tale she creates: it cannot deny death, the sealed eyes; the poem cannot finish in optimistic faith but in a question that both reanimates Arthur, as one called to enter another dimension, and wants not to let him go, taking to roads that leave his current home. The dead still participate in our imagination of them, the only way we can come to terms with their departure; and our poems become ceremonies to mourn departure through repetition. Memory displaced in the present, serves Bishop in the desire for the homemade, constituted by her re-created losses.

III

Bishop had been obsessed for years by the influence of her Uncle Arthur in her remaking the homemade. She opens a letter to Aunt Grace in 1957, "I'd love to have the portrait of my mother—I've wanted it, as you know, for years." Her aunt does send her a portrait of her mother, but along with it, one of her uncle Neddy—which winds up as the focus of the story published as "Memories of Uncle Artie" (1977). She questions: "Why on earth did Aunt Hat, send me the portrait of her late husband? My mother's might have been expected, but Uncle Neddy's came as a complete surprise; and now I can't stop thinking about him" (*CPr*, 229). From across the equator, the paintings arrive and exist in the present—in her memory trying to reconstruct the world they represent. Bishop's uncle is the village drunk, always refigured as a bit devilish and sinister, representing for the child Bishop a life of recklessness, but also, it seems, imaginative potential. Instead of to her mother's garden, Bishop returns to her uncle's tinsmith shop (the images associated with her uncle recur in the depiction of the blacksmith Nate of "In the Village"). She describes the site with loving detail and recognition for the homemade:

> From the entrance, with double doors, the shop starts out fairly bright; a large section is devoted to "store" galvanized pails and enameled pots and pans, two or three or more black kitchen ranges with nickel trimmings, farming implements, and fishing rods—the last be-

cause fishing was Uncle Neddy's passion. But the farther in one goes, the darker and more gloomy it becomes: the floor is covered with acrid-smelling, glinting, black dust and the workbench stretching across the far end is black, with glints of silver. Night descends as one walks back, then daylight grows as one reaches the dirty windows above the workbench. This night sky of Uncle Neddy's is hung with the things he makes himself: milk pails, their bottoms shining like moons; flashing tin mugs in different sizes; watering pots like comets, in among big dull lengths of stove pipe with wrinkled blue joints like elephants' legs dangling overhead. (236)

That Neddy's shop holds "the things he makes himself," that he "actually made" (237) to be used at home fascinates Bishop along with the fact that in the shop these things "were all out of place" (237): "Who would expect to see comfortable-looking kitchen stoves, with names like 'Magee Ideal' and 'Magic Home' on their oven doors, standing leaning sidewise, in a shop?"

Bishop's compulsion to reexamine this uncle's life rests upon his power within her imagination as artificer and creator; she says, "What I liked best was to watch Uncle Neddy heat the end of a rod to the melting point and dribble it quickly to join a wide ribbon of tin and make a mug." It is this join-ing, metaphoric of human connection over time that lets her think of herself as crafter: "Occasionally, Uncle Neddy would let me help him hold a stick of solder and dribble it around the bottom of a pail. This was thrilling, but oh, to be able to write one's name with it, in silver letters!" (238). Early on, then, she seeks to inscribe her name, to find her identity through the soldering and forging associated with this "black-sheep" uncle.

Aside from his foregrounded creativity, Neddy's dipsomania is mentioned throughout her memoir as a repressed but finally quite visible reality. She confesses:

All I knew of alcohol at that time was the homemade wines the ladies sometimes served each other, or the hot toddy my grandfather some-times made himself on freezing winter nights. But finally phrases like "not himself," "taken too much," "three seas over," sank into my con-sciousness and I looked at my poor uncle with new eyes, expectantly. There was one occasion when he had to be taken away from the home funeral of Mrs. Captain McDonald, an old woman everyone was very fond of. What at first passed for Uncle Neddy's natural if de-monstrative grief had got "out of hand." My grandmother moaned about this; in fact, she moaned so loudly in her bedroom across the hall from mine that I could hear almost every word. (247)

Is she looking at herself with new eyes, at her own recurrent problem with alcoholism? The grief that gets out of hand, the moaning—usually repressed—that can finally be heard, these are the elements picked out by memory. In "The Prodigal" (71), Neddy seems to have already appeared, as combination of drinker, visionary, exile:

> But sometimes mornings after drinking bouts
> (he hid the pints behind a two-by-four),
> the sunrise glazed the barnyard mud with red;
> the burning puddles seemed to reassure.
> And then he thought he almost might endure
> his exile yet another year or more.

An even more explicit identification with her uncle and his "disgrace"—and "the burning puddles"—comes through her never-published confessional poem, "A Drunkard"[13] (discussed in fascinating detail by Goldensohn in connection with Bishop's love poems), where Bishop tries to return to an originary cause of her own drinking. Trying to reconstruct an origin or beginning, experience immediately becomes metaphor. She tells the story of her experience of a Salem fire (reported as happening 26 June 1914) when her mother ignores her needs and demands (a moment comparable to the birth of desire, in Lacanian terms):

> I was terribly thirsty but mama didn't hear
> me calling her.   Out on the lawn
> she and some neighbors were giving coffee
> or food or something to the people landing in boats—
> I glimpsed her once in a while I caught a glimpse of her
> and called and called—no one paid any attention—

Her drinking, however, the story goes, has its genesis in a "reprimand," a submerged sexual curiosity within the chaos and disarray of the fire:

> I picked up a woman's long black cotton
> stocking. Curiosity. My mother said sharply
> *Put that down!* I remember clearly, clearly—

> But since that day, that reprimand
> that night that day that reprimand—
> I have suffered from abnormal thirst—
> I swear it's true—and by the age
> of twenty or twenty-one I had begun
> to drink, & drink—I can't get enough
> and, as you must have noticed,
> I'm half-drunk now . . .
>
> And all I'm telling you may be a lie . . .

The fire narrated in "The Drunkard" seems to have found a place within "In the Village," which foregrounds the lapses within memory through its use of the present tense to show the very process of remembering experience, in an episode occurring just before her mother's return to the sanatorium. The reprimand is absent, and instead, the fire temporarily assuages the fear of an eruption of the mother's scream, even seems to reassure:

> Wait. Wait. No one is going to scream.
> Slowly, slowly it gets daylight. A different red reddens the wall-paper. Now the house is silent. I get up and dress by myself and go downstairs. My grandfather is in the kitchen alone, drinking his tea. He has made the oatmeal himself, too. He gives me some and tells me about the fire very cheerfully. (270–71)

Still "listening for sounds from upstairs," the child and her grandfather have a kind of cheerful intimacy.

As noted in Chapter 1, Bishop's earlier drafts to "One Art" contain the telling phrases "all that I write is false. I'm writing lies now"; they indicate—as does her admission in the "clearly, clearly" recalled event of "The Drunkard" that "all I'm telling you may be a lie"—that truth and falsehood, especially when it comes to autobiography, may not be easily distinguished; to remember is always to create. Memory and fiction, as Bishop's later poems reveal, are not easily disentangled. And the creation of the self depends upon the uncertain and seemingly arbitrary selectivity of memory. Yet as memory confirms loss, it also permits the homemade, the shaping of a provisioning but adaptable imagination.

Another figure, like Uncle Neddy, of evident great importance to Bishop's mythology of the personal and homemade is her maternal grandmother, whose rocking chair Bishop represents as a "memory machine" (*CPr*, 243). The grandmother appears in the Neddy story as purveyor of wisdom and keeper of family history, telling her husband, "*You'd* never remember anything. But *I* won't forget. *I* won't forget." Because she becomes the source of recuperative comfort and the person members in the family turn to in confidence, the grandmother must carry a heavy burden, and as in her dealings with the drunken Artie, she responds with disguised pain. When asked by the child Bishop what she means by her "mysterious remark" repeated like a "chorus in [their] lives: "Nobody knows . . . *nobody knows* . . . !" the grandmother's reaction becomes both emotional expression and concealment: "She laughed as easily as she cried, and one very often turned into the other (a trait her children and grandchildren inherited)" (242), the heightened awareness of the awful and the cheerful. The past, in all its truths and forewarnings, is "only known to a grandmother," or so feels the child of "Sestina."

"Memories of Uncle Neddy" reflects, then, not only upon the character of her uncle and her relation to him, but also upon the nature of memory itself. When the paintings of her mother and uncle as children arrive, Bishop must question their reality, or the "proportion" between realism and artifice, not even sure if the images derived from other images or if an actual posing took place. She thinks back through the paintings, to make a connection with her own history, knowing her reconstruction will be dubious and uncertain:

> The paintings are unsigned and undated, probably the work of an itinerant portrait painter. Perhaps he worked from tintypes, because in the family album the little girl's dress appears again. Or did she have only the one dress, for dress-up? . . . (In the tintype the French wax doll appears, too, seated on her lap, big and stiff, her feet sticking out in small white boots beneath her petticoats, showing fat legs in striped stockings. She stares composedly at the camera under a raffish blond wig, in need of combing. The tintype man has tinted the cheeks of both the doll and my mother a clear pink. . . .)
>
> Or perhaps the painter did the faces—clearer and brighter than the rest of the picture, and in Uncle Neddy's case slightly out of proportion, surely—from "life," the clothes from tintypes, and the rest from his imagination. He may have arrived in the village with his canvases already filled in, the unrecognizable carpets, the round table and improbable chair, ready and waiting to be stood on and leaned on. (233–34)

Bishop's speculation upon the tintype man indicates the kind of imaginative memory necessary in re-creating the past, and her characteristic supply of intricate detail does not clarify or remove the inscrutable artifice of the pictures. Bishop's story is, in some sense, about removal, the taking out of context that occurs when we leave our "original" home. Often, Bishop writes in her letters to her Aunt Grace, to whom she dedicates "The Moose," of her homesickness: her decision to write "autobiography," to write the geography of the self, responds to such a feeling. The transplantation of her uncle's likeness to Rio appears to Bishop a wrenching movement, for her uncle never traveled while alive; in memory and in the picture—bombarded by the dew and molds of "extravagant rain"—he will still change. The story concludes:

> Uncle Neddy will continue to exchange his direct, bright-hazel, child's looks, now, with those of strangers—dark-eyed Latins he never knew, who never would have understood him, whom he would have thought of, if he had ever thought of them at all, as "foreigners." How late, Uncle Neddy, how late to have started on your travels! (250)

Actual travels, however, would never live up to those remembered by art, as the opening declaration of the earlier "Over 2,000 Illustrations" testifies, in medias res, in stymied retrospection: "Thus should have been our travels: / serious, engravable." Art does not preserve, but engraves and tints with its mnemonic function, unpredictable, unreliable, but necessarily in the service of forging the homemade.

Knowing that self—constructed through imagining memory—cannot be strictly defined except as enigmatical, "Sandpiper" (CP, 131), a kind of self-portrait, describes the bird as "finical, awkward, / in a state of controlled panic, a student of Blake." Bishop confesses to a myopia that impels her to close scrutiny, and to her loss of perspective within a "controlled panic," her obsessive seeking without object:

> The world is a mist. And then the world is
> minute and vast and clear. The tide
> is higher or lower. He couldn't tell you which.
> His beak is focussed; he is preoccupied,
>
> looking for something, something, something.
> Poor bird, he is obsessed!

The absolute indeterminacy and doubleness of the world of this "poor bird" color both Bishop's obsessive desire to return to a personal past in her later work, and her very technique, fixing upon details, yet finding no ultimate referent: the "something, something, something" must, I think, allude to the impossible entity of home both as poetic, psychological and literal figure.

Throughout, Bishop's writing has been self-reflexive, positing a poetics founded on loss and the homemade, but as she becomes apparently more autobiographic, her poetics also includes an interrogation of selfhood. Because she knows places can only be imagined, the same becomes true for our identities. We fashion our permeable selves through remembering them, finding them tentative shelter. The "empty wasps' nest" that she rescues as homey souvenir in "Santarém" becomes a correlative for the kind of fragile solidity Bishop prizes in artifacts (we've already encountered this wasp nest in Jerónimo's decorations of a much earlier poem), but she is aware that perhaps only her idiosyncratic subjectivity makes it such:

> In the blue pharmacy the pharmacist
> had hung an empty wasps' nest from a shelf:
> small, exquisite, clean matte white,
> and hard as stucco. I admired it
> so much he gave it to me.

"The blue pharmacy" startles with its imagistic surrealism; the nest seems more in place than medicine would in such a setting. As conclusion, Bishop narrates, *as if returning* to reality, "back on board" to her own unstaying:

> Then—my ship's whistle blew. I couldn't stay.
> Back on board, a fellow-passenger, Mr. Swan,
> Dutch, the retiring head of Philips Electric,
> really a very nice old man,
> who wanted to see the Amazon before he died,
> asked, "What's that ugly thing?"

Lacking Bishop's imperative sense of mortality, Swan, "the retiring head," out of his pond, will probably be unable to "see" the Amazon, synecdochic with the overlooked wasps' nest.

The nest is the signature of a constructed home, the remaining trace of a family of wasps—and as such resonates with the timeliness and beauty of its history, possessing the symbolic power of the provisional and changeable home the artist, or Bishop's version of one, must construct from the interior. Bachelard refers to the paradoxical quality of the nest which he says "is a precarious thing" which, however, "sets us to *daydreaming of security*" (102). Bishop, in these terms, unmasks the daydream of security, touched by those fond processes of the self trying to locate comforting spaces for psychic habitation.

IV

The portrait does not reply,
it stares; in my dusty eyes
it contemplates itself.
The living and dead relations

multiply in the glass.
I don't distinguish those
that went away from those
that stay. I only perceive
the strange idea of family

travelling through the flesh.

(Carlos Drummond de Andrade, from Bishop's
translation of "Family Portrait," in *CP*, 260–61)

I begin by quoting from this translation because its notion of family portraiture as endlessly self-reflexive, multiple, interpretive and "strange" is descriptive of Bishop's geography of the family—how dubious and necessary all our connections with others must be as we continue to fabricate and place a self.

By beginning *Geography III* with intermediary and inconsecutive "Lesson VI" and "Lesson X" from an 1884 geography primer, Bishop remembers by forgetting adult perspective and knowledge, and her art continues to be indebted to poetry as patchwork or assemblage, a topography implying "relative or transitory boundaries," in Kristevan terms. The questions of the lessons are simple and childlike but represent a challenge to geography, or at least, represent it for what it is: *a writing of the earth*. "Lesson IV" provides the

question and answer duo: *"What is the shape of the Earth?* / Round, like a
ball." Because our understanding of the earth is always a matter of metaphoric description, and as it is for her like the boy in her St. Elizabeths, a
checking to see if it is flat, the next lesson opens with the question, *"What is
a Map?"* Maps should orient us, but as "The Map" early on disclosed, mapping is an artistic, subjective affair: we lose all direction and grounding on its
flat surface. Her lesson "piece," appropriately then, floods us with unanswerable questions:

> *In what direction is the Volcano? The*
> *Cape? The Bay? The Lake? The Strait?*
> *The Mountains? The Isthmus?*
> *What is in the East? In the West? In the*
> *South? In the North? In the Northwest?*
> *In the Southeast? In the Northeast?*
> *In the Southwest?*

Sense of place is relative to perspective: as Crusoes, we must design our own
maps. While we attempt to define the self in terms of remembered place,
Bishop reminds us that our constructions are artificial. *Geography III* gives
us a new primer where each direction or island must be renamed, yet resists nameability.

Throughout, she resorts pointedly to preposition, showing the placement
of a self yet the continual slippage of such design. "In the Waiting Room"
(*CP*, 159–61) another autobiographic and self-consciously fabricated poem,
re-places Bishop as child in a very specific time and space to expose the illusory nature of all such categories (and as Lee Edelman points out in his discussion of the poem, the issue of the *National Geographic* Bishop cites does
not accurately reference the African images she supposedly sees in the 1918
edition of the magazine). By remembering a pivotal moment in her self-
consciousness, she also dismembers it: "being" is put in crisis. Language, the
poet shows us, tries to establish perspective and position, both always in the
process of fraying and deterioration. The poem presents a powerful confrontation of identity with mortality, and dismantles the familiar boundaries we
erect between the two.

The title and the first lines of the poem orient us through the most prosy
and simplest of phrasings; with such apparent clarity before us, we are unpre-
pared for what this text provides: a dangerous landslide, where sense of uni-

tary self becomes unanchored to the buoys of space and time, and so drifts away:

> In Worcester, Massachusetts,
> I went with Aunt Consuelo
> to keep her dentist's appointment
> and sat and waited for her
> in the dentist's waiting room.
> It was winter. It got dark
> early.

By the end of the poem, "in" has turned to "in it" and we are "Outside, / in," a much vaguer, but therefore, more accurate phrasing for the "inside-out" collapsing that occurs within the eerily paratactic narrative:

> Then I was back in it.
> The War was on. Outside,
> in Worcester, Massachusetts,
> were night and slush and cold,
> and it was still the fifth
> of February, 1918.

As the poem is, in part, an awakening to mortality, it makes sense that she closes with the calendar date. Every word, carefully measured out, signifies. The colloquialism, "the War was on," continues to expose the ambiguity of prepositions; before we were simply "in" Worcester, now we come "Outside, / in." To be "still the fifth" is ironic, since nothing lacks movement in this poem. Words that locate no longer have specificity, and she suggests, that as she comes "back in it," we are always already "in it," with no clear boundary between outside and inside: all artificial demarcations dissolve in this poem and we find ourselves "falling off / the round, turning world." The experience of vertigo suspends us in a state neither inside nor outside, and yet *in* both: language makes it impossible to really step *out*.[14]

Bishop's homey diction endows a word such as "inside" with multiple functions and positions throughout, until the word itself turns outside-in uncannily back upon itself with no referent. She begins, really, in a blur of undifferentiated objects and people, collapsing place with time, as her aunt is "inside / what seemed like a long time":

> The waiting room
> was full of grown-up people,
> arctics and overcoats,
> lamps and magazines.
> My aunt was inside
> what seemed like a long time
> and while I waited I read
> the *National Geographic*
> (I could read) and carefully
> studied the photographs:
> the inside of a volcano,
> black, and full of ashes;
> then it was spilling over
> in rivulets of fire.

The act of perusal, aside from making the poem an identificatory event for the reader of it, places the child in another world, but even the photographs attest to uncertain boundaries, the "inside" of the volcano coming outside, "spilling over."

When the child hears a scream from "inside," it becomes both her aunt's and her own. Consuelo offers no consolation; her name, instead, signifies the poem's basic polarity: *con*, "with" and *suelo*, "alone." While the child scorns her aunt's weakness, she must identify with her, and with all the other waiting figures; uncontrollably, she finds herself screaming in recognition of her mortality, her "waiting," a verb of uneasy suspension:

> Suddenly, from inside,
> came an *oh!* of pain
> —Aunt's Consuelo's voice—
> not very loud or long.
> I wasn't at all surprised;
> even then I knew she was
> a foolish, timid woman.
> I might have been embarrassed,
> but wasn't. What took me
> completely by surprise
> was that it was *me*:
> my voice, in my mouth.
> Without thinking at all

I was my foolish aunt,
I—we—were falling, falling,
our eyes glued to the cover
of the *National Geographic*,
February, 1918.

"I" slides into "we," and it miraculously becomes "our eyes" riveted by the magazine, which appears as the most solid article to hold on to. Yet the images within the *Geographic* themselves participate in the child's experience, contribute to the precipitation and unhinging of the self. Bishop's penchant for regarding painting as animate and timely recurs here with the borders of the photojournalism losing definition.

Osa and Martin Johnson
dressed in riding breeches,
laced boots, and pith helmets.
A dead man slung on a pole
—"Long Pig," the caption said.
Babies with pointed heads
wound round and round with string;
black, naked women with necks
wound round and round with wire
like the necks of light bulbs.
Their breasts were horrifying.

Our reading seems to move "round and round" and we anticipate the loss of stability that follows. The horror of sickness and death beside wealth and well-being absorbs the child's attention, compels her to make a connection between her reading *in time* and the volcanoes erupting, her incipient sexualization and the suffering women in the photographs, between the dead man and Osa and Martin.

I read it right straight through.
I was too shy to stop.
And then I looked at the cover:
the yellow margins, the date.

Reading "right" transports the child from the waiting room. Or does it?
Osa and Martin Johnson could be among those in the waiting room with

their "shadowy gray knees, / trousers and skirts and boots," just as we all pre-figure the "dead man slung on a pole" or the women with "horrifying breasts." The child again experiences an identification with the familiar alien, "the strange idea of family / travelling through the flesh." This pivotal moment of *Geworfenheit* occurs as recognition of the strangeness of the gen-dered self, its difference, as well as of the enmeshment of the self in and with others, its identity.

> I said to myself: three days
> and you'll be seven years old.
> I was saying it to stop
> the sensation of falling off
> the round, turning world
> into cold, blue-black space.
> But I felt: you are an *I*,
> you are an *Elizabeth*,
> you are one of *them*.
> *Why* should you be one, too?

The child articulates her age to place a boundary, to fix a position within the "round, turning world," but it is through language that she names herself and recognizes the crisis of identity hovered over by mortality. This is a moment that approximates the Lacanian entrance into the symbolic—the arrival of self-consciousness and sexual denomination, and the perpetual split and di-vision they entail. Discovering the self has, suddenly, as much to do with looking outside as looking inside, neither process definitive or familiar, yet somehow proleptic: "I scarcely dared to look / to see what it was I was." This self is improbable and impossible: "nothing / stranger could ever happen" than "being," made noticeable and strange because of those dark waves of "non-being" it borders.

> Why should I be my aunt,
> or me, or anyone?
> What similarities—
> boots, hands, the family voice
> I felt in my throat, or even
> the *National Geographic*
> and those awful hanging breasts—

held us all together
or made us all just one?

Discovery of the self converts to a discovery of female sexuality, a find that inextricably connects us all. The "cry of pain" unfurls the legacy of loss and knowledge of time enjoined upon selfhood that conjoins "us all together," and that renders all our knowledge shaky and provisional. That the pain could have gotten worse throws us into ontological uncertainty, a trembling unto death, our suspended position in the waiting room.

We can deny our connection with those in Africa, those in foreign landscapes, but Bishop recommends that we examine our "unlikely" likenesses. Place disappears through the child's imaginative sympathy, and Worcester collapses, temporarily, into Africa:

> The waiting room was bright
> and too hot. It was sliding
> beneath a big black wave,
> another, and another.

To be "back in it," in Worcester, suggests that we cannot get outside our temporal situation, our hurtling through space or our drowning beneath waves, any more than we can step beyond our language, our strangerliness. A "great truth" in her life, Bishop records the same events in "The Country Mouse" (c. 1961) and her reaction of angst:

> A feeling of absolute and utter desolation came over me. I felt . . . *myself*. In a few days it would be my seventh birthday. I felt, *I, I, I*, and looked at the three strangers in panic. I was *one* of them too, inside my scabby body and wheezing lungs. "You're in for it now," something said. How had I got tricked into such a false position? I would be like that woman opposite who smiled at me so falsely every once in a while. The awful sensation passed, then it came back again. "You are you," something said. "How strange you are, inside looking out. You are not Beppo, or the chestnut tree, or Emma, you are *you* and you are going to be *you* forever." It was like coasting downhill, this thought, only much worse, and it quickly smashed into a tree. *Why* was I a human being? (*CPr*, 32–33)

Bishop's childhood illnesses of eczema and asthma must contribute to her aggravated awareness of the body in time and the body being seen. The "three strangers" are both inalterably outside and potentially the three I's— "I, I, I"—she iterates to denote herself. Being an "I"—which means to be a "you"—depends upon the self-division induced by saying "I," and marks a "false position," because it assumes an illusory identity or wholeness only in the face of atomization and headlong disintegration. With this understanding, it is apparent how the world can be both "a mist" and uniquely "minute and vast and clear" ("Sandpiper," 131).

The terror of irreducible uniqueness is the isolation and separation it appears to signal. Gerard Manley Hopkins, whose poems for Bishop wonderfully imitated the mind in the act of thinking, in one of his philosophical meditations refers to a similar experience to her own of self-discovery, or recovering. But his sense of self, as completely strange and unlike any other thing, rests as an integrated whole due to some "extrinsic power," and not a cause for dread but of wonder:

> When I consider my selfbeing, my consciousness and feeling of myself, that taste of myself, and I and me above and in all things, which is more distinctive than the taste of ale or alum, more distinctive than the smell of walnut leaf or camphor, and incommunicable by any means to another man (as when I was a child I used to ask myself: What must it be to be someone else?) Nothing else in nature comes near this unspeakable stress of pitch, distinctiveness, and selving, this selfbeing of my own. Nothing explains it or resembles it, except so far as this, that other men to themselves have the same feeling. . . . But to me there is no resemblance: searching nature I taste self but at one tankard, that of my own being.[15]

All things are unique in Hopkins's conception of the world—and the most individuated, the self. What for Crusoe becomes an overwhelming burden, a nightmare of cataloguing "infinities of islands" with their individuated objects, "registering their flora, / their fauna, their geography" would be Hopkins's delight. But even with Hopkins, we remain stranded, unable to know what it is like to be any other "selfbeing." Bishop takes up this perspective (at home with self-pity), and couples it with another vision: instead of perceiving only endless difference, she hails likenesses. While the taste of a self may be as distinctive as ale or camphor, there is no distilled essence, no transcendental ego; the self divides and dissolves. It is partly the sensitized awareness of death, so irresistible in Bishop's work, that disbands unitary identity.

The sense of the world's irreality and instability can be an experience of sublimity, otherworldliness, as we shall see with "The Moose." In his discussion of the origins of his "Intimations of Immortality," William Wordsworth, fending off the experience of individuated self, cut off from nature, confesses: "Nothing was more difficult for me in childhood than to admit the notion of death as a state applicable to my own being." To install the self, one must admit mortality. The world may soothingly disintegrate in the Wordsworthian ego, until the world appears as unreal and immaterial, whereas the Bishopic ego dissolves into the world, and the self loses rigid substantiality. I have elsewhere discussed the Chodorowian implications of such a sense of self, wavering and uncertain, potentially more capable of seeing itself in relation than in isolation. But Bishop's discovery, here, of the absolutely individuated yet completely soluble identity, leads her, ultimately, to a more visionary understanding of her art and the uses of her personal resources. "One Art" offers a way of writing disaster by deferring it, or moreover, by generating a kind of art that recognizes the deferral and loss that compose our lives. In the uncertain space we occupy as an identity, we must project an imaginative home, re-create the homemade, if not through memory, then in fiction. In this manner, Bishop becomes a "visionary" without proposing a transcendental ego; we enter landscapes that are not timeless, but are precise and concrete without being denotative, without losing their evocative power.

A self-reflexive topography where time and place again collapse, or coincide, "12 O'Clock News" defamiliarizes a writer's desk as battlefield or alien civilization and burial site, the metamorphic place of the writer. As virtual borders, the poem uses two columns, mocking correspondence: one presenting the object, plain and simple such as "pile of mss." or "typewriter," and beside it more lengthy descriptions of it as apparition. Next to "ink-bottle," for example, Bishop writes that "it may well be nothing but a *numen*, or a great altar recently erected to one of their gods, to which, in their present historical state of superstition and helplessness, they attribute magical powers, and may even regard as a "savior," one last hope of rescue from their grave difficulties." She, thus, mocks the attempt to elevate writing or poetic language to the position of religion; it must always remain bound to the material and timely, even as we must be "visionary"—because we lack solid or fixed objects as well as certain and static memory, and our writing, like the places we inhabit, becomes ground for burial and resurrection, without the sacred rites.

Bishop supplies a model for such "vision" in her translation of Octavio Paz's "Objects & Apparitions" (*CP*, 275–76), dedicated to Joseph

Cornell. The poem takes up Cornell's various pieces of box art, and reveals their apparitional aspect: "things hurry away from their names," pointing beyond themselves, stirring up associations, never resting upon any final signification.

> Memory weaves, unweaves the echoes:
> in the four corners of the box
> shadowless ladies play at hide-and-seek.

Relationships are unexpected within the metonymy of the boxes: nothing can be just one thing, an "identity"; objects behave in flux:

> Theatre of the spirits:
> objects putting the laws
> of identity through hoops.

> "Grand Hôtel de la Couronne": in a vial,
> the three of clubs and, very surprised,
> Thumbelina in gardens of reflection.

> A comb is a harp strummed by the glance
> of a little girl
> born dumb.

Such art depends upon the viewer's interaction with it, her ability to discover connections, to transform objects into apparitions. "Apparition" connotes the spiritual, but really only indicates an unexpected becoming apparent, the uncanniness of having an appearance. Cornell's images come alive through Bishop's translation of Paz's words, but they do so only within a particular time, held in place only by the frail words that invoke them:

> The apparitions are manifest,
> their bodies weigh less than light,
> lasting as long as this phrase lasts.

Phrasing does not last, as "One Art" has shown, longer than the bodies it proposes or makes momentarily manifest. Translation, here, comments on its own activity: it is an admission of the alteration of self always taking place when we resort to language.

As its title indicates, "Poem" is also self-reflexive and concerns the intertwining of remembering and language. Although its "subject" is one of her uncle's paintings, the poem is about her experience reading and interpreting the picture in an imaginative mnemonics, a weaving and unweaving of memory. The only painting is the one being written through her perception of her uncle's work, which lets her "recognize the place":

> It must be Nova Scotia; only there
> does one see gabled wooden houses
> painted that awful shade of brown

The world *is* "painted"—she recognizes not the place but the perception of it, a thing worked up and imposed upon the never-to-be-determined thing itself. Since we cannot "relive duration," the picture makes the past a "clear" present, erases the boundary between now and then, not to disavow time but to present it as indeterminate, as only opaquely reflective:

> Up closer, a wild iris, white and yellow,
> fresh-squiggled from the tube.
> The air is fresh and cold; cold early spring
> clear as gray glass.

As did the landscape in "Brazil, January 1, 1502" which looked as if it was shaken from the frame, place here seems just now painted. Remembering involves the poet in admitting the place as painting and not the place itself, ultimately unknowable:

> Heavens, I recognize the place, I know it!
> It's behind—I can almost remember the farmer's name.
> His barn backed on that meadow. There it is,
> titanium white, one dab. The hint of steeple,
> filaments of brush-hairs, barely there,
> must be the Presbyterian church.
> Would that be Miss Gillespie's house?
> Those particular geese and cows
> are naturally before my time.

Her "naive" painting of the memory fuses the representation with the literal: yet it is as if the geese exist only as painting, as does the barn, steeple, house. When Bishop writes that she "know[s] it," we become immediately suspicious, for in her realm, nothing is "known" once and for all, our very language revealing the absence of ultimate referentiality.

Memory is hermeneutical, and it inevitably turns "life" into art until the three cannot be disentangled. The poet imagines a conversation as the process of memory trying to determine relations: *"Your Uncle George, no, mine, my Uncle George, / he'd be your great-uncle, left them all with Mother / when he went back to England."* Even with such hesitations and revisions, the painting as poem, however, brings her in communion, through homemade objects, with a relative she never even met:

> I never knew him. We both knew this place,
> apparently, this literal small backwater,
> looked at it long enough to memorize it,
> our years apart. How strange. And it's still loved,
> or its memory is (it must have changed a lot).
> Our visions coincided—"visions" is
> too serious a word—our looks, two looks:
> art "copying from life" and life itself,
> life and the memory of it so compressed
> they've turned into each other. Which is which?

Memory is indistinguishably bound up with our perception, and the art we turn life into. The parenthetical "(it must have changed a lot)" recognizes that their memory, and the painting, could not be accurate, and that memory changes too, over time. She rejects "vision" for "look," refusing to posit any "too serious" transcendent power to her perception; after all, they "both knew this place, / apparently," giving knowledge more of a shifting appearance than any essential entity.

Yet what joins her with her uncle is their hermeneutic efforts—this becomes the homemade, signature of their diachronic desire to make a place, preserve an intimate space turned synchronic:

> Life and the memory of it cramped,
> dim, on a piece of Bristol board,
> dim, but how live, how touching in detail
> —the little that we get for free,
> the little of our earthly trust. Not much.
> About the size of our abidance
> along with theirs: the munching cows,

the iris, crisp and shivering, the water
still standing from spring freshets,
the yet-to-be-dismantled elms, the geese.

Bishop rejects, of course, the heavenly and substitutes an "earthly trust." The image reduced upon the Bristol continues to exist in process, on the verge of mirroring and measuring "our abidance," our frail weathering of time. "Poem," throughout, relies upon an ecomonic metaphor to establish the idea of free investment and exchange, the only mode by which memory survives. The painting resembles a dollar bill, but "has never earned any money in its life"; its history of passage suggests that the painting acts as "collateral," a pledge that promises the fulfillment of an obligation:

Useless and free, it has spent seventy years
as a minor family relic
handed along collaterally to owners
who looked at it sometimes, or didn't bother to.

Our only hope, for Bishop, seems to be in the looking. Or in her ability to trouble us. Her poem fulfills in some sense the promissory note, the debt we owe the painting's desire, the hope to commemorate and memorialize an abode. But it is in our looking, in our reading of the poem, which allows our limited abidance. "The little that we get for free" comes to represent our investments in our homey industries, our making of our imaginative homes, our rewriting the earth. The uncle's painting exists in the present as long as we invest our "earthly trust"; Bishop's poem takes up the ranks of the "useless and free," the homemade object that is "live" and "touching in detail" through the act of reading.

Weaving and unweaving memory, the only way we come to it. Just as Crusoe's looking up the blanks in his literary memory leads us along the same track, if we turn to the issue of the *Geographic* so precisely dated by "In the Waiting Room," we cannot find it. Memory, for Bishop, is suspect and becomes an unfolding process that can only refer to a disintegrative consciousness. "The End of March" (*CP*, 179–80), with its very definite marking of time, reveals only the imaginative indecision at the basis of our remembering, and of our projecting the future to be continually shaped and reshaped. Hindsight and foresight converge, just as the memory of the painting in "Poem," handed down "collaterally," looks to be inspiration for present and eventual imaginings. "The End of March" turns upon Bishop's daydream of a future and imaginary home, more the idea of one (seemingly the only kind of home-made), entirely personal and cryptic:

> I wanted to get as far as my proto-dream-house,
> my crypto-dream-house, that crooked box
> set up on pilings, shingled green,
> a sort of artichoke of a house, but greener
> (boiled with bicarbonate of soda?),
> protected from spring tides by a palisade
> of—are they railroad ties?
> (Many things about this place are dubious.)

She can really only imagine and see the "proto-dream-house" in the poem, for "that day the wind was much too cold / even to get that far, / and of course the house was boarded up." The house exists only in prolepsis, conjectured through imagined memory. She tells us parenthetically that "many things about this place are dubious," a commonplace by now of Bishopian vision. Writing in the above passage as if she "knows" the house, her exactitude wavers, modifies itself through question, and we sense only the place's vegetative fantasticality: "a sort of artichoke of a house, but greener" provides a vivid image with "artichoke," but with the phrase "a sort of" and the addition of "but greener," more language just does not function as clarification.

Bachelard comments upon "the image of the *dream house*" which, in order to remain a nurturing force in the imagination, must remain "proto," to use Bishop's language. He writes:

> Maybe it is a good thing for us to keep a few dreams of a house that we shall live in later, always later, so much later, in fact, that we shall not have time to achieve it. For a house that was final, one that stood in symmetrical relation to the house we were born in, would lead to thoughts—serious, sad thoughts—and not to dreams. It is better to live in a state of impermanence than in one of finality. (61)

Bishop certainly concurs with such a sentiment. Her dream is, ultimately, of impermanence—her homemade thrives on the inconclusive and the impossible. The "artichoke" house is discontinuous from previous houses, remains a living thing within her imagination because never completed, arrived at, or substantiated any more than the self in process.

Only briefly can she inhabit a house that exists through dream and desire.

By questioning if the protective palisade surrounding her "home" is made from railroad ties, Bishop refers to her earlier "Chemin de Fer" with its ties "too close together / or maybe too far apart," and proposes for herself a solitary Crusoe existence in the "dubious" space of "there":

> I'd like to retire there and do *nothing*,
> or nothing much, forever, in two bare rooms:
> look through binoculars, read boring books,
> old, long, long books, and write down useless notes,
> talk to myself, and, foggy days,
> watch the droplets slipping, heavy with light.
> At night, a *grog à l'américaine*.
> I'd blaze it with a kitchen match
> and lovely diaphanous blue flame
> would waver, doubled in the window.

To live within this place approximates a living within the imagination: the house becomes a figure for turning inward, the casting off of the unnecessary and material; like the character of "In Prison," discussed in Chapter 2, she needs little external stimulation: it is even best that books are "boring," and so open to imaginative remaking. Each event within the minimalist "two bare rooms" can take on poetic significance, and as Crusoe's knife "reeked of meaning," so too would the conjurations and improvisations of the moment—sipping her own brew, watching the reflective rain slip in slowed motion, transfixed by "lovely diaphanous blue flame."

This "*dia*phanous" flame, struck uselessly, is synecdochic for Bishop's poetic technique in "The End of March." She imagines that it "would waver, doubled in the window," as do all her lines. Even within single lines, she startles by disjunctive splittings, making an assertion and then withdrawing it; notice the motility in these lines describing the amenities:

> There must be a stove; there *is* a chimney,
> askew, but braced with wires,
> and electricity, possibly
> —at least, at the back another wire
> limply leashes the whole affair
> to something off behind the dunes.
> A light to read by—perfect! But—impossible.

The definitely existing chimney is "askew, but braced," and the wires, connecting "the whole affair / to something off behind the dunes," seem about to split and snap. Bishop reveals the process of creating and amending her "proto-dream-house" which materializes as she walks toward it. But it is not only her dream house that has no re-solution or consistency. Even those things she does manage to reach and see evade comprehension. The wires that "limply leash" the home recur within the "lengths and lengths, endless, of wet white string" that she follows but cannot name for certain. Even as she says of these strings that "finally, they did end:" it is with a colon introducing the string as a "sodden ghost" whose "rising" and "falling back" upon the waves enacts her elegiac mourning for all those she has lost, the disappearance and reappearance act of fort-da, the "giving up the ghost." She questions and puzzles: "A kite string?—But no kite." The string connects up to no referent in this disorienting landscape where "a track of big dog-prints" are "so big / they were more like lion-prints." Correspondence waxes dubious—the kite string without the kite, desire without final fulfillment.

As an interface between winter and spring, the season of the poem doubles and wavers. Walking toward the house, the wind "numbed our faces on one side," and on the way back from the mythical house, our "faces froze on the other side." She says of the seascape: "Everything was withdrawn as far as possible, / indrawn: the tide far out, the ocean shrunken, / seabirds in ones or twos." Everything comes "in ones or twos." Doubled, the sea is "withdrawn" and "indrawn," suggesting outward and inward, but also words with potentially identical meaning when applied to personality.

Doubling the phrase "for just a minute" in the last stanza, Bishop brings into transitory correspondence the elements of her dreamscape; interpreting the cryptic string and paw-prints, she finds for them ideal referents:

> The sun came out for just a minute.
> For just a minute, set in their bezels of sand,
> the drab, damp, scattered stones
> were multi-colored,
> and all those high enough threw out long shadows,
> individual shadows, then pulled them in again.
> They could have been teasing the lion sun,
> except that now he was behind them
> —a sun who'd walked the beach the last low tide,
> making those big, majestic paw-prints,
> who perhaps had batted a kite out of the sky to play with.

Sudden and brief illumination, even visionary transfiguration, yet retains the ambiguity of discontinuity. The hope to arrive at the "proto-dream-house" is a kind of warm-up for the accidental, homemade revelations the poet trips upon within the processes of unknowing and uncertainty.

Remembering the homemade involves the envisioning of an inner home, neither solid nor immutable but reflective of the homeless ego. Yet the homemade, in Bishop's later pieces such as "Poem" and "The End of March," shows memory in the making of imaginative spaces. Dedicated to her beloved Aunt Grace and by implication to her lost Nova Scotia, "The Moose" (CP, 169–73), because written over a period of at least twenty years, refers to its own postponement as it recalls a New England bus ride, literalizing displacement and loss through a journey. If "In the Waiting Room" reflects more upon the strangeness of selfhood, "The Moose" considers that "strange idea of family / travelling through the flesh," the strangeness of our connections with others that persist over time, underlined by the "deaths, deaths, and sicknesses" that join us, and changed through memory.

Cinematic, the poem unfolds its topographical discoveries only gradually. The first clause of the poem stretches across five stanzas making three half-stops with semicolons, and strives to define location, delaying the arrival of the sentence's subject; her journeying syntax includes us in the bus ride and those homey accommodations we must make with the natural world:

> From narrow provinces
> of fish and bread and tea,
> home of the long tides
> where the bay leaves the sea
> twice a day and takes ·
> the herring long rides,
>
> where if the river
> enters or retreats
> in a wall of brown foam
> depends on if it meets
> the bay coming in,
> the bay not at home;
>
> where, silted red,
> sometimes the sun sets
> facing a red sea,
> and others, veins the flats'

lavender, rich mud
in burning rivulets;

on red, gravelly roads,
down rows of sugar maples,
past clapboard farmhouses
and neat, clapboard churches,
bleached, ridged as clamshells,
past twin silver birches,

through late afternoon
a bus journeys west,
the windshield flashing pink,
pink glancing off of metal,
brushing the dented flank
of blue, beat-up enamel;

The anaphoric "where" and repetition of "home" in the first two stanzas (in every stanza at least one word is repeated) draw the reader into a homemade landscape made apparent by the impressions coming and going, entering or retreating as the poem presses ahead. Displacement characterizes this poem, so much about the transitory and the relentless passage of time: "Goodbye to the elms, / to the farm, to the dog. / The bus starts." With the farewells made, the bus takes its passengers and us into a less known, less populated and human landscape as the fog "comes closing in." Geography as reassuring metaphor begins to lose its hold:

One stop at Bass River.
Then the Economies—
Lower, Middle, Upper;
Five Islands, Five Houses,
where a woman shakes a tablecloth
out after supper.

A pale flickering. Gone.
The Tantramar marshes
and the smell of salt hay.
An iron bridge trembles
and a loose plank rattles
but doesn't give way.

Arbitrary topographical division "gives way" to the phonemic allure of "Tantramar marshes," to imagistic and fragmentary perception. Only a sentence that denotes precarious position is complete in the above stanzas. The poem, like the bus trip, makes visible sharp, sudden but discontinuous visions such as "Two rubber boots show, / illuminated, solemn. / A dog gives one bark." Alliterative and hypnotic, the poem suspends waking consciousness within visionary hallucination as the bus moves into the "moonlight and mist" of the New Brunswick woods, a dreamscape that dwarfs individual human existence to "a pale flickering." Spatial journeying changes to mental "divagation" as the passengers fall to sleep. Bishop allows for a communal dream that is also a collateral memory of an "old conversation," not to be pinned down, emerging from "somewhere, / back in the bus," that strange idea of a family traveling through us:

> Grandparents's voices
>
> uninterruptedly
> talking, in Eternity:
> names being mentioned,
> things cleared up finally;
> what he said, what she said,
> who got pensioned;
>
> deaths, deaths and sicknesses;
> the year he remarried;
> the year (something) happened.
> She died in childbirth.
> That was the son lost
> when the schooner foundered.
>
> He took to drink. Yes.
> She went to the bad.
> When Amos began to pray
> even in the store and
> finally the family had
> to put him away.

By invoking a balladic "Eternity" of things going "to the bad" and muddled, yet landmark occurrences, fitted for the family album, Bishop reveals the cliché of memory (just as with "Brazil, January 1, 1502," she had exposed the cliché of tapestry), yet paradoxically, the narrative mirrors many of the poet's autobiographic concerns, if displaced: foundering, drinking, going mad, wanting "prayer," even as it seems most impossible or incongruous. Even as memory is conjectured to include the expected human failings and melo-drama, what finally binds the passengers (and us and Bishop) is our reitera-tive losses and mortality, the "deaths, deaths and sicknesses," but also the awe for the eternally resistant "(something)," the mystery of our existence. The two are inseparable, twined within our subtextual, indrawn conversa-tions:

> Yes . . ." that peculiar
> affirmative. "Yes . . ."
> A sharp, indrawn breath,
> half groan, half acceptance,
> that means "Life's like that.
> We know *it* (also death)."

Even estrangement becomes homey, *heimlich* and *unheimlich*; even as we af-firm, however, we do so "peculiarly," without full or clear knowledge. Bishop gives us a snapshot—converting bus to "old featherbed"—that takes on the "dim" homemade quality of her uncle's painting on Bristol.

> Talking the way they talked
> in the old featherbed,
> peacefully, on and on,
> dim lamplight in the hall,
> down in the kitchen, the dog
> tucked in her shawl.

Throughout, Bishop's lines have mesmerized with the stanza's rhymed third and sixth lines, but as we have come to the furthest point of imagined mem-ory, she lets the rhyme drop a line, displacing itself just before the bus comes to a sudden stop.

Distinctions between dream and real landscape, interior and exterior dis-solve with the startling appearance of the moose stepping into the human world, momentarily, from the dark and inscrutable woods, and partaking of both. The moment of confrontation binds the passengers, yet only, it would seem, as they cannot comprehend the moose, as they ascribe to it familiar and "safe" images, resorting to appropriate simile:

> Towering, antlerless,
> high as a church,
> homely as a house
> (or, safe as houses).
> A man's voice assures us
> "Perfectly harmless. . . ."

Enunciations and declarations blend. Language fails. But a wordless "joy" at the "awful" beyond what can be expressed takes over:

> Some of the passengers
> exclaim in whispers,
> childishly, softly,
> "Sure are big creatures."
> "It's awful plain."
> "Look! It's a she!"
>
> Taking her time,
> she looks the bus over,
> grand, otherworldly.
> Why, why do we feel
> (we all feel) this sweet
> sensation of joy?

Bishop inserts her most direct assertion, as is her custom, within parenthesis. Thus, she mutes the potential transcendence even while invoking it. The moose, Bishop's most female character I think, becomes a kind of vision, apparition of "the homely as a house"—beyond objectification, but "vision" might be too strong a word since she always disclaims a centralized ego that might lay claim to any absolute knowledge. For her, the otherworldly remains inaccessible, taking its own time; the momentary vision of something bringing us all together, making us all one, always breaks off. Bishop, like her driver, will "shift gears" to frame, for just a moment, the doubleness of the wholly natural with the human stain:

> For a moment longer,
>
> by craning backward,
> the moose can be seen
> on the moonlit macadam;

> then there's a dim
> smell of moose, an acrid
> smell of gasoline.

"Dim" and touching, the moose becomes remembered and sensed, an entity on the threshold position of "the moonlit macadam," not to be confined nor kept captive, to be felt in the protracted moment of Bishop's "craning backward."

"The Moose," as a poem that held Bishop's interest for more than a third of her career, is arguably one of her most evocative pieces, and allows us to see a topography of the self that cannot be limited to individual existence. The personal becomes the communal, and our remembering, like our poems, are moments of the homecoming: temporary alleviation of estrangement but also heightened awareness of the ultimate strangeness of "being" and "family." We memorialize and distort, language displacing us as we use it in the service of the homemade. The examination of personal history and self, then, does not implement fixed identity; within Bishop's poetics of loss, she can only acknowledge a fluid sense of being in the world. Poems are the provisional homes of our perception but cannot, finally, contain our experience. Within a stanza of "One Art," Bishop can let slip the "next-to-last, of three loved houses," knowing that we make our soluble homes from within—through arbitrary and elastic geographics.

Conclusion: "That Peculiar Affirmative"

It has been said by others, and by her, that she is a poet of the small, the humble, the unmonumental. And Bishop certainly is not a mythic poet in the vein of Eliot or Auden; she indirectly compares herself to Paul Klee in an interview with Ashley Brown: "he had 16 paintings going at once; *he* didn't have a formulated myth to look to, apparently, and his accomplishment was very considerable."[1] In the same interview she also rejects a "desire to get everything in its place." Yet even as she is "not interested in big-scale work as such" (Brown, 295), I hope that it is by now evident how very intensely Bishop engages the larger questions of human existence. Because of her awareness that nothing can have an impermeable place—and that it would not be desirable if it could—she does not propose confining answers or a coherent system of beliefs that might provide ultimate meaning or project an alternative world to the one we inhabit. Yet she is a major poet of our times, partly for her resistance to closure and ultimacy, for her intensive questions of epistemology and ontology. Her attraction to autobiography, diaries, letters, journals all turn back to the notion of the poet as investigator of the soul, prompting one to think of Saint Augustine; while there is always this kind of spiritual dimension in her quest(s), at the same time, she dissolves the dark night of the soul (the unbeliever asleep on the top of his mast, afraid to fall into a sea of knives) with the psychological one so that the celestial always partakes of the doubts and limitations of the terrestrial. Attention to the earthly is, of course, a commonplace of modern poetry, but Bishop complicates the notion of a secular self by interrogating gender categories, and definitions of the self in its different placements of home and of travel—no boundary we draw around identity can be safe, we discover, in her active, restless poetics.

While she approaches matters of the spirit with hesitation and with unorthodox skepticism and unbelieving, Bishop nevertheless engages matters of faith as vigorously as would her forefigures Herbert, Hopkins, and even Dickinson (she had meant to write a poem on the latter two.) As with the collagist Joseph Cornell, who was in fact a Christian Scientist, she does not abandon cosmic possibilities in her explorations of distinctive realities and apparently unrelated objects; like Cornell's, her objects become animate apparitions constellated to show interconnectivity and trespassable boundaries. I have argued that loss is a motivating current in her work; and personal loss becomes directly implicated in questions of faith, and the pain that comes with the loss of religious orthodoxy. "The Baptism" tells us what Lucy must write: "'*January 20th*: At last, I know my own mind,' she began, 'or rather I have given it up completely. Now I am going to join the church as soon as I can'"(*CPr*, 165). While such joining would probably be considered a definite kind of insanity by Bishop, she is not only ironic about her conversion figure. To know one's mind often means to give it up, and the discovery of a disintegrative self—much more founded on loss and movement than stability or stillness—also recommends Bishop's loving engagement and immersion within the world.

Throughout her career, Bishop struggles to discover a way to handle and write about (if both are not the same) the process of suffering. In a rather early letter to Lowell (8 August 1948), she addresses the difficulties in writing about suffering.[2] She likes Randall Jarrell's somewhat confessional "90 North," which ends in the bleakly existential summation, "Pain comes from the darkness / And we call it wisdom. It is pain." Yet she feels that with such suffering, "there's no use talking so much about it." Of her own solitude and ennui, she says it is the kind of anguish she is "most at home with & helpless about." She then acknowledges Eliot as the only one who can write "convincingly" about suffering, but complains that he "gets that oh-so resigned tone"; she follows with an objection to Auden's handling of pain in the ecphrastic "Musée des Beaux-Arts" as "plain inaccurate" as it depicts "the ploughman & people on the boat [who] will rush to see the falling boy any minute, they always do, though maybe not to help." In the same letter, she tells the story about the boy in New York who continues to play after hearing about death, records that she has begun writing "The Prodigal," and confesses to be enjoying *The Sorrows of Young Werther*. All of these details point to her obsessive interest in suffering, and though she says there's "no use talking so much about it," she recognizes its great importance for her. It becomes a matter of how to talk about the most personal issues and still be writing with the sense of being so much within a world exceeding the self, without becoming ostentatious or confessional, and this, as we have well seen, she achieves with increased effectiveness and sensitivity, somewhere between or beyond the poles of a perhaps overly self-conscious Jarrell and ironically distanced and didactic Auden.

Auden's poem about Brueghel's *Icarus* begins:

> About suffering they were never wrong,
> The Old Masters: how well they understood
> Its human position; how it takes place
> While someone else is eating or opening a window or just
>   walking dully along;

The sentiment about human meaninglessness is similar to Jarrell's. But Auden also affirms "The Old Masters," something Bishop will not do, especially in discussing painting. "Everything turns away / quite leisurely from the disaster," we learn; and this is just what she does not permit us to do. Instead, she demands engagement: the "dogs may go on with their doggy life," but it is empathy and compassion that makes this not entirely possible. Her "Poem," and the poem that prefigures it, "Large Bad Picture," both attest to quite a different view of suffering: it is one, as we have seen, that must consider the touching and live details of our earthly trusts, those endeavors to create objects, perhaps of limited aesthetic value in the museum, imbued with the personal history and inevitable suffering of the self, its family and landscape. We cannot walk dully along, avert our eyes, especially from death—if we want to be fully alive.

Phyllis Stowell perceptively suggests that "[Bishop's] last three poems, 'Santarém,' 'North Haven,' and 'Sonnet,' deal with death and the way death affects our perception of life."[3] That Santarém is a kind of swan song. Indeed, in her memorial poem for Lowell, "North Haven" (*CP*, 188–89), Bishop quite directly confronts her friend's death, probably more so than she has been able to write about the death of any significant other. It is not unlikely that she looks to her own death as a poet, in this poem of eulogy of Lowell's endless revising. ("The Moose," we recall, was written over a twenty-year period.) With a color that will appear more than once in "Santarém," she ends the poem:

> You left North Haven, anchored in its rock,
> afloat in mystic blue . . . And now—you've left

for good. You can't derange, or re-arrange,
your poems again. (But the Sparrows can their song.)
The words won't change again. Sad friend, you cannot
    change.

A "permanence" of changeless words has an uncomfortable ring in Bishop, but much of the pathos of the last line is the direct mourning for the loss of Lowell's changes, his revisions.

The poem began in an italicized present, a note held in homage to North Haven as a reflowering "place."

I can make out the rigging of a schooner
a mile off; I can count
the new cones on the spruce. It is so still
the pale bay wears a milky skin, the sky
no clouds, except for one long, carded horse's-tail.

"I can count" has, in its self-reference to metrics, similar evocative power to "I could read," spoken by the child of "In the Waiting Room." Are the things of the landscape in sympathy with us, or are they simply just what we can "make out" through language? This opening stanza presents a distinct vision, excepting for the cloud "one long, carded horse's-tail," a metaphor that brings together the natural with another metaphor, for poetic device—carding, the disentangling of wool or thread, preparing to spin. Mediating between the natural and the human has been a subject of Bishop before in "Five Flights Up" (*CP*, 181) as she spatializes the worlds of the guiltless dog, who "bounces cheerfully," and his owner who reprimands: "Obviously, he has no shame"—no sense of death either. These two realms of natural and human are less disjunctive in "The Moose," if only for a moment. And now in "North Haven" the split between the two is again addressed, and the "White-throated Sparrow's five note song, / pleading and pleading, brings tears to the eyes." Each pleading appears to be in sympathetic cry for Lowell, and also synchronous with his poetic process: "Nature repeats herself, or almost does: / *repeat, repeat, repeat; revise, revise, revise.*" Almost the same, over and over; yet different, revised. The parenthetical Sparrows of the last stanza will alter their song—almost as if in tune with the dead deranger. A natural world of harmonious perfection—mirror for lyric immutability—had never been Bishop's ideal either, as we have seen.

In the interview with Elizabeth Spires, she recounts that "The Moose," itself emblematic of a kind of carding over time, was "all true": "The bus trip took place before I went to Brazil. I went up to visit my aunt. Actually, I was on the wrong bus. I went to the right place but it wasn't the express I was supposed to get."[4] Accident and chance, the mysterious contributions to her life and poems; and then the revisions written over long stretches of time. Though "it took [her] a long time / finally to make [her] mind up to go home" ("The Prodigal," CP, 71) she does return, and as exile, with the deep knowledge of the essential displacement in human lives, the "deaths, deaths and sicknesses," along with the wholly mysterious, generative and, in this instance, feminine force of life connecting us all, "this sweet / sensation of joy." What gives Bishop her "peculiar affirmative" is her understanding of the ultimately double and impossibly mixed state of human existence: it is awful but cheerful, it is gruesome but delightful, it is tragic but comic, it is simple but complex, it is "high as a church, / homely as a house," it is grand but plain, and so forth without end. And this "peculiar affirmative" is rooted, as I have implied, in compassion for suffering, an ever-generous eye for the frail, the broken, the eyesores, the pink dogs, the homeless. Finally, Bishop's power holds contrary notions or aspects of existence simultaneously, without letting one submerge the other, and without hoping for a seamless suturing between them; proffering, instead, a loving counterpoint and interchange that does not exclude the knowledge of suffering loss and death, but is only enlivened by it.

"Santarém" epitomizes this achievement and the poetic devices repeated and revised throughout her career. It memorializes a place *as* mystery, constructed from dubious memory, as discussed in Chapter 5. The river becomes a kind of saint for remembering, in this poem that dramatizes Bishop's relinquishing of mastery in favor of open-ended meditation, of the up in the air. With her miraculous language she gives the illusion of simple and vivid description, but by the end of the poem, the meanings are loose of their referent places. The introductory question "Of course I may be remembering it all wrong / after, after—how many years?" conditions everything to follow, shrouding all statement with reservation and doubt. In "[t]hat golden evening" when "more than anything else [she] wanted to stay awhile / in that conflux of two great rivers, Tapajós, Amazon / grandly, silently flowing, flowing east," staying is, of course, what she knows as impossible, and finally, undesirable. Gingerly, her language constructs images only to unhinge and suspend them, until they float as if slightly off the page, at an inquiring distance from the words. Modification, equivocation, conditionals, obverse and mirror doublings, questions—these characterize what becomes—if very fleetingly—the most blatantly philosophical or abstract moment of the poem:

> Suddenly there'd been houses, people, and lots of mongrel
> riverboats skittering back and forth
> under a sky of gorgeous, under-lit clouds,
> with *everything* gilded, burnished along one side,
> and *everything* bright, cheerful, casual—*or so it looked.*
> I *liked the* place; I *liked the idea* of the place.
> *Two rivers.* Hadn't *two rivers* sprung
> from the Garden of Eden? No, that was four
> and they'd diverged. Here only two
> and coming together. *Even if* one were tempted
> to literary interpretations
> such as: life/death, right/wrong, male/female
> —such notions *would have* resolved, dissolved, straight off
> in that watery, dazzling dialectic. (emphasis mine)

This is as close to mythologizing as we get in Bishop—close enough for her to propose the rivers in the Garden of Eden as a parallel topos to Santarém. "Here only two / and coming together" is the stillest moment of paradox in the poem, and it cannot last; somehow it remains beyond interpretive sin, even beyond a language to describe it. Even so, Bishop remains within language, no matter how dissolving, in "dialectic."

We have seen division before in the early poems about art and gender; in the later ones, most explicitly figured in "The End of March," with the walk toward its dream of an impossible idea of home, as the "icy, offshore wind / numbed our faces on one side"; on the return from any arrival, "our faces froze on the other side." Wholeness, the way we are used to imagining it, is not, apparently, possible. The moment of culmination, the rivers coming together and still being "two" (finally the ties close together and far enough apart) occurs in Santarém. Stowell discusses the poem as creating "a place of union, wholeness, and the resolution of mind-made dichotomies and oppositions. It is a place in the imagination," but then "the recall staggers downward through a series of increasingly problematical observations" (48). Although I agree with a great deal of this essay's alert perceptions, including the sense of a spiraling "downward" movement, it is not a way down that is not also a way up. Stowell concludes that the poem "expresses a terrible split, an interior dichotomy between feeling and intellect, between an empathetic and actively assisting masculine figure, the pharmacist, and a negating one, Mr. Swan. It also reveals a conflict between imagination and a 'reality' devoid of human meaning or value—a reality at once insignificant and devastating" (48–49).

Yet this "terrible split" is, perhaps, not so neatly dissectable. "Back on board," Bishop does meet with Mr. Swan on a journey "to see the Amazon before he died," and his unstoppable blindness, but she still holds the "empty wasps' nest"—has seen it, "small, exquisite, clean matte white, / and hard as stucco," along with her perception of its mixed symbolism—as home, no longer home; as art object, imperfect and natural: a meeting or conflux of worlds. To end with Mr. Swan's rudely comic question "What's that ugly thing?" does not truly close the poem. His remark is of a piece with the imperfections that inform this flowing and flown, doubling existence. What appears as deflation can also be seen as peculiarly affirmed snags in the numinous skein woven by the poet's vision. The church, mock-elevated to Cathedral, seen from the river, thoughout, does not provide this kind of affirmation, but itself is part of one in this bright landscape, tinted with darkness, its "modest promenade and a belvedere / about to fall into the river." The poem later narrates that "the Cathedral'd / been struck by lightning. One tower had / a widening zigzag crack all the way down. / It was a miracle." The contractual casualness of "Cathedral'd" reflects a crack within orthodoxy—after all this is the landscape of the proselytes/Christians who owned slaves. It is the lightning crack, apparently attractive, that *is* the miracle, in its natural expertise in symbolic jolting. She has seen, slightly modified from the search among Edenic landscape, "Two rivers full of crazy shipping—people / all apparently changing their minds, embarking, / disembarking, rowing clumsy dories." Her tone is consistently compassionate toward the "crazy shipping—people" and their clumsy fluctuations, arrivals, and departures. When Bishop writes in the last stanza that "Then—my ship's whistle blew. I couldn't stay," she reveals, in this sudden temporal transition, the flimsiness of making up one's mind to go, and the poignancy of necessary passage. The "blew" triples with the "blue" of the pharmacy, and the strangely "*blue*" zebus; this is the "mystic blue" of meditation and imagination, also here a valedictory signal. She couldn't stay; Lowell has "left / for good." This is not resignation, but "half groan, half acceptance." Pain becomes wisdom here.

Personal loss, as the foregoing has demonstrated, permeates Bishop's perception of the world, of her role as artist, lover, and "seer." While bringing into view the unanswerable questions of suffering and faith, "Santarém" is a

kind of conflux of poetic impulses, with much of the innovations of the earlier career running beside those breakthroughs of the later. There exist no
seamless continuity and linear development in Bishop's work (there is always
the flux of arrival and departure, embarking and disembarking), but rather
fundamental concerns—with loss, with isolation and connection, with
charting a feminist encounter with tradition—as recurrent as the rhymes of
her villanelle. Fort, da. We begin with loss. Returning with a peculiar affirmative.

Notes

Introduction

1. Brett C. Millier, *Elizabeth Bishop: Life and the Memory of It* (Berkeley and Los Angeles: University of California Press, 1993).

2. Randall Jarrell, *Poetry and the Age* (New York: Knopf, 1953), 235.

3. Anne Stevenson, *Elizabeth Bishop* (New York: Twayne, 1986); Thomas J. Travisano, *Elizabeth Bishop: Her Artistic Development* (Charlottesville: University of Virginia Press, 1988), 7.

4. Jerome Mazzaro, *Postmodern American Poetry* (Urbana: University of Illinois Press, 1980), 28.

5. Lynn Keller, *Re-making It New: Contemporary American Poetry and the Modernist Tradition* (Cambridge: Cambridge University Press, 1987), 99–100.

6. Bonnie Costello, *Elizabeth Bishop: Questions of Mastery* (Cambridge: Harvard University Press, 1991).

7. For other pivotal sources of postmodern thought, see also Roland Barthes, *The Pleasure of the Text* (New York: Hill and Wang, 1977); Jacques Derrida, *Writing and Difference* (Chicago: University of Chicago Press, 1978) and *Margins of Philosophy* (Chicago: University of Chicago Press, 1982); Michel Foucault, *Language, Counter-Memory, Practice* (Ithaca: Cornell University Press, 1977); Luce Irigaray, *Speculum of the Other Woman* (Ithaca: Cornell University Press, 1985); Julia Kristeva, "Revolution and Poetic Language," in *The Kristeva Reader*, ed. Toril Moi (New York: Columbia University Press, 1986); and Jean-François Lyotard, *The Postmodern Condition* (Minneapolis: University of Minnesota Press, 1984).

8. Sheri Benstock reminds us that "avant-garde" modernism exists alternative to high modernism, which "constructed itself on a political agenda of exclusion"; this other modernism may include the work of high modernists but is generally more experimental and subversive in terms of gender; see her "Expatriate Sapphic Modernism" in *Lesbian Texts and Contexts: Radical Revisions*, ed. Karla Jay and Joanne Glasgow (New York: New York University Press, 1990), 186. Also see *The Gender of Modernism*, ed. Bonnie Kime Scott (Bloomington: Indiana University Press, 1990), an anthology that makes evident the way modernism is gendered and not the universal, neutral category it has been defined as by many of its male practitioners.

9. Ihab Hassan, "The Culture of Postmodernism," in *Modernism: Challenges and Perspectives*, ed. Monique Chefdor, Ricardo Quinones, and Albert Wachtel (Urbana: University of Illinois Press, 1986).

10. Ludwig Wittgenstein, *On Certainty* (New York: Harper and Row, 1972); *Philosophical Investigations* (New York: Macmillan, 1970).

11. Elizabeth Bishop, *Complete Poems* (New York: Farrar, Straus and Giroux, 1979). All poetry citations to be taken from this volume, abbreviated as *CP*.

12. David Kalstone, *Becoming a Poet: Elizabeth Bishop with Marianne Moore and Robert Lowell* (New York: Farrar, Straus, and Giroux, 1989).

13. Craig Owens, "The Discourse of Others: Feminists and Postmodernism," in *The Anti-Aesthetic: Essays on Postmodern Culture*, ed. Hal Foster (Seattle: Bay Press, 1983), 62.

14. For an overview of feminist literary theory, in both its Anglo-American and French versions, see Toril Moi, *Sexual / Textual Politics* (New York: Methuen, 1985); for discussion of French feminism alone, see Elizabeth Grosz, *Sexual Subversions* (Sydney: Allen and Unwin, 1989); and for explicit discussions of the intersection of feminism and postmodernism, see *Feminism / Postmodernism*, ed. Linda J. Nicholson (New York: Routledge, 1990), and Judith Butler, *Gender Trouble* (New York: Routledge, 1990).

15. Jane Flax, "Postmodernism and Gender Relations," in *Feminism / Postmodernism*, ed. Linda J. Nicholson (New York: Routledge, 1990).

16. Nancy Fraser and Linda J. Nicholson, "Social Criticism Without Philosophy," in *Feminism/Postmodernism*, ed. Linda J. Nicholson, 33.

17. Lillian Faderman, *Odd Girls and Twilight Lovers: A History of Lesbian Life in Twentieth-Century America* (New York: Penguin, 1991).

18. Adrienne Rich, "The Eye of the Outsider: Elizabeth Bishop's *Complete Poems*" (1983), in her *Blood, Bread, and Poetry* (New York: Norton, 1986), 134.

19. Jeredith Merrin, *An Enabling Humility: Marianne Moore, Elizabeth Bishop, and the Uses of Tradition* (New Brunswick: Rutgers University Press, 1990).

20. Betsy Erkkila, *The Wicked Sisters: Women Poets, Literary History, and Discord* (New York: Oxford University Press, 1992).

21. Lorrie Goldensohn, *Elizabeth Bishop: The Biography of a Poetry* (New York: Columbia University Press, 1991).

22. Ashley Brown, "An Interview with Elizabeth Bishop," in *Elizabeth Bishop and Her Art*, ed. Lloyd Schwartz and Sybil Estess (Ann Arbor: University of Michigan Press, 1983), 296.

Chapter 1

1. See Bonnie Costello, *Elizabeth Bishop: Questions of Mastery*. She recognizes the tension between the desire for mastery and the inability to achieve it, but nevertheless sees Bishop as "joining" in the ecphrastic tradition, "which ascribes to the plastic and graphic media the virtues of permanence, presence, inexhaustible expressiveness" (215). Bishop's "One Art," in particular, "explores the concept of mastery" and achieves a provisional, "limited mastery" (1). Also see Sharon Cameron, *Lyric Time: Dickinson and the Limits of Genre* (Baltimore: Johns Hopkins University Press, 1979), who expresses an argument similar to mine in reference to Dickinson's work as she addresses the loss and absence at the center of writing: "for all poems, are not so much past or present as they are referential in tense, and what they refer to is no longer there" (187). At the same time, she continues to see the lyric, in general, as "an attempt to cure imperfections" (140), as a defiance of temporality and as an attempt to transcend it—strategies that perhaps work for an analysis of Dickinson but that will be countered by Bishop.

2. Elizabeth Bishop, *The Collected Prose* (New York: Farrar, Straus and Giroux, 1979). All prose citations taken from this volume, abbreviated as *CPr*. Elizabeth Bishop, trans., *Minha Vida De Menina*, referred to here by its English title *The Diary of Helena Morley* (London: Victor Gollancz, 1957).

3. David Perkins, *A History of Modern Poetry: Modernism and After* (Cambridge: Harvard University Press, 1987), 357.

4. M. L. Rosenthal sees the term "confessional" as useful in describing Robert Lowell's

Life Studies as a "culmination of the Romantic and modern tendency to place the literal Self more and more at the center of the poem" (27); explicit references to sexual guilt, alcoholism, mental illness, divorce—all usually made in the first person and generally pointing to the author himself—mark the text as quintessentially confessional. *The New Poets: American and British Poetry Since World War II* (New York: Oxford University Press, 1967).

5. Thomas Travisano, "Emerging Genius: Elizabeth Bishop and *The Blue Pencil, 1927–1930*," *Gettysburg Review* 5 (Winter 1992): 40.

6. Karl Malkoff, *Escape from the Self: A Study in Contemporary American Poetry and Poetics* (New York: Columbia University Press, 1977), 99.

7. See Lorrie Goldensohn's *Elizabeth Bishop: The Biography of a Poetry* for further exploration of the connections between Bishop's art and life.

8. Nancy Chodorow, *The Reproduction of Mothering* (Berkeley and Los Angeles: University of California Press, 1978), 168. Chodorow's model has been subject to criticism by postmodern feminists on the grounds that she posits a cross-cultural, universal, and essentialist notion of the self and therefore produces a too reductive masculine / feminine binarism; see especially Judith Butler, "Gender Trouble" (329) and Nancy Fraser and Linda J. Nicholson, "Social Criticism without Philosophy" (29–30) in *Feminism and Postmodernism*, ed. Nicholson. However, while Chodorow's theory is fallible as "universal," it nevertheless presents itself as one built upon the knowledge that gender categories are socially constructed. I think her notion of a constructed feminine identity—as it emerges through Western models of the family reproduced—is compatible with a postmodern view of the self as tenuous and definable only through its relations. I employ her model as useful description not essentialist definition. Admittedly, Chodorow's use of object-relations theory becomes more difficult to support as she underlines the development of self, as if it were an entity capable of full integration and continuity. For elaboration of her theory, see her *Feminism and Psychoanalytic Theory* (New Haven: Yale University Press, 1989).

9. Chodorow's model of gender development has been shown to be quite apt in describing possible relationships among lesbians; see Joyce Lindenbaum's "The Shattering of an Illusion: Competition in Lesbian Relationships," *Feminist Studies* 11, no. 1 (Spring 1985): 85–103.

10. For fuller biographical information, see Brett Millier's *Elizabeth Bishop: Life and The Memory of It*. Through thorough research into letters and manuscripts unavailable before, Millier has constructed a very persuasive account of the poet's life, supplying numerous details and bridging significant gaps in the poet's history. She vividly reveals that Bishop's traumas and losses were not confined to childhood but were replicated throughout her life: Bob Seaver, a young man she knew during college apparently committed suicide because she refused to marry him (112); after stressful, difficult times and separations in her relationship to Bishop, Lota took an "accidental" overdose upon their reunion in New York in 1967 (395); other traumatic events included her involvement in a car accident in Burgundy in 1937 when one of her closest friends, Margaret Miller, lost an arm and later was hospitalized for mental illness (124). Millier suggests that there seems to be a pattern in Bishop's life that leads her to become involved with those who demonstrate mental disturbance, thus resurrecting her repressed relationship with her troubled mother. Millier further narrates with sensitivity Bishop's ongoing struggles with alcoholism, asthma, and depression, careful to show the possible interrelations between them. For a more critical biography, see David Kalstone's *Becoming a Poet: Elizabeth Bishop with Marianne Moore and Robert Lowell*. Also see Goldensohn, which includes Bishop's own autobiographical sketch as preface.

11. Earlier drafts of poems seem more readily autobiographical such as those of "One Art" to be discussed in the Conclusion. Seventeen drafts (1975) are in the Elizabeth Bishop Collection at Vassar College Library (Poughkeepsie, New York).

12. Peter M. Sacks, *The English Elegy: Studies in the Genre from Spenser to Yeats* (Baltimore: Johns Hopkins University Press, 1985), 6.

13. John Bowlby, *Attachment and Loss* (New York: Basic Books, 1982).

14. John Bowlby, "Childhood Mourning and its Implications," in *The Making and Breaking of Affectional Bonds* (New York: Tavistock, 1979).

15. "William T. Bishop," *Worcester Magazine*, p. 643. Bishop Collection, Vassar College.

16. Patricia Yaeger, *Honey-Mad Women* (New York: Columbia University Press, 1988).

17. David Kalstone, *Five Temperaments* (New York: Oxford University Press, 1977), 10–11.

18. Jerome Mazzaro, *Postmodern American Poetry*, 28.

19. Hélène Cixous, "The Laugh of the Medusa," trans. Claudia Reeder, *New French Feminisms*, ed. Elaine Marks and Isabelle de Courtivron (New York: Schocken), 103.

20. Thomas J. Travisano, *Elizabeth Bishop: Her Artistic Development*, 20.

21. See Carolyn G. Heilbrun, *Writing a Woman's Life* (New York: Norton, 1988), for a more extensive exploration of the "difference" in woman's biographical writings; diaries and letters seem to be more honest accounts—arenas where a woman's daily life may be better understood—because they allow for narratives repressed by more public appearances in print.

22. Helena McNeil, "Elizabeth Bishop," *Visions and Voices*, ed. Helen Vendler (New York: Random House, 1987), 420.

23. Millier, 287.

24. From the manuscript archives at the Houghton Library, Harvard University. Letter to Robert Lowell, 22 March 1955.

25. From "Autobiographical Sketch" (1961), Bishop Collection, Vassar College.

26. Robert Dale Parker, *The Unbeliever: The Poetry of Elizabeth Bishop* (Urbana: University of Illinois Press, 1988), 59.

27. J. D. McClatchy, "'One Art': Some Notes," in *Elizabeth Bishop Criticism and Interpretation*, ed. Harold Bloom (New York: Chelsea, 1985).

28. J. D. McClatchy, "Interview with James Merrill," in *Writers at Work*, 6th ser., ed. George Plimpton (New York: Viking, 1984), 310.

29. Elizabeth Spires, "The Art of Poetry XXVII: Elizabeth Bishop," *Paris Review* 23 (Summer 1981): 64.

30. Sigmund Freud, *Beyond the Pleasure Principle*, trans. James Strachey (New York: Norton, 1961), 9.

31. Sigmund Freud, "Mourning and Melancholia," in *General Selections from the Work of Sigmund Freud*, trans. John Rickman (New York: Doubleday, 1957), 126.

32. Jacques Lacan, "The Signification of the Phallus," in *Ecrits*, trans. Alan Sheridan (New York: Norton, 1977), 287.

33. Jacques Lacan, "The Mirror Stage," in *Ecrits*, 6.

34. "The Agency of the Letter in the Unconscious," in *Ecrits*.

35. Juliet Mitchell and Jacqueline Rose, eds., *Feminine Sexuality: Jacques Lacan and the école freudienne* (New York: Norton, 1982), 51.

36. Julia Kristeva, *Desire in Language: A Semiotic Approach to Literature and Art*, trans. Thomas Gora, Alice Jardine, and Leon S. Roudiez (New York: Columbia University Press, 1980), 125.

37. Drafts 1–17 (1975), Bishop Collection, Vassar College.

38. Adrienne Rich, "Contradiction: Tracking Poems," in Rich, *Your Native Land, Your Life* (New York: Norton, 1986), 98.

Chapter 2

1. T. E. Hulme, "Romanticism and Classicism," in *Speculations*, ed. Herbert Read (New York: Harcourt, 1924), 113–40.

2. de Gourmant, *Natural Philosophy of Love*, trans. and with a postscript by Ezra Pound (New York: Rarity Press, 1931), 169, as cited in Sandra M. Gilbert and Susan Gubar, *No Man's Land*, vol. 2, *Sexchanges* (New Haven: Yale University Press, 1989).

3. George Starbuck, "The Work!: A Conversation with Elizabeth Bishop," in *Elizabeth Bishop and Her Art*, ed. Schwartz and Estess, 312–30. Bishop discusses her uneasiness with feminism, hinting at a fear that it might separate male from female too distinctly, but then confesses: "One gets so used, very young, to being 'put down' that if you have normal intelligence and have any sense of humour, you very early develop a tough, ironic attitude" (324). Though she speaks of "one," she obviously references her role as female artist (312–30). In a later interview with Elizabeth Spires (28 June 1978), she says outright, "I've always considered myself a strong feminist" (80); see Spires, "The Art of Poetry XXVII: Elizabeth Bishop."

4. Ann Winslow, ed., *Trial Balances* (New York: Macmillan, 1935).

5. Rudolf Arnheim, "The Perception of Maps," in *New Essays in the Psychology of Art* (Berkeley and Los Angeles: University of California Press, 1986), 199.

6. T. S. Eliot, "Hamlet and His Problems," in *Selected Prose of T. S. Eliot*, ed. Frank Kermode (New York: Harcourt Brace Jovanovich, 1975), 48.

7. Robert Lowell, "From Thomas, Bishop, and Williams," in *Elizabeth Bishop and Her Art*, ed. Schwartz and Estess, 187–88.

8. Betsy Erkkila, *The Wicked Sisters*.

9. Marianne Moore, "Poetry," in *The Complete Poems* (New York: Macmillan, 1982), 267. Further citations taken from this volume referred to as Moore, *CP*.

10. Marianne Moore, "Archaically New," in *The Collected Prose of Marianne Moore* (New York: Viking, 1986), 328.

11. Robert Lowell, "From Thomas, Bishop, and Williams."

12. T. S. Eliot, "Tradition and the Individual Talent," in *Selected Essays, 1917–1930* (New York: Harcourt, 1932), 87.

13. Bonnie Costello, *Marianne Moore* (Cambridge: Harvard University Press, 1981), 61.

14. From an unpublished manuscript, Bishop Collection, Vassar.

15. Wallace Stevens, "The Noble Rider and the Sound of Words," in *The Necessary Angel* (New York: Knopf, 1951), 32.

16. Max Ernst, "Surrealist Situation of the Object," in *The Manifestoes of Surrealism*, by André Breton (Ann Arbor: University of Michigan Press, 1969).

17. Michel Foucault, "What is an Author?" in *Textual Strategies*, ed. Josue V. Harari (Ithaca: Cornell University Press, 1979), 142.

18. Bishop's literary and personal relationship with Marianne Moore and Robert Lowell is well documented in Kalstone, *Becoming A Poet*. Also see Lynn Keller's "Words Worth a Thousand Postcards: The Bishop / Moore Correspondence," wonderfully complete in charting Bishop's mentorship with Moore and growing independence from the older writer. *American Literature* 55 (October 1983): 405–29.

19. In an unpublished letter to Robert Lowell, Bishop writes, significantly, that she has "always had a day dream of being a light-house keeper, absolutely alone, with no one to interrupt my reading or just sitting" (27 July 1960, Houghton Library, Harvard University). Such a sentiment draws our attention to Bishop's attraction to solitude as a means of escape.

20. Millier, 123–26.

21. Letter to Robert Lowell (30 June 1948, Houghton Library, Harvard University).

22. Henry David Thoreau, *Walden* (London: J. M. Dent, 1962), 155.

23. Eudora Welty, "Why I live at the P.O." in *The Collected Stories* (New York: Harcourt Brace, 1980), 109.

24. Stevens, *The Necessary Angel*, 20.

25. Toril Moi, *Sexual / Textual Politics* (New York: Methuen, 1985), 140.

26. Butler, "Gender Trouble, Feminist Theory, and Psychoanalytic Discourse," in *Feminism / Postmodernism*, ed. Linda J. Nicolson (New York: Routledge, 1991), 324–40.

27. Hugh Kenner, A *Homemade World: The American Modernist Writers* (New York: Knopf, 1975).

28. Judith Fetterley, *The Resisting Reader: A Feminist Approach to American Fiction* (Bloomington: Indiana University Press, 1978).

29. Patrocinio P. Schweickart, "Reading Ourselves: Toward A Feminist Theory of Reading," in *Speaking of Gender*, ed. Elaine Showalter (New York: Routledge, 1989).

30. Alice Walker, "In Search of Our Mothers' Gardens," in *In Search of Our Mothers' Gardens* (New York: Harcourt Brace, 1983), 241.

31. Claude Lévi-Strauss, *The Savage Mind* (Chicago: University of Chicago Press, 1968).

32. Richard Mullen, in "Elizabeth Bishop's Surrealist Inheritance," provides an excellent overview of surrealist techniques in Bishop's poetry—in both showing her link with ideas behind the movement and her deviation from them. *American Literature* 54 (March 1982): 63–80.

33. André Breton, "Second Manifesto of Surrealism," in his *Manifestoes of Surrealism*, trans. Richard Seaver and Helen R. Lane (Ann Arbor: University of Michigan Press, 1969).

34. Keller, *Re-making It New*, 135.

35. Elizabeth Bishop, "Letter to Anne Stevenson," in *Elizabeth Bishop and Her Art*, ed. Schwartz and Estess, 288.

36. Morris W. Croll, "The Baroque Style in Prose," in his *Style, Rhetoric, and Rhythm* (Princeton: Princeton University Press, 1943).

Chapter 3

1. Alan Williamson does call Bishop a "poet of feeling" and he also considers some of the poems in *A Cold Spring* as love poems. Yet he considers her, in contrast with my own conclusions about such lyrics, as possessing "the ground-conviction that reciprocal love is, about metaphysically impossible" and that Bishop, rather than perceiving relationship, is "obsessed with distance between human beings" and is "inclined to see the connections as illusory." "The Poet of Feeling," in *Elizabeth Bishop and Her Art*, ed. Schwartz and Estess, 97–100.

2. Millier, *Elizabeth Bishop: Life and the Memory of It*.

3. Lee Edelman, "The Geography of Gender: Elizabeth Bishop's 'In the Waiting Room,' " *Contemporary Literature* 26 (Summer 1985): 196.

4. Adrienne Rich, "The Eye of the Outsider" (1983).

5. Lloyd Schwartz has discovered an unpublished love poem, not "shadowed by her more customary silences" (86) with the provocative stanza:

> —Cold as it is, we'd
> go to bed, dear,
> early, but never
> to keep warm.

He wisely notes that all of her "love poems" have a "distinctive erotic charge." "Elizabeth Bishop and Brazil," *New Yorker* (30 September 1991): 85–97.

6. In their inclusive study of women's writing in both the nineteenth and twentieth centuries, Sandra M. Gilbert and Susan Gubar only discuss Bishop briefly in *No Man's Land*, vol. 1, *The Place of the Woman Writer in the Twentieth Century* (New Haven: Yale University Press, 1987), 211–14. See also interview, George Starbuck, "The Work!"

7. Hélène Cixous, "The Laugh of the Medusa."

8. Adrienne Rich, "Compulsory Heterosexuality and Lesbian Existence," in her *Blood, Bread and Poetry*, 23–75.

9. Roland Barthes, *A Lover's Discourse*, trans. Richard Howard (New York: Farrar, Straus and Giroux, 1978).

10. In Alicia Suskin Ostriker, *Stealing the Language: The Emergence of Women's Poetry in America* (New York: Beacon, 1986).

11. Margaret Homans, *Women Writers and Poetic Identity: Dorothy Wordsworth, Emily Brontë, and Emily Dickinson* (Princeton: Princeton University Press, 1980).

12. Letter to Robert Lowell (11 July 1957).

13. John Dewey, *Human Nature and Conduct* (New York: Holt, 1922).

14. Letter to Robert Lowell (14 August 1947).

15. William Carlos Williams, *Spring and All*, in his *Imaginations* (New York: New Directions, 1971).

16. Sandra M. Gilbert and Susan Gubar, *No Man's Land: The Place of the Woman Writer in the Twentieth Century*.

17. "Vaguely Love Poem," unpublished manuscript, Bishop Collection, Vassar College.

18. Carol Gilligan, *In a Different Voice: Psychological Theory and Women's Development* (Cambridge: Harvard University Press, 1982).

19. "Review of Emily Dickinson's *Letters to Dr. and Mrs. Josiah Gilbert Holland*," unpublished manuscript, Bishop Collection, Vassar College.

20. Hariette Chessman, *The Public is Invited to Dance: Representation, the Body, and Dialogue in Gertrude Stein* (Stanford: Stanford University Press, 1989), 82.

21. Julia Kristeva, *Tales of Love*, trans. Leon S. Roudiez (New York: Columbia University Press, 1987).

22. Rita Felski, *Beyond Feminist Aesthetics* (Cambridge: Harvard University Press, 1989).

23. Anne Rosalind Jones, "Writing the Body: Toward an Understanding of Feminine Ecriture," in *The New Feminist Criticism*, ed. Elaine Showalter (New York: Pantheon, 1985), 365.

24. Lispector, "Three Stories of Clarice Lispector," trans. Elizabeth Bishop, *Kenyon Review* (Summer 1964): 501–11.

Chapter 4

1. Ralph Waldo Emerson, journal entry, 13 July 1833 (pp. 110–11), in *Emerson in His Journals*, ed. Joel Porte (Cambridge: Belknap Press of Harvard University Press, 1982).

2. David Kalstone, *Becoming a Poet*, 196.

3. Letter to Robert Lowell (14 December 1957).

4. Ibid., 11 December 1957.

5. Ibid., January 1948.

6. Ibid., 11 July 1948; 31 December 1948.

7. Ibid., 8 July 1955.

8. Ibid., 26 November 1951.

9. Ibid., 28 July 1953.

10. Ralph Waldo Emerson, "Circles," in *Essays and Lectures* (New York: Library of America, 1983).

11. Claude Lévi-Strauss, *Tristes Tropiques*, trans. John Russell (New York: Atheneum, 1972), 396.

12. Jacques Derrida, *The Post Card: From Socrates to Freud and Beyond*, trans. Alan Bass (Chicago: University of Chicago Press, 1987).

13. Letter to Lowell (30 October 1960); E. H. Gombrich, *Art and Illusion: A Study in the Art of Pictoral Presentation* (London: Phaidon, 1968).

14. Letter to Lowell (15 February 1960).

15. Sir Kenneth Clark, *Landscape into Art* (New York: Harper and Row, 1949).

16. Robert Dale Parker, *The Unbeliever*, 96.

17. Jane Shore, "Elizabeth Bishop: The Art of Changing Your Mind," *Ploughshares* 5 (1979), 182.

18. Tzvetan Todorov, *The Conquest of America: The Question of the Other*, trans. Richard Howard (New York: Harper and Row, 1984), 4.

19. Robert Pinsky, poetry reading at Sunset Recreation Center, University of California, Los Angeles, May 1990.

20. Charles Wagley, *Amazon Town* (New York: Knopf, 1964).

21. George Starbuck, "The Work!" 312–13.

22. Elizabeth Bishop and the Editors of *Life*, *Brazil* (New York: Time, 1962), 11–12.

23. Quoted in Candace W. MacMahon, *Elizabeth Bishop: A Bibliography, 1927–1979*, 70.

24. Bishop was extremely interested in Joseph Cornell's work, including his Medici series, which focused upon children who, he felt, had to grow up too soon and in painful circumstances. See Sandra Leonard Starr, *Joseph Cornell: Art and Metaphysics* (New York: Castelli, Feigen, and Corcoran, 1982).

25. Gaston Bachelard, *The Poetics of Space*, trans. Maria Jolas (Boston: Beacon, 1969), xxxi.

26. Kalstone, *Becoming a Poet*, 187.

27. Letter to Lowell (14 April 1962).

Chapter 5

1. Letter to Robert Lowell (18 March 1948).

2. Gaston Bachelard, *The Poetics of Space*, 3.

3. Richard Poirier, *A World Elsewhere*, 8–9.

4. She tells George Starbuck how "Crusoe" got started: "I reread the book and discovered how really boring *Robinson Crusoe* was, which I hadn't realized," 319.

5. Renée R. Curry, "Augury and Autobiography: Bishop's 'Crusoe in England,'" *Arizona Quarterly* 47 (Autumn 1991): 70–91.

6. William Wordsworth, *Wordsworth's Poetical Works*, ed. E. de Selincourt (Oxford: Clarendon Press, 1944), 507.

7. Julia Kristeva, "Revolution in Poetic Language," in *The Kristeva Reader*, 96.

8. Spires, "The Art of Poetry XXVII: Elizabeth Bishop," 75.

9. Letter to Lowell (8 September 1948).

10. Paul Fussell, *Poetic Meter and Poetic Form* (New York: Random House, 1979), 145.

11. Sigmund Freud, "The 'Uncanny'" in *On Creativity and the Unconscious: Papers on the Psychology of Art, Literature, Love, and Religion*, ed. Benjamin Nelson and trans. Joan Riviere (New York: Harper and Row, 1958).

12. Helen Vendler, "Domestication, Domesticity, and the Otherworldly," in *Elizabeth Bishop and Her Art*, ed. Schwartz and Estess.

13. "The Drunkard," unpublished material, Bishop Collection, Vassar College.

14. Lee Edelman in "Geography of Gender: In the Waiting Room" discusses, as well, the poem's overturning of binary oppositions and hierarchies in terms of the child's dis-position in gender and language.

15. Hopkins, *The Hopkins Reader*, ed. John Pick (London: Oxford University Press, 1953), 297.

Conclusion

1. Ashley Brown, "An Interview with Elizabeth Bishop," in *Elizabeth Bishop and Her Art*, ed. Schwartz and Estess.

2. Letter to Lowell (8 August 1948).

3. Phyllis Stowell, "The Question of Santarém," *Studia Mystica* 11 (Spring 1988): 35–51.

4. Spires, "The Art of Poetry XXVII: Elizabeth Bishop," 62.

Select Bibliography

Arnheim, Rudolph. "The Perception of Maps." In her *New Essays in the Psychology of Art*, 194–202. Berkeley and Los Angeles: University of California Press, 1986.

Bachelard, Gaston. *The Poetics of Space*. Translated by Maria Jolas. Boston: Beacon, 1969.

Barthes, Roland. *A Lover's Discourse*. Translated by Richard Howard. New York: Farrar, Straus and Giroux, 1978.

———. *The Pleasure of the Text*. New York: Hill and Wang, 1977.

Benstock, Sheri. "Expatriate Sapphic Modernism." In *Lesbian Texts and Contexts*, ed. Karla Jay and Joanne Glasgow, 183–203. New York: New York University Press, 1990.

Bishop, Elizabeth. *The Collected Prose*. New York: Farrar, Straus and Giroux, 1979.

———. *The Complete Poems: 1927–1979*. New York: Farrar, Straus and Giroux, 1979.

———, trans. *Minha Vida De Menina*. London: Victor Gollancz, 1957.

———, ed. *An Anthology of Twentieth-Century Brazilian Poetry*. Middletown, Conn.: Wesleyan University Press, 1972.

———. *Brazil*. New York: Time, 1962.

Bowlby, John. *Attachment and Loss*. New York: Basic Books, 1982.

———. "Childhood Mourning and its Implications." In his *The Making and Breaking of Affectional Bonds*. New York: Tavistock, 1979.

Breton, André. "Second Manifesto of Surrealism." In his *Manifestoes of Surrealism*, trans. Richard Seaver and Helen R. Lane, 119–94. Ann Arbor: University of Michigan Press, 1969. (Essay originally published 1930).

Brown, Ashley. "An Interview with Elizabeth Bishop." In *Elizabeth Bishop and Her Art*, ed. Lloyd Schwartz and Sybil Estess, 289–302. Ann Arbor: University of Michigan Press, 1983.

Butler, Judith. *Gender Trouble*. New York: Routledge, 1990.

———. "Gender Trouble, Feminist Theory, and Psychoanalytic Discourse." In *Feminism / Postmodernism*, ed. Linda T. Nicholson, 324–40. New York: Routledge, 1991.

Cameron, Sharon. *Lyric Time: Dickinson and the Limits of Genre*. Baltimore: Johns Hopkins University Press, 1979.

Chessman, Hariette. *The Public is Invited to Dance: Representation, the Body, and Dialogue in Gertrude Stein*. Stanford: Stanford University Press, 1989.

Chodorow, Nancy. *Feminism and Psychoanalytic Theory*. New Haven: Yale University Press, 1989.

———. *The Reproduction of Mothering.* Berkeley and Los Angeles: University of California Press, 1978.

Cixous, Hélène. "The Laugh of the Medusa." Translated by Claudia Reeder. In *New French Feminisms,* ed. Elaine Marks and Isabelle de Courtivron, 245–64. New York: Schocken, 1980.

Clark, Sir Kenneth. *Landscape into Art.* New York: Harper and Row, 1949.

Costello, Bonnie. *Elizabeth Bishop: Questions of Mastery.* Cambridge: Harvard University Press, 1991.

———. *Marianne Moore.* Cambridge: Harvard University Press, 1981.

Croll, Morris W. "The Baroque Style in Prose." In his *Style, Rhetoric, and Rhythm,* 207–33. Princeton: Princeton University Press, 1943.

Curry, Renée R. "Augury and Autobiography: Bishop's 'Crusoe in England.'" *Arizona Quarterly* 47 (Autumn 1991): 70–91.

Derrida, Jacques. *Margins of Philosophy.* Chicago: University of Chicago Press, 1982.

———. *The Post Card: From Socrates to Freud and Beyond.* Translated by Alan Bass. Chicago: University of Chicago Press, 1987.

———. *Writing and Difference.* Chicago: University of Chicago Press, 1982.

Dewey, John. *Human Nature and Conduct.* New York: Holt, 1922.

Edelman, Lee. "The Geography of Gender: Elizabeth Bishop's 'In the Waiting Room.'" *Contemporary Literature* 26 (Summer 1985): 175–96.

Eliot, T. S. "Hamlet and His Problems." In *Selected Prose of T. S. Eliot,* ed. Frank Kermode, 45–49. New York: Harcourt Brace Jovanovich, 1975.

———. "Tradition and the Individual Talent." In *Selected Essays, 1917–1930,* 3–11. New York: Harcourt, 1932.

Emerson, Ralph Waldo. "Circles." In his *Essays and Lectures.* New York: Library of America, 1983.

———. *Emerson in His Journals.* Edited by Joel Porte, 110–11. Cambridge: Belknap Press of Harvard University Press, 1982.

Erkkila, Betsy. *The Wicked Sisters: Women Poets, Literary History and Discord.* New York: Oxford University Press, 1992.

Ernst, Max. "Surrealist Situation of the Object." In *The Manifestoes of Surrealism,* by André Breton. Translated by Richard Seaver and Helen R. Lane, 275–78. Ann Arbor: University of Michigan Press, 1969.

Faderman, Lillian. *Odd Girls and Twilight Lovers: A History of Lesbian Life in Twentieth-Century America.* New York: Penguin, 1991.

Felski, Rita. *Beyond Feminist Aesthetics.* Cambridge: Harvard University Press, 1989.

Fetterley, Judith. *The Resisting Reader: A Feminist Approach to American Fiction.* Bloomington: Indiana University Press, 1978.

Fitzgerald, F. Scott. *The Great Gatsby.* New York: Bantam, 1925.

Flax, Jane. "Postmodernism and Gender Relations." In *Feminism / Postmodernism,* ed. Linda J. Nicholson, 39–62. New York: Routledge, 1991.

Foucault, Michel. *Language, Counter-Memory, Practice.* Ithaca: Cornell University Press, 1977.

———. "What is an Author?" In *Textual Strategies,* ed. Josue V. Harari, 141–60. Ithaca: Cornell University Press, 1979.

Freud, Sigmund. *Beyond the Pleasure Principle.* Translated by James Strachey. New York: Norton, 1961.

———. "Mourning and Melancholia." In *A General Selection from the Works of Sigmund Freud,* trans. John Rickmann, 124–40. New York: Doubleday, 1957. (Essay originally published 1917)

————. "The 'Uncanny.'" In *On Creativity and the Unconscious: Papers on the Psychology of Art, Literature, Love, and Religion*, ed. Benjamin Nelson and trans. Joan Riviere, 122–61. New York: Harper and Row, 1958.

Fussell, Paul. *Poetic Meter and Poetic Form*. New York: Random House, 1979.

Gilbert, Sandra M., and Susan Gubar. *No Man's Land*. Vol. 1, *The Place of the Woman Writer in the Twentieth Century*. New Haven: Yale University Press, 1987.

————. *No Man's Land*. Vol. 2, *Sexchanges*. New Haven: Yale University Press, 1989.

Gilligan, Carol. *In a Different Voice: Psychological Theory and Women's Development*. Cambridge: Harvard University Press, 1982.

Goldensohn, Lorrie. *Elizabeth Bishop: The Biography of a Poetry*. New York: Columbia University Press, 1991.

Gombrich, E. H. *Art and Illusion: A Study in the Art of Pictoral Presentation*. London: Phaidon, 1968.

Grosz, Elizabeth. *Sexual Subversions*. Sydney: Allen and Unwin, 1989.

Hassan, Ihab. "The Culture of Postmodernism." In *Modernism: Challenges and Perspectives*, ed. Monique Chefdor, Ricardo Quinones, and Albert Wachtel, 304–23. Urbana: University of Illinois Press, 1986.

Heilbrun, Carolyn G. *Writing a Woman's Life*. New York: Norton, 1988.

Homans, Margaret. *Women Writers and Poetic Identity: Dorothy Wordsworth, Emily Brontë, and Emily Dickinson*. Princeton: Princeton University Press, 1980.

Hopkins, Gerard Manley. *The Hopkins Reader*. Edited by John Pick. London: Oxford University Press, 1953.

Hulme, T. E. "Romanticism and Classicism." In *Speculations*, ed. Herbert Read, 113–40. New York: Harcourt, 1924.

Irigaray, Luce, "Ce sexe qui n'en pas un." Translated by Claudia Reeder. In *New French Feminisms*, ed. Elaine Marks and Isabelle de Courtivron, 99–106. New York: Schocken, 1980.

————. *Speculum of the Other Woman*. Ithaca: Cornell University Press, 1985.

Jarrell, Randall. *Poetry and the Age*. New York: Knopf, 1953.

Jones, Anne Rosalind. "Writing the Body: Toward an Understanding of Feminine Ecriture." In *The New Feminist Criticism*, ed. Elaine Showalter, 361–77. New York: Pantheon, 1985.

Kalstone, David. *Becoming a Poet: Elizabeth Bishop with Marianne Moore and Robert Lowell*. New York: Farrar, Straus and Giroux, 1989.

————. *Five Temperaments*. New York: Oxford University Press, 1977.

Keller, Lynn. *Re-making it New: Contemporary American Poetry and the Modernist Tradition*. Cambridge: Cambridge University Press, 1987.

————. "Words Worth a Thousand Postcards: The Bishop / Moore Correspondence." *American Literature* 55 (October 1983): 405–29.

Kenner, Hugh. *A Homemade World: The American Modernist Writers*. New York: Knopf, 1975.

Kristeva, Julia. *Desire in Language: A Semiotic Approach to Literature and Art*. Translated by Thomas Gora, Alice Jardine, and Leon S. Roudiez. New York: Columbia University Press, 1980.

————. "Revolution and Poetic Language." In *The Kristeva Reader*, 90–123. New York: Columbia University Press, 1986.

————. *Tales of Love*. Translated by Leon S. Roudiez. New York: Columbia University Press, 1987.

Lacan, Jacques. "The Agency of the Letter in the Unconscious." In his *Ecrits*, trans. Alan Sheridan, 146–78. New York: Norton, 1977.

————. "The Mirror Stage." In his *Ecrits*, trans. Alan Sheridan, 1–7. New York: Norton, 1977.

————. "The Signification of the Phallus." In *Ecrits*, trans. Alan Sheridan, 281–91. New York: Norton, 1977.

Lévi-Strauss, Claude. *The Savage Mind*. Chicago: University of Chicago Press, 1968.

————. *Tristes Tropiques*. Translated by John Russell. New York: Atheneum, 1972.

Lindenbaum, Joyce. "The Shattering of an Illusion: Competition in Lesbian Relationships." *Feminist Studies* 11, no. 1 (Spring 1985): 85–103.

Lispector, Clarice. "Three Stories of Clarice Lispector." Translated by Elizabeth Bishop. *Kenyon Review* 26, no. 3 (Summer 1964): 501–11.

Lowell, Robert. "From Thomas, Bishop, and Williams." In *Elizabeth Bishop and Her Art*, ed. Lloyd Schwartz and Sybil Estess, 186–89. Ann Arbor: University of Michigan Press, 1983.

————. "On Skunk Hour." In *Elizabeth Bishop and Her Art*, ed. Lloyd Schwartz and Sybil Estess, 199. Ann Arbor: University of Michigan Press, 1983.

Lyotard, Jean-François. *The Postmodern Condition*. Minneapolis: University of Minnesota Press, 1984.

MacMahon, Candace W. *Elizabeth Bishop: A Bibliography, 1927–1979*. Charlottesville: University of Virginia Press, 1980.

Malkoff, Karl. *Escape from the Self: A Study in Contemporary American Poetry and Poetics*. New York: Columbia University Press, 1977.

Mazzaro, Jerome. *Postmodern American Poetry*. Urbana: University of Illinois Press, 1980.

McClatchy, J. D. "'One Art': Some Notes." In *Elizabeth Bishop Criticism and Interpretation*, ed. Harold Bloom, New York: Chelsea, 1985.

————. "Interview with James Merrill." In *Writers at Work*, 6th ser., ed. George Plimpton, 281–312. New York: Viking, 1984. (Interview conducted summer and fall 1981)

McNeil, Helena. "Elizabeth Bishop." In *Visions and Voices*, ed. Helen Vendler, 394–425. New York: Random House, 1987.

Merrin, Jeredith. *An Enabling Humility: Marianne Moore, Elizabeth Bishop, and the Uses of Tradition*. New Brunswick: Rutgers University Press, 1990.

Miller, Nancy. "Arachnologies: The Woman, The Text, and the Critic," in her *The Poetics of Gender*, 270–95. New York: Columbia University Press, 1987.

Millier, Brett. *Elizabeth Bishop: Life and the Memory of It*. Berkeley and Los Angeles: University of California Press, 1993.

Mitchell, Juliet, and Jacqueline Rose, eds. *Feminine Sexuality: Jacques Lacan and the école freudienne*. New York: Norton, 1982.

Moi, Toril. *Sexual / Textual Politics*. New York: Methuen, 1985.

Moore, Marianne. "Archaically New." In *The Collected Prose of Marianne Moore*, ed. Patricia C. Willis, 327–29. New York: Viking, 1986.

————. *The Complete Poems of Marianne Moore*. New York: Macmillan, 1982.

Mullen, Richard. "Elizabeth Bishop's Surrealist Inheritance." In *American Literature* 54 (March 1982): 63–80.

Nicholson, Linda J. *Feminism / Postmodernism*. New York: Routledge, 1990.

Ostriker, Alicia Suskin. *Stealing the Language: The Emergence of Woman's Poetry in America*. New York: Beacon, 1986.

Owens, Craig. "The Discourse of Others: Feminists and Postmodernism." In *The Anti-Aesthetic: Essays on Postmodern Culture*, ed. Hal Foster, 57–77. Port Townsend: Bay Press, 1983.

Parker, Robert Dale. *The Unbeliever: The Poetry of Elizabeth Bishop*. Urbana: University of Illinois Press, 1988.

Pearce, Roy Harvey. *The Continuity of American Poetry*. Princeton: Princeton University Press, 1961.

Perkins, David. *A History of Modern Poetry: Modernism and After*. Cambridge: Harvard University Press, 1987.

Pinsky, Robert. Poetry reading at Sunset Recreation Center, University of California, Los Angeles, May 1990.

———. *The Situation of Poetry: Contemporary Poetry and Its Traditions*. Princeton: Princeton University Press, 1976.

Poirier, Richard. *A World Elsewhere: The Place of Style in American Literature*. New York: Oxford University Press, 1966.

Rich, Adrienne. "Compulsory Heterosexuality and Lesbian Existence." In her *Blood, Bread and Poetry*, 23–75. New York: Norton, 1986. (Essay originally published 1980)

———. "The Eye of the Outsider: Elizabeth Bishop's *Complete Poems*." In her *Blood, Bread and Poetry*, 124–35. New York: Norton, 1986. (Essay originally published 1983)

———. *Your Native Land, Your Life*. New York: Norton, 1986.

Rosenthal, M. L. *The New Poets: American and British Poetry after World War II*. New York: Oxford University Press, 1967.

Sacks, Peter M. *The English Elegy: Studies in the Genre from Spenser to Yeats*. Baltimore: Johns Hopkins University Press, 1985.

Schwartz, Lloyd. "Elizabeth Bishop and Brazil." *New Yorker* (30 September 1991): 85–97.

———, and Sybil Estess, eds. *Elizabeth Bishop and Her Art*. Ann Arbor: University of Michigan Press, 1983.

Schweickart, Patrocinio P. "Reading Ourselves: Toward a Feminist Theory of Reading." In *Speaking of Gender*, ed. Elaine Showalter, 17–44. New York: Routledge, 1989.

Scott, Bonnie Kime, ed. *The Gender of Modernism*. Bloomington: Indiana University Press, 1990.

Shore, Jane. "Elizabeth Bishop: The Art of Changing Your Mind." *Ploughshares* 5 (1979): 178–91.

Spires, Elizabeth. "The Art of Poetry XXVII: Elizabeth Bishop." *Paris Review* 23 (Summer 1981): 56–83.

Starbuck, George. "The Work!: A Conversation with Elizabeth Bishop." In *Elizabeth Bishop and Her Art*, ed. Lloyd Schwartz and Sybil Estess, 312–30. Ann Arbor: University of Michigan Press, 1983.

Starr, Sandra Leonard. *Joseph Cornell: Art and Metaphysics*. New York: Castelli, Feigen, and Corcoran, 1982.

Stevens, Wallace. "The Noble Rider and the Sound of Words." In his *The Necessary Angel*, 1–36. New York: Knopf, 1951.

Stevenson, Anne. *Elizabeth Bishop*. New York: Twayne, 1966.

Stowell, Phyllis. "The Question of Santarém." *Studia Mystica* 11 (Spring 1988): 35–51.

Thoreau, Henry David. *Walden*. London: J. M. Dent, 1962.

Todorov, Tzvetan. *The Conquest of America: The Question of the Other*. Translated by Richard Howard. New York: Harper and Row, 1984.

Travisano, Thomas J. *Elizabeth Bishop: Her Artistic Development*. Charlottesville: University of Virginia, 1988.

———. "Emerging Genius: Elizabeth Bishop and *The Blue Pencil*, 1927–30." *Gettysburg Review* 5 (Winter 1992): 32–47.

Vendler, Helen. "Domestication, Domesticity, and the Otherworldly." In *Elizabeth Bishop and Her Art*, ed. Lloyd Schwartz and Sybil Estess, 32–48. Ann Arbor: University of Michigan Press, 1983.

Wagley, Charles. *Amazon Town*. New York: Knopf, 1964.

Walker, Alice. *In Search of Our Mothers' Gardens*. New York: Harcourt Brace, 1983.

Welty, Eudora. "Why I live at the P.O." In *The Collected Stories*, 89–110. New York: Harcourt Brace, 1980.

Williams, William Carlos. *Spring and All*. In *Imaginations*, 85–151. New York: New Directions, 1971.

Williamson, Alan. "The Poet of Feeling." In *Elizabeth Bishop and Her Art*, ed. Lloyd Schwartz and Sybil Estess, 98–108. Ann Arbor: University of Michigan Press, 1983.

Winslow, Ann, ed. *Trial Balances*. New York: Macmillan, 1935.

Wittgenstein, Ludwig. *On Certainty*. New York: Harper and Row, 1972.

———. *Philosophical Investigations*. New York: Macmillan, 1970.

Wordsworth, William. *Wordsworth's Poetical Works*. Edited by E. de Selincourt. Oxford: Clarendon Press, 1944.

Yaeger, Patricia. *Honey-Mad Women*. New York: Columbia University Press, 1988.

Index